Coincraft
Britain's Coin Shop

Coincraft
Britain's Coin Shop - since 1955
45 Great Russell Street, LONDON
WC1B 3LU
(opposite the British Museum)

Tel: 020 7636 1188
Web www.coincraft.com
Email info@coincraft.com

Coincraft has been helping collectors for the past 70 years. Our shop across the street from the famous British Museum has been here for almost 50 years. Every three weeks we issue two different catalogues of coins and banknotes for sale at fixed prices. We have 18 full time staff and experts to help you with your collecting wishes. Our shop is open Monday to Friday 9:30-5:00 excluding Bank Holidays and you are welcome to come in and have a look.

We handle and have handled some of the rarest and choicest British and world coins. We were the first company to offer the finest known 1819 George III Sovereign. In modern issues, for example, we can offer King Charles III Proof Coronation Sovereigns in lots of 100 pieces. All in their original cases of issue.

We handle everything you might want from Greek and Roman coins to some of the latest issues. We have over 4,000,000 coins and banknotes in stock.

We are a family owned and family run business. We only sell to collectors, we do not sell anything for investment. We have been called 'old fashioned' and we take this as a compliment. If you want to business in an old fashioned way with an old fashioned company then maybe Coincraft is for you.

Send for a complimentary copy of The Phoenix, our 24 page A3 full colour newspaper / catalogue, which comes out every three weeks. See why our collectors say, 'Coincraft makes collecting fun again'.

TOP PRICES PAID

ROYAL GOLD
Established 1979

PO Box 123, Saxonwold,
Johannesburg 2132,
South Africa
Tel: +27 11 483 0161
WhatsApp: +27 76 196 2425
Email: info@royalgold.co.za

Authorised Partner of the South Africa Mint

www.royalgold.co.za

SOVEREIGN RARITIES LTD

DEALERS in RARE COINS from 1000 YEARS of BRITISH HISTORY
Resident British Coin Specialist STEVE HILL the author of this book.

George III, 1817  — George IV, 1821  — George IV, 1828

William IV, 1831, proof  — Victoria, 1839, proof  — Victoria, 1880, proof

Victoria, 1887, proof  — Victoria, 1893, proof  — Edward VII, 1902, matt proof

George V, 1916, Canada  — George VI, 1937, proof  — Elizabeth II, 1958

Elizabeth II, 1989, proof  — Elizabeth II, 2021, proof  — Charles III, 2024, proof

17-19 MADDOX STREET, LONDON, W1S 2QH
TEL: +44 (0)20 3019 1185   INFO@SOVR.CO.UK

WWW.SOVR.CO.UK

PAUL DAVIES

— WE STILL NEED TO BUY —

WORLD GOLD COINS
MODERN BRITISH GOLD AND SILVER
PROOF COINS
WE ARE ALWAYS KEEN TO BUY ALL DATES
OF PROOF SOVEREIGNS

PLEASE CONTACT US IF YOU HAVE ANYTHING TO SELL

PAUL DAVIES

PO BOX 17, ILKLEY, WEST YORKSHIRE, LS29 8TZ, ENGLAND
PHONE: 01943 603116 | Email: paul@pauldaviesltd.co.uk

LIFE MEMBER

Regular Exhibitor at U.K Coin Fairs

BNTA

WORLD & ANCIENT COINS

Heritage Brings Top Prices for Gold Sovereigns

Australia: Victoria gold Proof Pattern
Sovereign 1853-SYDNEY
PR63 Ultra Cameo NGC
Realized $384,000

Australia: George V gold
Sovereign 1920-S
MS64+ NGC
Realized $552,000

Canada: George V gold
Sovereign 1916-C
MS66 PCGS
Realized $156,000

Great Britain: George III gold
Proof Pattern 5 Pounds 1820
PR63+★ Ultra Cameo NGC
Realized $504,000

Great Britain: Victoria gold
Proof "Una and the Lion"
5 Pounds 1839
PR66★ Ultra Cameo NGC
Realized $1,440,000

Great Britain: Victoria gold
"Shield" Sovereign 1841
MS65+ PCGS
Realized $96,000

Great Britain: George VI gold Matte
Proof Sovereign 1937
PR64 PCGS
Realized $72,000

Great Britain: Edward VIII gold
Proof Pattern 5 Pounds 1937
PR67 Ultra Cameo NGC
Realized $2,280,000

South Africa: George V gold
Sovereign 1923-SA
MS66 PCGS
Realized $52,800

Inquiries: Heritage Auctions UK, Ltd.
+44 (0)207 493 0498 | HA.com/UK or UK@HA.com

DALLAS | NEW YORK | BEVERLY HILLS | CHICAGO | PALM BEACH
LONDON | PARIS | GENEVA | BRUSSELS | AMSTERDAM | HONG KONG | TOKYO

Always Accepting Quality Consignments in 50+ Categories
Immediate Cash Advances Available
1.75 Million+ Online Bidder-Members

HERITAGE AUCTIONS
THE WORLD'S LARGEST NUMISMATIC AUCTIONEER

BP 20%; see HA.com 74771

COLIN COOKE

P.O. Box 602, Altrincham WA14 5UN
Telephone: 0161 927 9524
website: www.colincooke.com   email: coins@colincooke.com

Please get in touch to request a complimentary copy of our monthly illustrated sales list and separate Farthing List

www.colincooke.com

Colin Cooke Coins is founded on long-established traditions of honesty, integrity and accurate grading of merchandise, always dedicated to total customer satisfaction.

PLEASE GET IN TOUCH IF YOU HAVE ANY COINS TO SELL OR REQUIRE FURTHER INFORMATION

CHARDS
COIN AND BULLION DEALER
— SINCE 1964 —

Why Choose Us?

60 Years Experience

After sixty prosperous years, you can be reassured that you are dealing with a business that is here to stay.

Family Business

We pride ourselves in providing a level of service that's tailored to you, with care, attention and the highest ethical standards that a corporate body cannot always match.

LBMA Full Member

The LBMA govern the London Bullion Market, the world's largest precious metals market. As full members with global partners, we commit to secure and ethical transactions.

Fully Insured

Our specialist insurance through Lloyd's of London covers against any potential risks associated with orders, deliveries and our vaulting service giving customers peace of mind.

UK Showrooms

Strategically positioned in London's Hatton Garden and Blackpool's South Shore, our offices offer personalised, face-to-face consultations in two locations.

Auditing & Accounts

In partnership with Azets, a top 10 UK auditor, we provide third-party verification of our financials and vaulted assets to deliver exemplary customer confidence.

01253 343081 · chards.co.uk · 32-36 Harrowside, Blackpool, Lancashire, FY4 1RJ

ST. JAMES'S AUCTIONS

0% COMMISSION
FOR LOTS THAT SELL FOR OVER £1000

SINGLE PIECES OR COLLECTIONS
PURCHASED OR FOR AUCTION
GENEROUS AND INTEREST FREE ADVANCES AVAILABLE

George III, SOVEREIGN 1818, GRADED MS64
SOLD JUNE 2024 FOR £25,200 (inc. Premium)

10 CHARLES II STREET, LONDON SW1Y 4AA
PHONE: +44(0)20 7930 7888
info@stjauctions.com | www.stjauctions.com

The Standard Catalogue of THE GOLD SOVEREIGN SERIES

by
Steve Hill
(based on the original by Michael A. Marsh)

Edited by Carol Hartman
and the Editorial Team
of COIN NEWS

TOKEN PUBLISHING LTD
Exeter

© 2024 Token Publishing Limited
8 Oaktree Place, Manaton Close, Matford Business Park, Exeter, Devon EX2 8WA

Telephone: 01404 46972
email: info@tokenpublishing.com
Website: http://www.tokenpublishing.com

All rights reserved.

The rights of Token Publishing Ltd to be identified as the publishers of this work has been asserted in accordance with section 77 and 78 of the Copyright, Design and Patents Act 1988.

No part of this publication may be reproduced, stored in a retrieval system or transmitted in any form or by any means, either electronic, mechanical, photocopying, recording or otherwise, without the prior permission of the publishers. Whilst every care has been taken in compiling this work, the publishers do not accept any responsibility for errors and omissions or for any consequences caused thereby.

First edition 1980
Second edition 1999
Jubilee edition 2002
Revised edition 2017
Second revised edition 2021
Third revised edition 2024

ISBN 978-1-908828-69-9

Printed in England by Short Run Press, Exeter

Dedicated
to
John W. Mussell

Contents

Acknowledgements	vi
Editor's Preface	vii
Abbreviations used in this edition	viii

THE "ORIGINAL" SOVEREIGN SERIES 1

THE SOVEREIGN 1
- Henry VII, 1485–1509 5
- Henry VIII, 1509–47 10
- Edward VI, 1547–53 14
- Mary, 1553–54 18
- Elizabeth I, 1558–1603 20
- James I, 1603–25 27

THE HALF-SOVEREIGN 31
- Henry VIII, 1509–47 32
- Edward VI, 1547–53 35
- James I, 1603–25 43

THE "MODERN" SOVEREIGN SERIES 45

THE FIVE POUNDS 49
- George III, 1760–1820 50
- George IV, 1820–1830 52
- Victoria, 1837–1901 54
- — Una and the Lion 54
- — Jubilee Head 58
- — Old or Veiled Head 60
- Edward VII, 1901–10 61
- George V, 1910–36 62
- Edward VIII, 1936 64
- George VI, 1936–52 65
- Elizabeth II, 1952–2022 66
- Charles III, 2022– 78

THE TWO POUNDS 81
- George III, 1760–1820 82
- George IV, 1820–30 84
- William IV, 1830–37 88
- Victoria, 1837–1901 90
- — Jubilee Head 91
- — Old or Veiled Head 93
- Edward VII, 1901–10 94
- George V, 1910–36 95
- Edward VIII, 1936 96
- George VI, 1936–52 97

THE TWO POUNDS continued
    Elizabeth II, 1952–2022.. 98
    Charles III, 2022– 109

THE SOVEREIGN 113
    George III, 1760–1820 115
    George IV, 1820–30 119
    William IV, 1830–37 125
    Victoria, 1837–190 131
    — Young Head Shield reverse 136
    — — Melbourne and Sydney Branch Mint Shield Sovereigns 146
    — — St George reverse. 152
    — — Sydney Branch Mint *AUSTRALIA* reverse 157
    — Jubilee Head 161
    — Old or Veiled Head 168
    Edward VII, 1901–10 173
    George V, 1910–36 181
    Edward VIII, 1936 193
    George VI, 1936–52. 194
    Elizabeth II, 1952–2022.. 197
    Charles III, 2022– 213
    — Struck on the day 217

THE HALF-SOVEREIGN 219
    George III, 1760–1820 221
    George IV, 1820–30 223
    William IV, 1830–37 228
    Victoria, 1837–1901. 231
    — Young Head Shield reverse 232
    — — Branch Mints 243
    — — *AUSTRALIA* reverse 245
    — Jubilee Head half-sovereigns 251
    — Old or Veiled Head 257
    Edward VII, 1901–10 263
    George V, 1910–36 268
    George VI, 1936–52. 275
    Elizabeth II, 1952–2022.. 277
    Charles III, 2022– 288

THE QUARTER-SOVEREIGN 292
    Elizabeth II, 1952–2022.. 293
    Charles III, 2022– 296

Finally 298
Engravers of the Sovereign.. 305
Bibliography 306
Addendum. The melting of gold sovereigns by the Bank of England in 1930–31 307

Acknowledgements

The publishers are deeply indebted to Steve Hill for his enthusiasm and expertise in compiling this third revised edition. Thanks are also due to the many collectors and dealers who have shared their knowledge to enable this publication to remain the most important source of information for the enthusiast as well as the beginner. We are also grateful to the following for their unstinting assistance with the information for this publication:

> Keith Bayford of KB Coins
> Dr Kevin Clancy of the Royal Mint
> Andrew Crellin of Sterling & Currency
> Paul Davies
> Eric Eigner of Drake Sterling Numismatics
> David Fletcher
> Howard Hodgson
> David Iverson
> Mark Rasmussen
> Dave Robinson
> Les Robinson of Top End Coins
> Dr K. A. Rodgers

Thanks are also due, alphabetically, for this new revised 2024 edition, to the following numismatists for a variety of reasons in their own areas of interest: Tony Davis, Geraint Evans, Dr Stewart Gilbert, James Korp, Andrew Leak, Cameron Maclean, Bernard Taylor, Alberto Tricca and Graham Warboys.

Our thanks are also due to the many auction houses and others who have allowed us to use their illustrations, especially Baldwins, Lawrence Chard, Noonans, Heritage Auctions, Sovereign Rarities, Spink (in particular for supplying rare images for the new Hammered section) and many others who prefer to remain anonymous.

Editor's preface to the third revised edition

Welcome to the third Token Publishing Ltd imprint of Michael Marsh's *The Gold Sovereign* and *The Gold Half Sovereign*, since 2017 published together as one volume.

These two books, first published in 1980, quickly became essential reference works in the numismatic world and have long been regarded as the most important resource on the gold Sovereign and Half Sovereign, not only the history of the coins, but their development numismatically with every variety, type, date and mintmark of the Sovereign and Half Sovereign since 1817 catalogued.

Over a period of nearly 30 years Michael ensured that all new strikes and newly discovered varieties were recorded making these books the most comprehensive of their type. Sadly, the author passed away in 2006 so the last available editions (posthumously published by Michael's wife Tessa in the year of his death) did not include any recent strikes, or indeed some of the stunning varieties that have come to light through such sales as the Bentley Collection in 2012/2013 and subsequently. To this end, when given the opportunity to reprint Michael's works, we approached an acknowledged expert to update and amend the original text; someone who could both correct any small errors that might have come to light thanks to recent discoveries and also ensure that all the new issues, and hitherto unknown variants, were covered. That expert was Steve Hill, formerly of Spink and Baldwin's (where he catalogued the superb Bentley Collection), and now of Sovereign Rarities Ltd. We are indebted to him for all his hard work on that first edition which, as far as was able, stuck to the author's original text, numbering system, et al—making it an update of a classic and not a brand new work. One new area was, of course, the inclusion Quarter Sovereigns that hadn't been in existence when Michael wrote the original works.

The second edition carried on in the same vein. However, this time around, Steve not only revised and checked the details on the Sovereigns, Half sovereigns and Quarters and included all the new strikes and varieties that had come to light, but he has also added two brand new sections. For the very first time, the Five Sovereign and Double Sovereign coins, with their own numbering system based on Marsh's original were included, making the book the definitive guide to the entire modern sovereign series from the Five down to the Quarter. Such was the impact of these additions that the book was awarded the International Association of Professional Numismatists (IAPN) Book of the Year in 2022.

Since publication of that second edition three years ago, a host of new strikes have come out of the Royal Mint in Llantrisant and, in addition, a large number of new varieties have surfaced. ALL are included in this new book.

However, it isn't only new "modern" Sovereigns that have a place in this third edition. For the very first time, the book goes back to where it all began—to 1489, the reign of King Henry VII and the striking of the very first coin to bear the name "Sovereign". Now, at last, every coin (excluding some patterns) that have used the moniker "Sovereign" somewhere in its name in the past 535 years is featured, making this truly the "Standard Catalogue" to the Gold Sovereign Series.

We have, once again, also included a separate price guide, something Michael did not have in the original work, but which has proved popular. It is important to note though that valuations are not this book's primary function as prices, especially of gold, do vary and we recommend that for a more in-depth look at coin values, readers consult the COIN YEARBOOK, published by Token Publishing Ltd. As pricing can be a minefield, we have endeavoured to help collectors gauge the value of their collection even if no up-to-date price guide is available, giving each of the coins listed in this volume a rarity code. That rarity scale is something that Michael did include in the original books, and it is as used and trusted today as it was over four decades ago.

Eagle-eyed readers will note that the numbers used, although still consistent with the Marsh original, are now referred to as the Hill numbers. Steve has worked tirelessly on these books over the past eight years and has added so much to them that it is fair to say this new edition is more his work than Michael's. We will always be indebted to Michael, his name will always be associated with the book, however, the work as it stands simply could not have happened without Steve's efforts, and that deserves to be acknowledged; indeed, we note a number of leading auction houses are already referring to "Hill" number in their catalogues.

Abbreviations used in this publication

Numismatic terms used

VF and EF are accepted UK coin grades for Very Fine and Extremely Fine
Obv. Obverse
Rev. Reverse

Mintmarks

I	Bombay (India) Branch Mint	M	Melbourne (Australia) Branch Mint
C	Ottawa (Canada) Branch Mint	S	Sydney (Australia) Branch Mint
SA	South Africa Branch Mint	P	Perth (Australia) Mint

Reference numbers used:

DISH   David Iverson and Steve Hill (*The Jubilee Head Gold Sovereign 1887–1893* by David Iverson, edited by Steve Hill, Baldwins, 2015, updated Sovereign Rarities 2018). Or any of the Jubilee Head publications by David Iverson, edited by Steve Hill. (*The Jubilee Head Gold Half-Sovereign*, published by Sovereign Rarities 2019, *The Jubilee Head Gold Two Pounds of 1887*, published by Sovereign Rarities 2020.

L&S   Linecar and Stone (*English Proof and Pattern Crown Size Pieces 1658–1960*) by Howard W. A. Linecar and Alex G. Stone, published by Spink 1968.

M   Michael Marsh (*The Gold Sovereign*).

WR   Wilson and Rasmussen (*English Pattern Trial and Proof Coins in Gold 1547–1968* by Alex Wilson and Mark Rasmussen, Alexander Publishing, 2000).

In the tables the following letters have been used to indicate the rarity rating:

C3	Extremely common
C2	Very common
C	Common
N	Normal
S	Scarce
R	Rare
R2	Very rare
R3	Extremely rare
R4	11–20 examples estimated to have survived
R5	5–10 examples estimated to have survived
R6	3 or 4 examples known to exist
R7	1 or 2 examples known to exist

Legends that appear on the coins in various forms—these all translate as King (or Queen) of All the Britons By the Grace of God, Defender of the Faith, Emperor (or Empress) of India:

DEI GRATIA
D:G:BRITANNIAR:REX F:D:
D:G:BRITT:REG:F:D:
BRITANNIARUM REGINA FID: DEF:
DEI.GRA.BRITT.REGINA.FID.DEF.IND.IMP.
D:G:BR:OMN:REX:F:D:IND:IMP:

The following initials sometimes appear on the coin as described in the text, with or without stops:

BM	Edgar Bertram Mackennal		MG	Mary Gillick
BP	Benedetto Pistrucci		MJ	Martin Jennings
DeS	George William De Saulles		PJD	Paul Day
HP	Thomas Humphrey Paget		RDM	Raphel David Maklouf
IRB	Ian Rank-Broadley		TB	Thomas Brock
JBM	Jean Baptiste Merlen		TN	Timothy Noad
JEB	Joseph Edgar Boehm		WW	William Wyon
JC	Jody Clark		WWP	William Wellesley Pole

THE "ORIGINAL" SOVEREIGN SERIES

THE SOVEREIGN

The first time the name "Sovereign" was used for a denomination of currency in England was during the reign of Henry VII (1485–1509). We know that during Henry's reign there were in fact five different varieties of gold coins struck called sovereigns, and we are indebted to a fine paper by Professor Philip Grierson that was published in the *British Numismatic Journal* of 1964 which reveals much about these coins.[1] It also tells us which was the earliest, and thus the first of our gold coins to bear the name of "sovereign" (pictured above[2]). This query had arisen because none of the five types struck bore a date, as was usual in the 15th century.

For some 500 years before Henry VII the coinage had consisted almost entirely of silver pennies and 240 of them weighed one pound, known as the pound sterling. During this period attempts were made to establish a gold coinage and in 1344 Edward III issued the gold double florin with a value of 6 shillings, together with the florin and the half florin, but this was superseded later the same year by the noble valued at 6 shillings and 8 pence (6*s*. 8*d*.), accompanied by its halves and quarters.

In 1465 during the reign of Edward IV the noble was replaced by the angel, also valued at 6*s*. 8*d*., and the short-lived ryal of 10 shillings was also introduced, together with its halves and quarters, although it only lasted until the end of the reign. Thus the angel remained the only English gold coin until the reign of Henry VII when the new English sovereign came into existence by a Royal commission dated October 28, 1489. This instructed the Mint to strike a gold double ryal worth 20*s*. which would be called a sovereign. Each would be struck in 240 grains (15.55 grams or 0.5 troy ounces) of .995 fine gold alloy.

The sovereign marked a new era in English coinage, both in its size and because for the first time the pound sterling was presented as a single coin. The obverse of the sovereign features the King seated facing on a Gothic throne and holding in his hands an orb and sceptre. The legends on these coins reads variations of HENRIC DI GRA REX ANGLIE ET FRANC DNS IBAR (which translates as "Henry by the Grace of God King of England and France, Lord of Ireland"). The reverse depicts a large double rose having on it the royal escutcheon bearing the arms of France and England quarterly, and surrounded by the legend IHS AUTEM TRANSIENS PER MEDIUM ILLORUM IBAT (which translates as "Jesus passing through their midst went His way").

The Mint engraver at this time was Michael Flynt and so it is likely that the first new sovereign was his design and work, although the design of the new coin has been commonly credited to a Flemish engraver: Alexandre de Bruchsells. He was undoubtedly responsible for some innovative coin designs introduced by Henry VII. However, as the late Howard Linecar pointed out, Bruchsells was appointed as engraver at the Dutch mint in 1494 while the sovereign commenced issue five years earlier. At best Bruchsells' contribution may have been to improve renderings of the original design used on Henry's later sovereign issues. Nevertheless, without doubt it must be said the first sovereign is rich in beauty and is a magnificent example from the Tudor period. It is also of the highest rarity because it is the only known example of its kind. Since 1915 the coin has been in the British Museum collection.

The other four sovereigns struck for Henry are all of similar design but the fifth and final type shows a portcullis, symbol of the House of Beaufort, beneath the feet of the enthroned monarch. Its presence stresses Henry's claim to the English crown through his mother, Margaret Beaufort, great-granddaughter of John of Gaunt, the third of five surviving sons of Edward III. This basic design would change little on most of the sovereigns struck by Henry's successors.

Henry VIII included the sovereign as part of his first coinage in 1509. He continued the same design style and value as those of his father, i.e. 15.55g of .995 fine gold.

The quality of early Tudor gold was such that there was a steady outflow across the Channel to Europe. In order to limit this drain on the country's finances, the face value of all gold coins was increased by 10 per cent in 1526. This made the sovereign worth 22 shillings. A few months later it was revalued further to 22 shillings 6 pence.

The latter portion of Henry's reign saw the open debasing of English gold and silver coinage to supply the king with the finance for his wars and lifestyle. The gold denominations suffered less than the silver.

In 1544 the gold fineness of the 20 shillings sovereign was reduced to .958 and its weight to 12.96g. In subsequent years the weight was cut further to 12.44g and the fineness lowered first to 0.917 and then 0.833.

Henry's debased sovereigns can be readily recognised. On the reverse the shield-on-Tudor-rose is replaced by the royal arms with lion and dragon supporters and the monogram "HR" in a panel below.

Throughout the years of Edward VI's reign his advisors, led by John Dudley, Duke of Northumberland, sought to redress his father's coin debasements. The silver coins were their primary concern so from 1547 to 1551 Henry's debased gold coins continued to be struck. Among these posthumous issues was a .833 fine sovereign. Edward's first coinage in his own name included a 6.22g half sovereign denominated as 10 shillings, but not a sovereign.

From 1549 to 1550 an 11.01g 0.917 fine 20 shillings sovereign was struck showing Edward enthroned. He wears doublet and hose instead of robes and holds a sword instead of a sceptre. The reverse continues to bear the Royal arms and supporters as is the case for all of Edward's later sovereigns.

In 1550 a full weight, 15.55g sovereign was produced struck in .995 fine gold and denominated as 30 shillings. This revaluation was necessary to approximately relate the intrinsic value of the coin's gold to that of the debased silver. Again the King was shown enthroned on the obverse. These coins are extremely rare.

Subsequently an 11.01g .917 fine gold 20 shillings sovereign was issued alongside the 30 shillings. The obverse design was innovative. Edward is shown as a half-length profile figure, crowned, in armour and holding a sword. The contrasting obverse designs ensured there was no confusion as to the face value of either sovereign.

With the reign of Edward local mints ceased to operate and henceforth all English gold and silver would be struck at the Tower Mint with the exception of the period of the Civil War and during the Great Recoinage of 1816.

Queen Mary issued a single, full weight, 15.55g sovereign struck in .995 fine gold. Like her brother's corresponding coin it was also valued at 30 shillings. Mary's are the only Tudor sovereigns to be dated: MDLIII and MDLIIII although some are undated. During her joint reign with her husband Philip of Spain no sovereigns were struck.

THE ORIGINAL SOVEREIGN

Henry VIII second coinage sovereign of 20s 6d.

Henry VIII debased third coinage sovereign.

Edward VI second period sovereign.

Edward VI third period sovereign.

Mary's sovereign of 30 shillings.

Elizabeth I sovereign of 30 shillings.

(Images are not shown to scale.)

One of Elizabeth's first acts on ascending to the throne was to complete the returning of the nation's coinage to the standards set by her grandfather, Henry VII. She did so despite both active and passive opposition from members of her Council who no doubt appreciated this policy could impact on their own wealth.

As with Edward's advisors Elizabeth realised that no permanent change could be achieved until all the debased silver was stripped from circulation. It was to this end she directed her primary efforts.

In her gold issues she set in stone the distinctions begun under Edward VI between .995 "Fine Gold" coins and those struck in "Crown Gold" of .917 fineness.

This saw the production of the full weight, 15.55g Fine Gold sovereign initially denominated as 30 shillings circulating alongside an 11.01g 20 shillings struck in Crown Gold and termed a "pound".

Elizabeth was the last Tudor monarch. With her death James VI of Scotland's House of Stuart acceded to the English throne in 1603 as James I of England. As a consequence James did not rock the boat but for his first issues continued the same denominations, standards and fineness as those of Elizabeth. This first issue included an 11.01g Crown Gold 20 shillings sovereign.

This coin and its accompanying half-sovereign and half-crown would be the first gold coins of England to show the monarch styled as: ANG . SCO. FRAN. ET . HIB . REX [King of England, Scotland, &c]. On the reverse the Royal Arms were amended to incorporate the Scottish lion rampant and the Irish harp in the second and third quarters.

Only in the second year of his reign did James restyle himself: MAG . BRIT. FRAN . ET, HIBER . REX [King of Great Britain &c]. This second style would never make it to a sovereign. After 115 years James' first and only sovereign would be the last struck until the coin re-emerged in 1817 in heavily modified form.

For a more in-depth coverage of the history of the sovereign, the reader is referred to the excellent Royal Mint publication *The History of the Sovereign, Chief Coin of the World* by Dr Kevin Clancy.[3]

Four sovereigns of Henry VII which were issued in quick succession after the first was struck in 1489.

Notes/References
1. Professor Philip Grierson, "The Origin of the English Sovereign and the Symbolism of the Closed Crown", *British Numismatic Journal*, London 1964, pp. 118–34.
2. Courtesy of Trustees of The British Museum.
3. Dr Kevin Clancy, *The History of the Sovereign, Chief Coin of the World*, Royal Mint, 2016.

HENRY VII (1485–1509)

The first gold Sovereign was struck in fine gold of 23 carats 3 ½ grains, at a 20 Shilling face value and full weight of 15.552g; all coins were struck at the Royal Mint within the Tower of London. Sovereign production commenced from October 28, 1489, but no accounts were made for five years so more accurate dates and outputs are unknown for type I and II.

Type I commenced from October 28, 1489.

Type II commenced circa November 1492.

Type III is issued from Spring 1493 to Autumn of 1495.

Type IV with mintmark dragon on reverse is issued from Michaelmas 1502 to Spring of 1504.

Type V with mintmark crosslet on reverse from Spring 1504 to circa November 1505 and with mintmark pheon reverse from November 20, 1505 to April 1509.

Description and details of Henry VII sovereign, type I

Obverse: Full body figure of King, crowned and robed, seated facing on wood throne, holding orb and sceptre, crown with jewelled arches breaking inner beaded circle, mint mark cinquefoil and legend in surrounding Latin, HENRIC DI GRA REX ANGL z FRANC z DNS IBARNE.

Reverse: Jewelled arched crown with cross and fleur de lis ornaments, over quartered shield of English lions and fleur de lis, upon Tudor rose with small leaves, beaded circles and legend with mint mark cinquefoil surrounding reads IHS AVTE TRANCIES PER MEDIV ILLORV IBAT.
See H1 in tabulation.

Description and details of Henry VII sovereign, type II

Obverse: Full body figure of King, crowned and robed, seated facing on low back throne, holding orb and sceptre, diapered background of fleur de lis, arched crown with top cross breaking inner beaded circle, legend surrounding in Latin, HENRICVS DI GRACIA REX ANGLIE ET FRANC DNS IBAR.

Reverse: Quartered shield of English lions and fleur de lis, upon Tudor rose with leaves, all upon ten arc tressure, English lion and French fleur de lis in alternate spandrels, beaded circles and legend with mint mark cross fitchee surrounding reads IHS AVTEM TRANSCIENS PER MEDIVM ILLORVM IBATHE.
See H2 in tabulation.

Description and details of Henry VII sovereign, type III

Obverse: Full body figure of King, crowned with flowing robe, holding orb and sceptre, seated facing on ornate wide throne with high back and greyhound and dragon on side pillars, nine fleur de lis around perimeter of throne, single arched crown with top cross intruding inner beaded circle, legend of tall letters surrounding in Latin with mint mark dragon, HENRICVS DEI GRACIA REX ANGLIE ET FRANCIE DNS IBAR.

Reverse: Quartered shield of English lions and fleur de lis, upon multi lobed Tudor rose with large leaves, all upon ten arc tressure, English lion and French fleur de lis in alternate spandrels, beaded circles and legend with mint mark dragon surrounding reads IHESVS AVTEM TRANSIENS PER MEDIVM ILLORVM IBAT.

See H3 in tabulation.

Description and details of Henry VII sovereign, type IV

Obverse: Full body figure of King, crowned and robed, holding orb and sceptre, seated facing on large ornate wide throne with high back canopy that reaches toward rim of coin at top, 11 fleur de lis around perimeter of throne, beaded circle and legend surrounding in Latin with mint mark lis, HENRICVS DEI GRA REX ANGL ET FRAN DNS HIBN.

Reverse: Quartered shield of English lions and fleur de lis, upon multi lobed Tudor rose with large leaves, all upon ten arc tressure, English lion and French fleur de lis in alternate spandrels, beaded circles and legend with mint mark dragon surrounding reads IHESVS AVTEM TRANSIENS PER MEDIVM ILLORVM IBAT.
See H4–H5 in tabulation.

Description and details of Henry VII sovereign, type V

Obverse: Full body figure of King, crowned and robed, holding orb and sceptre, seated facing on throne with ornate back and wide cross topped pillars either side, chained portcullis below King's feet to bottom of coin, roped circle surrounds design with trefoil alternating with pellet decoration, single arched crown and cross intrudes legend surrounding in Latin with mint mark lis, HENRICVS DEI GRACIA REX ANGLIE ET FRANC DNS HIB.

Reverse: Quartered shield of English lions and fleur de lis, upon multi lobed Tudor rose with large leaves, all upon ten arc scrolled tressure, roped circles and legend with mint mark crosslet or pheon surrounding reads IHESVS AVTEM TRANSIENS PER MEDIVM ILLORVM IBAT.
See H6–H10 in tabulation.

For all types I to V—the abbreviated Latin legends translate as on obverse: Henry by the Grace of God, King of England and France, Lord of Ireland.

On the reverse: But Jesus, passing through the midst of them, went His way (Luke 4:30 from the Bible).

The mintmark of dragon that appears in types III and IV was reserved exclusively for use on the gold Sovereign denomination.

For further reading on the dawn of the English Sovereign see "The Coinage of Henry VII" part 3 by W. J. W. Potter and E. J. Winstanley, *British Numismatic Journal* 1963 Volume 32 and "The Origins of the English Sovereign and the Symbolism of the Closed Crown" by Philip Grierson, *British Numismatic Journal* 1964 Volume 33, both available to read at www.britnumsoc.org.

For further reading on the entire run of hammered Sovereigns and Half-Sovereigns see *The Herbert Schneider Collection of English Gold Coins* volumes one 1257–1603, and two 1603–20th Century by Peter Woodhead, published by Spink.

SOVEREIGNS OF HENRY VII, 1485–1509

Type V sovereign (image courtesy of Spink).

SOVEREIGNS OF HENRY VII

No.	Descriptive comments	Rarity	Dating and/or rarity
H1	Type I arched crown on head mm cinquefoil	R7	1489 Unique in British Museum
H2	Type II mm cross fitchee	R6	1492 2 in Museums, 2 held privately
H3	Type III mm dragon	R4	1493–95 16 known to Potter & Winstanley in 1963 (P&W)
H4	Type IV mm lis obv., mm dragon rev.	R3	1502–04 19 known to P&W
H5*	Type IV same mint marks but with no obv. inner circle	R7	only one known to P&W
H6	Type V mm lis obverse, mm crosslet rev.	R5	1505–09 9 with crosslet known to P&W
H7	Type V Piedfort Double Sovereign mm lis / crosslet	R7	unique weight circa 30g
H8	Type V Piedfort Treble Sovereign mm lis / crosslet	R7	unique weight 51.10g
H9	Type V mm lis obverse, mm pheon rev.	R4	1505–09 6 with pheon known to P&W
H10	Type V Piedfort Double Sovereign mm lis / pheon	R7	unique weight 30.46g

* This variety H5 noted by Potter and Winstanley was later written up as invalid in the 1972 *British Numismatic Journal* by the late Ian Stewart (later Lord Stewartby) in a short note on page 181, having examined this coin in the British Museum Collection, he concluded the coin had been doctored to erase the inner circle.

H prefix = Hammered Sovereign; "mm" = mint mark; "obv." = obverse; "rev." = reverse

HENRY VIII (1509–47)

The fine gold Sovereign continues through the first two coinages of Henry VIII and then progresses through a period of gradual debasement in the three year, third coinage in the twilight of his reign.

First Coinage 1509–26—accurate dating of the Sovereign within this period is unknown.

Struck at the Royal Mint within the Tower of London in fine gold at 20 Shillings face value and full weight 15.552g—Similar to type V of Henry VII.

Second Coinage 1526–44

Struck at the Royal Mint within the Tower of London in fine gold at 22 Shillings and Sixpence face value and full weight 15.552g.

Third Coinage 1544–47

There was a reorganisation at the Royal Mint within the Tower from 1544 splitting coin production across two separate workshops known as Tower I (Under-treasurer Sir Martin Bowes) and Tower II (Under-treasurer Thomas Knight) both of which struck gold, though there does not seem to be a differentiation between the Tower issues to tell which Sovereign is from which workshop, though in the succeeding reign of Edward VI, the Sovereign only comes from Tower I as the mint marks are separately assigned according to the minting hub.

From 1545 minting activity commences at Southwark (Under-treasurer Sir John York) in southeast London, for the first time since the time of the Norman Kings; and latterly from 1546 at the major English port of Bristol with Under-treasurer Sir William Sharington, whose initials WS appear ligatured together as its mint mark.

Dating for the mints and debasement:

An indenture for Tower I and Tower II to coin 22 carat gold was issued on March 27, 1545.

A commission for the mint of Southwark was issued on September 6, 1545 to coin 22 carat gold.

Indentures are issued on April 1, 1546 for Tower I, Tower II, Southwark and Bristol to issue gold at 20 carat fineness.

Third coinage, type I Sovereign—struck at Tower of London in 23 carat gold at 20 Shillings face value, on a large module flan at a full weight of 12.96g in 1544.

Third coinage, type II Sovereigns—Tower, Southwark and Bristol mints—struck in varying carat of gold as debased period comes into force, from 23 to 22 to as low as 20 carats and full weight decreasing from 12.96g to 12.44g (weight and fineness split as Type IIa and IIb).

For further reading on the gold of Henry VIII, see "The Coinages of Henry VIII and Edward VI" by C. A. Whitton, available to read at www.britnumsoc.org.

Description and details of Henry VIII sovereign, First Coinage

Obverse: Full body figure of King, crowned and robed, holding orb and sceptre, seated facing on throne with ornate back and wide cross topped pillars either side, chained portcullis below King's feet to bottom of coin, multi arc tressure surrounds design with trefoils on cusps and pellets in spandrels, single arched crown and cross intrudes legend surrounding in Latin with mint mark crowned portcullis with chains, HENRICVS DEI GRACIA REX ANGLIE ET FRANC DNS HIB.

Reverse: Quartered shield of English lions and fleur de lis, upon multi lobed Tudor rose with large leaves, all upon ten arc beaded and linear double tressure, English lion and fleur de lis in alternate spandrels, roped circles and legend with mint mark crowned portcullis with chains surrounding reads, IHESVS AVTEM TRANSIENS PER MEDIVM ILLORVM IBAT.

See H11 in tabulation.

Description and details of Henry VIII sovereign, Second Coinage
Obverse: Full body figure of King, crowned and robed, holding orb and sceptre, seated facing on throne with ornate back and wide cross topped pillars either side, chained portcullis below King's feet to bottom of coin, multi arc tressure surrounds design with trefoils on cusps and pellets in spandrels, single arched crown and cross intrudes legend surrounding in Latin with mint mark sunburst or lis, HENRICVS DEI GRACIA REX ANGLIE ET FRANC DNS HIB.
Reverse: Quartered shield of English lions and fleur de lis, upon multi lobed Tudor rose with large leaves, all upon ten arc beaded and linear double tressure, English lion and fleur de lis in alternate spandrels, roped circles and legend with mint mark sunburst, lis or arrow surrounding reads IHESVS AVTEM TRANSIENS PER MEDIVM ILLORVM IBAT.
See H12–H14 in tabulation.

Description and details of Henry VIII sovereign, Third Coinage—Type I
Obverse: Full body figure of King, with large bearded head, crowned and robed, holding orb and sceptre, seated facing on throne with ornate back and wide cross topped pillars either side, rose below King's feet to bottom of coin, multi arc tressure surrounds design with trefoils on cusps and pellets in spandrels, single arched crown and cross intrudes legend surrounding in Latin with mint mark lis, HENRIC 8 DI GRA ANGLIE FRANCIE ET HIBE REX.
Reverse: Crowned quartered shield of arms with alternating English lions and fleur de lis, crowned lion supporter to left, dragon supporter to right, HR ligatured on banner below, arch of crown and cross breaks inner roped circle toward top of coin, legend with mint mark lis surrounding reads IHESVS AVTEM TRANSIENS PER MEDIVM ILLORV IBAT.
See H15 in tabulation.

Description and details of Henry VIII sovereign, Third Coinage—Type II
Obverse: Full body figure of King, with in proportion thinner bearded head, crowned and robed, holding orb and sceptre, seated facing on throne with ornate back and bird-like wide lis topped pillars either side, rose below King's feet to bottom of coin, single arched crown and cross intrudes legend surrounding in Latin with mint mark (lis, pellet in annulet, S, E or WS ligatured), HENRIC 8 DI GRA AGL FRANCIE ET HIBERN REX (or similar).
Reverse: Crowned quartered shield of arms with alternating English lions and fleur de lis, crowned lion supporter to left, dragon supporter to right, HR ligatured on banner below, arch of crown and cross breaks inner roped circle toward top of coin, legend surrounding with same mint mark as obverse reads IHS AVTEM TRANSIENS PER MEDIVM ILLOR IBAT.
See H16–H24 in tabulation.

Third Coinage Tower type II
Sovereign mm lis.

SOVEREIGNS OF HENRY VIII, 1509–47

Third Coinage Southwark
mm S both sides.

Legend translations—the abbreviated Latin legends translate as on obverse: Henry by the grace of God, King of England and France, Lord of Ireland, for first two coinages. Third coinage changes to Henry the Eighth by the grace of God, King of England, France and Ireland in reaction to the passing of the Crown of Ireland Act in 1542.

On the reverse: But Jesus, passing through the midst of them, went His way (Luke 4:30 from the Bible).

SOVEREIGNS OF HENRY VIII

No.	Descriptive comments	Rarity	Dating and/or rarity
H11	First coinage mm crowned portcullis	R3	issued within 1509–26
H12	Second coinage mm sunburst	R7	issued 1537–38
H13	Second coinage mm lis	R2	issued 1538–41
H14	Second coinage mm lis obv., with mm arrow rev.	R3	issued 1541–42
H15	Third Coinage Type I Tower, large module, full round face mm large lis	R5	issued 1544
H16	Third Coinage Type IIa Tower, small module, mm small lis, 23 carat 12.96g	R4	issued 1544–47
H17	Third Coinage Type IIb Tower, mm lis, 22 or 20 carat, 12.44g, trefoil stops*	R2	1544–47
H18	Third Coinage Type IIb Tower, mm lis, 22 or 20 carat, 12.44g, sleeve stops*	R2	1544–47
H19	Third Coinage Type IIb Tower mm pellet in annulet, rev. lis, 12.44g	R5	1544–47
H20	Third Coinage Southwark mm S, trefoil stops	N	issued 1545–47
H21	Third Coinage Southwark mm S obv. / mm E rev. E below shield	R5	issued 1545–47
H22	Third Coinage Southwark mm E obv. / mm S rev	R5	issued 1545–47
H23	Third Coinage Southwark mm E, with E below rev. shield, sleeve stops**	S	issued 1545–47
H24	Third Coinage Bristol mm WS ligatured obv. only, trefoil stops	R5	issued 1547

* Examples of these coins occasionally turn up with the stops in the legend muled, meaning with trefoils one side and sleeves on the other, for which two obv./rev. combinations are therefore possible.
** The letter E mint mark and E below shield are Gothic style with rounded backs.

EDWARD VI (1547–53)

This reign commences with a posthumous coinage still in the name of his Father.

Posthumous issue in the name of Henry VIII from 1547—struck at 20 carats gold and 20 Shillings face value, full weight of 12.44g. There is a brief Posthumous Coinage of gold Sovereigns at the Tower of London and Bristol mints of the same design format as the last Henry VIII Type II, H25 and H26 respectively, but both mint issues defined by having Roman uppercase lettering. The Tower mint Sovereign having a lis florencée mint mark (lis with feelers projecting each side) which was only used for this senior denomination. This posthumous coinage continues through the first period of coinage in the reign of Edward VI from April 1547 to January 1549. See H25–H26 in tabulation.

Second Period coinage January 1549 to April 1550—Sovereigns struck at Tower I or Southwark according to mint marks used at 22 carat fineness and 20 Shillings face value, full weight 10.977g. See H27–H30 in tabulation.

Third Period coinage 1550–53

A dual coinage of Sovereigns coexist within this period with Edward's continuing efforts to restore the fineness to the coinage. A fine gold issue of Sovereigns in 23 carat gold at a face value of 30 Shillings and the traditional full weight of 15.55g, of a similar design to his Father's earliest issue and Grandfather's Sovereigns, of which there are records of the King using as coins for presentation and payment in his progress around England, as listed by Christopher Challis in his book "Tudor Coinage". See H31–H33 in tabulation.

The other lighter weight, lower fineness issue is the "crown" gold issue in 22 carat of a gold Sovereign of 20 Shillings face value and full weight of 11.31g.

The Bristol Mint having disposed of William Sharington in December 1548 for embezzlement, (replaced by Sir Thomas Chamberlain from January), ceased production by October 1549 and was closed on March 25, 1550 (Lady Day). The Southwark Mint closes in August 1551, and a commission of October 1551 unifies Tower II with Tower I, with Tower II ceasing production and defunct as of the Spring of 1552. The only other mint to produce gold coins but not Sovereigns, is the Durham House Mint in London off the Strand (Under-Treasurer Sir Martin Bowes), which commenced production in January 1549, but had likely closed by December of that year, the records for which do not survive. Therefore, by the end of this reign only the Royal Mint in the Tower of London was in operation.

Description and details of Edward VI sovereign, Second Period

Obverse: Full body figure of crowned boy King facing seated on throne with wide cherub topped side pillars with floor depicted at feet, all within linear circle with legend surrounding, mint mark arrow, none or Y, EDWARD VI DEI GRA AGL FRAN ET HIB REX or similar.

Reverse: Crowned quartered shield of arms with alternating English lions and fleur de lis, crowned lion supporter to left, dragon supporter to right, ER ligatured on banner below, roped circle and legend surrounding with mint mark arrow or Y reads IHS AVTEM TRANSIENS PER MEDIVM ILLOR IBAT.

See H27–H30 in tabulation.

Description and details of Edward VI sovereign, Third Period— Fine gold Thirty Shilling Sovereign at 23 carats and full weight 15.552g

Obverse: Full body figure of King, crowned and robed, holding orb and sceptre, seated facing on throne with ornate back and wide decorated lis topped pillars either side, portcullis below King's feet to bottom of coin, multi arc tressure surrounds design with trefoils on cusps and pellets in spandrels, single arched crown and cross intrudes legend surrounding in Latin with mint mark ostrich head or tun, EDWARD VI D G ANGLIE FRANCIE Z HIBERNIE REX.

Reverse: Quartered shield of English lions and fleur de lis, upon Tudor rose with large leaves, all upon ten arc beaded and linear double tressure, lis at each cusp, roped circles and legend with mint mark ostrich head or tun surrounding reads IHESV AVTEM TRANSIENS PER MEDIVM ILLORVM IBAT. The mint mark ostrich head was used exclusively for this fine gold coinage which also included Angels and is thought could be a rebus for the High Treasurer Sir Edmund Peckham.

See H31–H33 in tabulation.

THE GOLD SOVEREIGN SERIES

Description and details of Edward VI sovereign, Third Period—Crown gold Twenty Shilling Sovereign at 22 carats and full weight 11.314g

Obverse: Half-length armoured crowned King facing right, holding orb and sword upright with blade resting on shoulder, all within linear and beaded circle with legend surrounding, mint mark y or tun at top with legend reading EDWARD VI D G AGL FRAN Z HIB REX.

Reverse: Crowned quartered shield of arms with alternating English lions and fleur de lis, crowned lion supporter to left, dragon supporter to right, ER ligatured on banner below, roped circle and legend surrounding with mint mark Y or tun reads IHS AVTEM TRANCI PER MEDI ILLOR IBAT or similar.

See H34–H35 in tabulation.

Third Period Sovereign with mm y.

Third Period Sovereign with mm tun.

Legend translations—the abbreviated Latin legends translate as on obverse: Edward the Sixth by the grace of God, King of England France and Ireland.

On the reverse: But Jesus, passing through the midst of them, went His way (Luke 4:30 from the Bible).

SOVEREIGNS OF EDWARD VI

No.	Descriptive comments	Rarity	Dating and/or rarity
H25	Posthumous Issue Tower mm lis florencée Roman lettering	R5	issued 1547–49
H26	Posthumous Issue Bristol mm WS ligatured Roman lettering, rosette stops	R5	issued 1547–49
H27	Second period, King seated facing on throne mm arrow, square pellet stops, 10.977g	S	issued 1549
H28	Second period, King seated facing on throne mm arrow rev. only	R2	issued 1549
H29	Second period, King seated facing on throne Southwark mm Y	S	issued 1549–50
H30	Second period, Treble Sovereign 3x weight 33g Southwark mm Y	R7	issued 1549–50
H31	Fine gold coinage mm ostrich head, 15.552g	R6	issued 1551
H32	Fine gold coinage piedfort Double Sovereign mm ostrich head	R7	issued 1551
H33	Fine gold coinage mm tun	R7	issued 1551-53
H34	Third period, Crown gold issue King half-length in armour mm tun*	N	issued 1550–53
H35	Third period, Crown gold issue King half-length in armour mm Y**	S	issued 1550–53

* this issue always seems to depict each of the crowned lion and dragon supporters with a phallus.

** Similarly to the above footnote, the mm Y pieces can have phallus' depicted on the supporters, but also without like all the second period Sovereigns with the same reverse design.

There exists a series of gold pattern coins of Edward VI of the same modular size (Half-Sovereign diameter) but of varying weights that equate with denominations of Sovereign, Half-Sovereign and Crown, plus some smaller module Halfcrowns. They all feature designs with the bare head cuirassed similar to that in the second period of his Half-Sovereign coinage, coupled with a reverse of a crowned Tudor rose with stem and leaves. The Sovereign weight design along with all the others are listed in *English Pattern Trial and Proof Coins in Gold 1547–1968* Wilson and Rasmussen, and the pattern for a Sovereign is number W. R. 3—unique in the Hunterian Museum Collection.

MARY (1553–54)

Mary 1553-dated fine Sovereign.

The reign of Mary Tudor sees only fine gold coinage issued, with the Sovereign denomination only in the period before her marriage to Philip of Spain, upon which, until the end of the reign, there is no coin larger than the gold Angel issued. Significantly, the first-dated Sovereigns appear in this reign, dated 1553 and much more rarely for 1554, the date appearing in Roman numerals at the end of the obverse legend. The fineness of the gold is restored to what it once was under her grandfather at 23 carats 3 ½ grains (0.995 fine) with the Sovereign at 30 Shillings and full weight of 15.552g.

SOVEREIGNS OF MARY, 1553–54

Description and details of Mary sovereign

Obverse: The design is similar to her predecessor's fine Sovereigns with a full body figure of Queen with eyes closed, crowned and robed, holding orb and sceptre, seated facing on throne with ornate back and wide decorated lis topped pillars either side, portcullis below the Queen's feet to bottom of coin, multi arc tressure surrounds design with trefoils on cusps and pellets in spandrels, arched crown and cross intrudes legend surrounding in Latin, with mint mark pomegranate or halved rose and castle after Queen's name, MARIA D G ANG FRA Z HIB REGINA MDLIII (or MDLIIII).

Reverse: Quartered shield of English lions and fleur de lis, upon full Tudor rose with large leaves, roped circles and legend surrounding with mint mark after DNO reads, A DNO FACTV EST ISTV Z EST MIRA IN OCVL NRIS, the types of stops and their formation can vary.

See H36–H39 in tabulation.

Mary 1554-dated fine Sovereign.

The abbreviated Latin legends translate as on obverse: Mary by the grace of God, Queen of England France and Ireland 1553 (or 1554).

On the reverse: This is the Lord's doing and it is marvellous in our eyes (Psalm 118.23 from the Bible).

SOVEREIGNS OF MARY

No.	Descriptive comments	Rarity
H36	1553 in Roman numerals mm pomegranate	S
H37	1553 in Roman numerals mm halved rose and castle obv., pomegranate rev.	R6
H38	1553 in Roman numerals mm halved rose and castle both sides	R5
H39	1554 in Roman numerals mm pomegranate	R5

ELIZABETH I (1558–1603)

Elizabeth I Second Issue fine Sovereign.

Queen Elizabeth I continues the fine gold coinage tradition by issuing a fine gold Sovereign at 30 Shillings face value and 15.552g full weight. This largest gold denomination is produced for the first two issues of coinage for this reign from 1558–62, and then has a break until the sixth issue from 1583–95 running through a total of seven mint marks across all three periods of issue.

For further detailed reading see "Notes on the Gold Coins of Elizabeth I" by Brown and Comber—*British Numismatic Journal Volume* 59, 1989; and for the catalogue of the most complete collection of these ever formed see the "George Holloway Collection of Fine Sovereigns of Elizabeth I", Dix Noonan and Webb Auction 198, November 17, 2021. Numismatist and friend, the late George Holloway, kept detailed notes on this specific series over 40 years of collecting only this denomination for this one reign, giving one of the most accurate reflections we have of true rarity from his census of surviving examples in museums and private collections, as well as revealing all die combinations and varieties, the majority of which are listed herewith.

Description and details of Elizabeth sovereign, First Issue—mint mark lis struck January 1, 1559 (1558 old style) to July 31, 1560

Obverse: Full body figure of Queen with eyes open, crowned and robed, holding orb and sceptre, seated facing on throne with ornate back consisting of a lattice with pellet in each compartment, with five pellet vertical upon each side bar, wide decorated lis topped pillars either side, portcullis below Queen's feet to bottom of coin, no side chains, multi arc tressure surrounds design with trefoils on cusps and pellets in spandrels, arched crown and cross intrudes legend surrounding in Latin with mint mark lis, ELIZABETH D G ANG FRA Z HIB REGINA.

Reverse: Quartered shield of English lions and fleur de lis, upon full Tudor rose with large leaves, roped circles and legend surrounding with mint mark lis, A DNO FACTV EST ISTV Z EST MIRA IN OCVL NRIS. The words MIRA, OCVL and NRIS can be further abbreviated see tabulation.
See H40 in tabulation.

For all this reign's issues the abbreviated Latin legends translate as on obverse: Elizabeth by the grace of God, Queen of England France and Ireland.

On the reverse: This is the Lord's doing and it is marvellous in our eyes (Psalm 118.23 from the Bible).

FIRST ISSUE SOVEREIGNS OF ELIZABETH I

No.	Descriptive comments	Rarity	Dating
H40	first issue mm lis, rev. legend with MIRA OCVL NRIS	R5	1558–60
H40A	first issue mm lis, rev. legend with MIRABI OCV NRIS	R6	1558–60
H40B	first issue mm lis, rev. legend with MIRABI OCV NRI	R7	1558–60

Note. The late George Holloway noted only eight examples of all three of these types seem to exist.

THE GOLD SOVEREIGN SERIES

Description and details of Elizabeth sovereign, Second Issue, mint mark crosslet struck December 1, 1560 to October 31, 1562

Obverse: Similar to first issue, whole crown on head now intrudes legend area, vertical side bars of throne back with larger pellets, portcullis below feet now with side chains and large ringlets, with substitution of the "Z" in legend each side with word "ET" and with chains added to the portcullis below the Queen's feet. Legend reads ELIZABETH D G ANG FRA ET HIBE REGINA.

Reverse: Some reuse of the first issue reverse die seen with overstruck mint mark variety. Of a similar design to first issue, legend reads DNO FACTV EST ISTV ET EST MIRA IN OCVL NRIS or can read MIRAB IN OCVLIS.

See H41–H42 in tabulation.

SECOND ISSUE SOVEREIGNS OF ELIZABETH I

No.	Descriptive comments	Rarity	Dating and/or rarity
H41	Second issue mm crosslet, struck over lis on rev.	R4	1561–62 Holloway records 10 known
H42	Second issue mm crosslet clear both sides	R5	Holloway records 9 known

Note. H41 this variety has reverse legend with MIRA IN OCVL
H42 this variety has reverse legend with MIRAB IN OCVLIS

Fine gold Sovereigns were not included and therefore not struck for what is currently known as the third, fourth and fifth issues of Elizabeth's coinage.

Description and details of Elizabeth sovereign, Sixth Issue

Obverse: Similar to previous issue except the portcullis chain rings are smaller and there is a pellet on each crossover junction in the portcullis itself, the tressure that surrounds the obverse design of alternating trefoils on cusps and pellets in spandrels around the perimeter of roped circle, now continues across the throne back, except for the earliest mint mark A varieties. Legend reads ELIZABETH D G ANG FRA ET HIB REGINA.

Reverse: Of a similar design to two previous issues, legend reads DNO FACTV EST ISTV ET EST MIRAB IN OCVLIS NRS or sometimes last word NRIS, or for mm tun only OCVL.

Mint Marks: This is the most populous surviving issue of collecting for the hammered gold Sovereign, for which a different kind of tabulation is used to help identification based on mint mark variation in combination with throne back ornamentation. The mint mark varies between die varieties and sometimes a succeeding obverse or reverse will have its mintmark struck over that on a die of the preceding issue, sometimes on both sides of the coin resulting in varying combinations. The other interesting variation is the throne back on which the Queen is seated which always has a lattice on the cushioned back with varying ornamentation. This is bordered each side with a vertical side bar on which varying ornamentation or none at all appears in a repeating pattern. The first two issues of fine Sovereign listed above for example having pellet ornamentation in the lattice and in the vertical side bars.
See H43–H60 in tabulation.

Mint mark gothic A: December 1, 1583 to February 13, 1585, some early mint mark A have a throne back of a lattice with pellet in annulet decoration in compartments, with side bar verticals of three fleur de lis alternating with quatrefoil of pellets. Latter mint mark A Sovereigns have pellets in the throne back lattice and the side bars.
See H43–H44 in tabulation.

Mint mark escallop: February 14, 1585 to May 30, 1587, the most populous surviving mint mark as a whole for the entire run of this denomination. Some mint mark escallop have a throne back with larger pellets in the lattice compartments, and other dies of this mint mark have a repeating pattern of an annulet alternating with either one or two horizontal pellets in vertical side bar decoration of the throne back. Another variety has pellet in annulet decoration in the lattice compartments and a further variety has the vertical side bar repeating pattern with two fleur de lis alternating with pairs of horizontal pellets.
See H45–H56 in tabulation.

Variety H53 mm escallop with NRIS reverse legend.

THE GOLD SOVEREIGN SERIES

Description and details of Elizabeth sovereign, Sixth Issue *continued*

Mint mark crescent: June 1, 1587 to circa January 31, 1590. One die struck over escallop with annulets in lattice of throne back and repeating pattern of fleur de lis alternating with pairs of horizontal pellets in the vertical side bars. Another variety of the crescent over escallop obverse has annulets in the side bars instead of the lis. The pure crescent only obverse mintmark variety has plain vertical side bars to the throne back as does the succeeding mint mark hand.
See H57–H58 in tabulation.

Mint mark hand: Circa February 1, 1590 to circa January 31, 1592, similar to latter variety of previous mint mark of crescent, with pellets in lattice and plain vertical side bars to throne back.
See H59 in tabulation.

Variety H59 mm hand.

Mint mark tun: Circa 1st February 1592 to 10th June 1593 when the fine issue Sovereign ceases and this mint mark otherwise continues until 1595 on other denominations. This final mint mark of tun obverse has small pellets in lattice compartments of throne back and in the vertical side bars. See H60 in tabulation.

Variety H60 mm tun.

The Fine Gold Sovereign was only minted in Elizabeth's first, second and sixth issues of coinage. In the sixth issue, the Sovereign is often termed a Double Noble in the official indentures.

After this last issue of the hammered fine Sovereign the 20 Shilling "Pound" becomes the largest gold denomination, but this is struck in 22 carat gold. There is even an experimental machine-made Pound made on the presses of Elloye Mestrelle that still exists today in the British Museum Collection (Wilson & Rasmussen 11). The final hammered gold Sovereigns as a senior denomination are issued a decade later than the last of Elizabeth I, at the start of the reign of Stuart King James I.

The tabulation headings for the sixth issue below are different in their detail to previous, and based on these obverse identifiers of throneback lattice and ornamentation of side bars:

SIXTH ISSUE SOVEREIGNS OF ELIZABETH I

No.	Mint mark variation	lattice ornamentation	Repeating vertical side bar ornamentation	Rarity	Comment by Holloway
H43	Gothic A, struck over crosslet on rev.	pellet in annulet	lis above four pellets	R6	3 known from one die combination
H44	Gothic A	pellet	pellets	R3	19 known across 2 die varieties
H45	Escallop, struck over A both sides	pellet	pellets	R4	17 known from one die combination
H46	Escallop, struck over A on obv.	pellet	pellets	R2	18 known across 2 die varieties
H46A	Escallop / A on obv. with NRIS rev. legend	pellet	pellets	R4	9 known from one die combination
H47	Escallop, struck over A on rev.	annulet	annulet above two pellets	R5	6 known from one die combination
H48	Escallop, struck over A on rev.	pellet	annulet above two pellets	R5	6 known from one die combination
H49	Escallop	pellet	pellets	S	68 known across 3 die varieties
H50	Escallop	pellet	annulet above one pellet	R3	19 known from one die combination
H51	Escallop, rev. legend NRIS for NRS	pellet	annulet above one pellet	R5	6 known from one die combination
H52	Escallop	pellet	annulet above two pellets	R3	24 known across 4 die varieties
H53	Escallop, rev. legend NRIS for NRS	pellet	annulet above two pellets	R3	18 known from one die combination
H54	Escallop	pellet in annulet	pellets	R5	5 known across 2 die varieties
H55	Escallop	annulet	lis above two pellets	R4	9 known across 3 die varieties
H56	Crescent, struck over escallop both sides	annulet	annulet above two pellets	R7	Known only from a single example
H57	Crescent, struck over escallop both sides	annulet	lis above two pellets	R7	Known only from a single example
H58	Crescent, struck over escallop on rev.	pellet	plain	R4	10 known from one die combination
H59	Hand, struck over crescent both sides	pellet	plain	R5	8 known from one die combination
H60	Tun, the rev. legend has shorter "OCVL"	small pellets	small pellets	N	100 known across 2 die varieties

Notes to tabulation above:
H43 the reverse legend ends with NRIS as last abbreviated word.
H44 can have either a pellet or a colon either side of the obv. mint mark A, the single pellet variety being of the higher rarity.
The following Escallop obv. mint marks have a colon each side—H45, H46, H49.
The following Escallop obv. mint marks have a pellet each side—H48, H50, H53, H54.
The following Escallop obv. mint marks have a pellet only before—H47, H51, H52, H55.
H49 has some colon punctuation in legend instead of pellets.
H52 there is an additional die variety with an extra stop in word "EST" on reverse giving "ES.T"
H55 there is an additional die variety with no stop after "ET" on the reverse legend reading.
H57 and H58 always have no stop after "ET" on reverse legend reading.
Comment by late George Holloway—as listed in sale catalogue of his collection mentioned in notes earlier, the most complete indication we have at present on the die varieties and rarities of these specific coins.

JAMES I (1603–25)

The son of Mary Queen of Scots, and King James VI of Scotland since his mother's abdication in 1567, James I of England continued the gold Sovereign as a 22 carat "crown" gold issue for his first coinage only of 1603–04, and therefore at a face value of 20 Shillings and full weight of 11.14g, through two bust types similar in design to the final coinage of Edward VI 50 years before.

Description and details of James I sovereign

Obverse: Half-length armoured figure of crowned King facing right holding orb and sceptre, crown breaks inner beaded circle with legend surrounding, mint mark thistle or lis at start of legend, IACOBVS D G ANG SCO FRAN ET HIB REX,

Reverse: Reverse with crowned quartered shield of arms incorporating English and French arms dimidiated appearing in two opposing quarters, Scottish lion to upper right, Irish harp to lower left, I to left and R to right, double arched crown above to top of coin breaking inner beaded circle, legend commences with same mint mark as obverse, EXVRGAT DEVS DISSIPENTVR INIMICI.
See H61–H63 in tabulation.

Mint mark thistle: Issued May 21, 1603 until May 22, 1604 with first or second bust.

Mint mark lis: Issued May 23, 1604 until November 10, 1604 with second bust.

First bust: With less ornate armour than second and a facial profile and beard that is proud of the body profile, lis head on sceptre partially breaks through inner beaded circle.

Second bust: With more ornate armour and with a facial profile that is more in line with the body profile with beard blending into armour below, lis head of sceptre reaches fully into legend area as high as lettering and crown beside it.

The abbreviated Latin legends translate as on obverse: James by the grace of God, King of England, Scotland, France and Ireland.
On the reverse as: Let God arise and let His enemies be scattered (Psalm 68, 1 from the Bible), as chosen by the King himself.

FIRST ISSUE SOVEREIGNS OF JAMES I

No.	Descriptive comments	Rarity	Dating and/or rarity
H61	First coinage first bust mm thistle	R2	issued first part of 1603-04
H62	First coinage second bust mm thistle	R	issued latter part of 1603-04
H63	First coinage second bust mm lis	S	issued 1604

Interim Period until the modern Sovereign

As James I was also King James VI of Scotland, his second coinage changed format to a similar coin now struck in 22 carat gold at 20 Shillings face value called the Unite, as he had brought both Kingdoms together for the first time. At the same time a fine gold coinage continued with introduction of a 30 Shilling Rose Ryal with the King depicted in a similar way to the earlier Sovereigns, and this coinage continues to 1619 when a third phase is entered. The third coinage introduces the 22 carat 20 Shilling "Laurel" changing the design to now show the King in Roman attire with a laurel wreath upon his head; whilst the larger fine gold Rose Ryal has a revised more intricate and neater design of the King on the throne which continues to the end of the reign.

The Interim period from the reign of Charles I to George III sees the transition from hammered to machine made coinage finally adopted from 1662. Charles I revives the 22 carat Unite at 20 Shillings commencing with the coronation type of 1625 and then onward as a denomination through to the Civil War period and the puritan Commonwealth until the Restoration of Charles II in 1660 with the final hammered issues. Amazingly, in the Civil War period, Charles I introduces the largest hammered gold denomination in the English series, the mighty Triple Unite of Three Pounds face value issued first in 1642 at Shrewsbury, but shortly after and for the next two years till 1644 at Oxford. The coin was perhaps based on the largest Scottish denomination ever issued, the 1575–76 20 Pound piece by his Father King James VI and was a showpiece of the King's power whilst in his new Royalist capital at Oxford, as well as a spendable coin that was highly coveted by the higher ranks in his army and within Royalist circles.

Moving into the Commonwealth period after the regicide, the hammered Unite of 20 Shillings continues with shield designs both sides and with the legends for the first time in plain English. Oliver Cromwell comes to prominence from 1653 onwards and the first machine-made 20 Shilling piece is one that bears his portrait dated 1656 when the presses and machinery of Peter Blondeau are employed to make a milled coinage in the 1656–58 period.

Upon the Restoration of King Charles II the final hammered coinages of 1660–62 are produced which feature 22 carat 20 Shilling pieces engraved by Thomas Simon, with one final swan-song as a machine-made, milled coin dated 1662, struck in a limited number of some 3,400 pieces. It is at this juncture that the denomination is revised into a smaller format at 20 Shillings as a gold Guinea (for further reading see Roderick Farey's sister publication *A Guide to the Guinea* under this publisher). The new denomination with its multiples and fraction continues successfully with various changes in face value, until finally fixed at One Pound and One Shilling in 1717 with Isaac Newton as Mint Master and runs right through until the final-dated issue of 1813 under George III, issued in part to pay the troops involved in the Napoleonic Wars. Then we have the advent of the modern Sovereign in currency 22 carat gold from 1817 onwards as depicted in the remainder of this book.

THE HALF-SOVEREIGN

The first Half-Sovereign ever issued of King Henry VIII (enlargement, actual size 30mm).
A unique example, courtesy of the Fitzwilliam Museum.

The gold Half-Sovereign commences production in the third coinage of Henry VIII. Previously the gold "Ryal" of 15 Shillings was issued as the half denomination of the Fine Gold Sovereign in the reign of King Henry VII, only for type II with mint mark cross fitchee and is not issued again until the first coinage of King Henry VIII with mint mark crowned portcullis. There is then a break in the Ryal denomination until the 15 Shilling face-value issue in fine gold for Queens Mary and Elizabeth. They are therefore, not listed in this publication as they are not denominated as Half-Sovereigns.

It is important to note that when Henry began his reign the Sovereign had a value of 20 shillings and weighed 240 grains, and the Ryal a value of ten shillings with a weight of 120 grains. It was in 1543 that a new indenture was made with the Master of the Mint that the fineness of the coins be reduced to 23 carats fine gold and one carat alloy. The new Sovereigns would be current for 20 shillings with a weight of 200 grains, fineness 23 carats, and the Half-sovereign was introduced for the first time to replace the Ryals at a value of ten shillings. In 1544 the standard of fineness was further debased while the weight of the Sovereign was lowered to 192 grains and the weight of the Half-sovereign to 96 grains, although Half-sovereigns weighing a little more are known to exist.

The obverse of this new Half-sovereign features the crowned King facing and seated in his chair of state holding his sceptre and orb, and with a large rose at his feet. The reverse displays a small royal shield quartered and containing the arms of France and England, supported on either side by a lion and a dragon. The letters H R appear at the bottom. The mint mark appears within the legend centrally placed at the top on both obverse and reverse of the coin.

The Half-sovereign continued to be used in similar form for the reign of Edward VI 1547–53, the young boy who succeeded his father at only nine years of age. His first series of four gold coins carried the image and name of his father, Henry VIII. However, the exception was the gold Half-sovereign which features the youthful Edward himself. The later coinage which was issued in three distinct periods in the young King's own name also featured a Half-sovereign, the last of which portrays a splendid portrait of the crowned King resplendent in armour holding a sword and orb.

HENRY VIII (1509–47)

The Half-Sovereign as a denomination starts in the Third Coinage of King Henry VIII (1544–47) with the unique survivor of the earliest type illustrated at the start of this section, which is housed in the Fitzwilliam Museum. The full weight of a Ten Shilling face value Half-Sovereign when first issued at 23 carat fineness in the type IIb phase of the third coinage was full weight 6.480g. See H100 in tabulation.

There was a reorganisation at the Royal Mint within the Tower from 1544 splitting coin production across two separate workshops known as Tower I (Under-treasurer Sir Martin Bowes) and Tower II (Under-treasurer Thomas Knight) both of which struck gold, though there does not seem to be a differentiation between the Tower issues to tell which Half-Sovereign is from which workshop (though in the succeeding reign of Edward VI the Half-Sovereign has different mint marking according to which Tower branch they emanate from). See H100–H107 in tabulation.

From 1545 minting activity commences at Southwark (Under-treasurer Sir John York) in southeast London for the first time since the time of the Norman Kings. See H108–H114 in tabulation.

Lastly, from 1546, gold coinage emanates from the major English port of Bristol with authority in place from Under-treasurer Sir William Sharington whose initials WS appear ligatured together as its mint mark. See H115–H116 in tabulation.

Dating for the mints and debasement:

An indenture for Tower I and Tower II to coin 22 carat gold was issued on March 27, 1545 with the Half-Sovereign of ten shillings at 6.221g.

A commission for the mint of Southwark was approved on September 6, 1545 to coin 22 carat gold with production commencing from the 15th.

Indentures are issued on April 1, 1546 for Tower I, Tower II, Southwark and Bristol to issue gold at 20 carat fineness.

Note the obverse legend in this coinage has number 8 for Henry's numerals, all lettering of Gothic form, unless stated, and stops can vary from saltires, to trefoils, to "sleeves" (curved device known heraldically as a manche). This coinage also depicts the change of Henry's obverse legend changing his status from "Lord" to "King" of Ireland according to the Crown of Ireland Act passed in 1542.

Description and details of Henry VIII half-sovereign

Obverse: Full body figure of King facing seated on ornate throne, holding orb and sceptre, rose below his feet, beaded circles with legend surrounding HENRIC 8 DI GRA AGL FRANCIE ET HIBER REX, or similar reading.

Reverse: Crowned quartered shield of arms with lion and dragon supporters, HR on banner below between them, legend surrounding IHS AVTEM TRANSIENS PER MEDIVM ILLOR IBAT, lettering styles, spelling and punctuation can differ.

Henry VIII Tower mm pellet in annulet, annulet on obv circle.

Henry VIII Southwark mm E both sides and below shield.

Henry VIII Southwark mm S both sides and below shield.

The abbreviated Latin legends translate as on obverse: Henry the Eighth by the grace of God, King of England, France and Ireland.

On the reverse: But Jesus, passing through the midst of them, went His way (Luke 4:30 from the Bible).

HALF-SOVEREIGNS OF HENRY VIII

No.	Descriptive comments	Rarity	Dating
H100	Third coinage Tower mm lis, 23 carat gold, 6.480g, small Roman lettering, saltire stops	R7	issued 1544–45
H101	Third coinage Tower mm pellet in annulet*, 22 or 20 carat gold, 6.221g, Roman letters with saltire stops, ET in legend for "and"	R5	issued 1545–47
H102	Third coinage Tower similar to above, Z in legend for "and"	R2	issued 1545–47
H103	Third coinage Tower, similar, Roman letters, trefoil stops, Z type "and"	R	issued 1545–47
H104	Third coinage Tower, similar, Roman letters, defective saltire stops, Z type "and"	R2	issued 1545–47
H105	Third coinage Tower, similar with annulet added to end of inner circle both sides**	R3	issued 1546–47
H106	Third coinage Tower with annulet added to end of inner circle on one side**	R4	issued 1546–47
H107	Third coinage Tower, Gothic lettering with sleeve stops	R3	issued 1546–47
H108	Third Coinage Southwark mm S both sides, 22 or 20 carat gold	R	issued 1545–47
H109	Third Coinage Southwark with E below shield mm S	S	issued 1545–47
H110	Third Coinage Southwark with E below shield mm S no sceptre	R4	issued 1545–47
H111	Third Coinage Southwark with E below shield mm E	R	issued 1545–47
H112	Third Coinage Southwark with mm E struck over arrow on obverse	R4	issued 1545–47
H113	Third Coinage Southwark with E below shield mint mark S obv. / E rev.	R2	issued 1545–47
H114	Third Coinage Southwark with E below shield mint mark E obv. / S rev.	R2	issued 1545–47
H115	Third Coinage Bristol mm WS ligatured both sides, trefoil stops	R2	issued 1546–47
H116	Third Coinage Bristol mm WS ligatured obverse only, gothic lettering	R3	issued 1546–47

* Sometimes the letter C in legend is actually a reversed D on one or both sides.
** This annulet may refer to the reduction to 20 carat fineness of gold from April 1546.

The Southwark Mint also mixes lettering styles of Roman and Gothic with trefoil or saltire stops at 6.221g full weight, some of the curved back E mm coins have sleeve stops.

The Bristol Mint uses Gothic Lombardic lettering and are 20 carat gold, the dies were made in London and sent for use at the Port's mint.

EDWARD VI (1547–53)

Posthumous issue in the name of Henry VIII from 1547—struck in 20 carat gold and Ten Shillings face value, full weight of 6.221g, which continues through the first period of coinage in the reign of Edward VI from April 1547 to January 1549. Followed by coinage in Edward's name of a similar design to posthumous issue, April 1547–January 1549 struck in 20 carat gold fineness. The Tower I and Tower II division is now identifiable to Half-Sovereigns as defined by their mint marks.

Second Period coinage January 1549 to April 1550—Half-Sovereigns struck at Tower I and II according to mint marks used at 22 carat fineness and 20 Shillings face value, full weight 5.489g.

Third Period coinage 1550–53

Crown gold 20 Shilling Half-Sovereign at 22 carats and 11.314g.

The Bristol Mint ceased production by October 1549 and was closed on March 25, 1550 (Lady Day); the Southwark Mint closes in August 1551 and a commission of October 1551 unifies Tower II with Tower I with Tower II ceasing production and defunct as of the Spring of 1552. The only other mint to produce gold coins is the Durham House Mint in London, off the Strand, which commenced production in January 1549 (1548 old style), but had likely closed by December of that year, the records for which alas do not survive. Therefore, by the end of this reign only the Royal Mint in the Tower of London was in operation.

First Posthumous Period 1547–49

Also known as Posthumous Coinage of King Henry VIII as still in his name while lower fineness coinage prevails.

The facing full figure portrait is now of the boy King Edward VI on the throne holding orb and sceptre. Lettering is now Roman upper case with pellet stops at Tower I and mainly lozenge type stops for Tower II.

Posthumous Tower I issue see H117–H124 in tabulation, mint marks arrow and lis.

Posthumous Tower II issue see H125–H137 in tabulation, mint marks grapple, martlet and lis and K below shield.

Southwark issue see H138–H150 in tabulation, mint marks E and S.

Bristol issue see H151 in tabulation, mint mark WS ligatured.

Description and details of Henry VIII Posthumous Issue Half-Sovereign under Edward VI, First Period

Obverse: Full body figure of boy King Edward VI facing seated on ornate throne, holding orb and sceptre, rose below his feet, beaded circles and legend surrounding in the name of his late Father, HENRIC 8 DI GRA AGL FRANCIE ET HIBER REX or similar reading.

Reverse: Crowned quartered shield of arms with lion and dragon supporters, HR on banner below between them, legend surrounding, HIS AVTEM TRANSIENS PER MEDIVM ILLOR IBAT, lettering styles, spelling and punctuation can differ.

The abbreviated Latin legends translate as on obverse: Edward the Sixth by the grace of God, King of England France and Ireland.

On the reverse: But Jesus, passing through the midst of them, went His way (Luke 4:30 from the Bible)

Posthumous issue Tower I,
mm arrow.

Posthumous issue Tower II,
no mm with K below shield.

Posthumous issue Tower II, mm grapple
obv. with grapple below shield.

Posthumous issue Tower II,
mm lis both sides.

HALF-SOVEREIGN OF EDWARD VI, 1547–53

Posthumous issue Southwark, mm E both sides.

POSTHUMOUS HALF-SOVEREIGNS OF EDWARD VI

No.	Descriptive comments	Rarity
H117	Third coinage of Henry VIII / Posthumous Tower I mule; obverse gothic lettering with sleeve stops mm pellet in annulet / rev. mm arrow, roman lettering with lozenge stops	R6
H118	Posthumous Tower I / Third coinage of Henry VIII mule; obverse no sceptre mm arrow roman lettering with lozenge stops / rev. mm pellet in annulet, gothic lettering with sleeve stops	R6
H119	Posthumous Tower I, mm arrow, lozenge stops	N
H120	Posthumous Tower I, no obv. mm, mm arrow on rev. only	S
H121	Posthumous Tower I, mm arrow, pierced cross stops, ligatured ET for Z in legend	R3
H122	Posthumous Tower I, mm arrow, saltire stops	N
H123	Posthumous Tower I, mm arrow obv., lozenge stops / mm lis rev., pellet stops	R6
H124	Posthumous Tower I, mm lis obv. of Tower II / mm arrow rev. Tower I	R6
H125	Posthumous Tower II, K below shield, mm K on reverse only, lozenge stops	R
H126	Posthumous Tower II, K below shield, no mint marks, lozenge stops	R2
H127	Posthumous Tower II, K below shield, mm E on obv. only	S
H128	Posthumous Tower II, K type obv. without mm, muled with mm grapple rev.	R6
H129	Posthumous Tower II, with grapple below shield and as mm both sides, pellet stops	R
H130	Posthumous Tower II, with grapple below shield, mm grapple obv. only, pellet stops	R2
H131	Posthumous Tower II, with grapple below shield, mm grapple rev. only	R2
H132	Posthumous Tower II, with grapple below shield, no mint marks, lozenge stops	R2
H133	Posthumous Tower II, no obv. mm, rev. with mm grapple over K and K below shield, saltire stops	R6
H134	Posthumous Tower II, mm martlet pellet stops	R2
H135	Posthumous Tower II, mm martlet saltire stops	R
H136	Posthumous Tower II, mm martlet obv. / mm lis rev.	R4
H137	Posthumous Tower II, mm lis, pellet stops	R2
H138	Posthumous Southwark, Portrait of Henry VIII, mm curved back gothic E, obv. only, Roman letters, lozenge stops*	R5
H139	Posthumous Southwark, Portrait of Edward VI, mm Roman E both sides, lozenge stops	N
H140	Posthumous Southwark, mm E both sides, pierced cross stops with saltires	R3
H141	Posthumous Southwark, mm E both sides, pellet stops	R4
H142	Posthumous Southwark, mm E rev. only	R2
H143	Posthumous Southwark, mm E obv. only, K below shield on rev.	R
H144	Posthumous Southwark, mm gothic curved E obv. sleeve stops / mm Roman E rev. lozenge stops	R2
H145	Posthumous Southwark, E below shield mm E both sides, lozenge stops	C
H146	Posthumous Southwark, E below shield mm E obv. / retrograde mm E on rev.	R3
H147	Posthumous Southwark, E reversed below shield, mm E both sides	R4
H148	Posthumous Southwark, E below shield mm E on rev. only, obv. lozenge stops, rev. saltire stops	R2
H149	Posthumous Southwark, no sceptre on obv., E below shield, mm E on rev. only	R3
H150	Posthumous Southwark, no mm obv. muled with Southwark third coinage rev. of Henry VIII with mm S on rev. only	R5
H151	Posthumous Bristol, mm WS ligatured obv. only, gothic lettering, trefoil stops	R5

* All posthumous issue Half-Sovereigns are in Henry's name with image of the boy King Edward VI on throne, except for H138 at Southwark.

First Period Coinage in Edward's Own Name.

Similar design to posthumous issue, April 1547–January 1549 struck in 20 carat gold fineness.

Tower I issue see H152 in tabulation with mint mark arrow.

Southwark issue see H153–H156 in tabulation with mint mark E.

Description and details of Edward VI Half-Sovereign, First Period in His Own Name

Obverse: Full body figure of boy King Edward VI facing seated on ornate throne, holding orb and sceptre, rose below his feet, beaded circles and legend surrounding, EDWARD 6 DI GRA AGL FRANCIE ET HIBER REX or similar reading.

Reverse: Crowned quartered shield of arms with lion and dragon supporters, HR on banner below between them, legend surrounding, HIS AVTEM TRANSIENS PER MEDIVM ILLOR IBAT, lettering styles, spelling and punctuation can differ.

Southwark EDWARD 6 legend, mm E with gothic or Roman E below shield.

FIRST PERIOD HALF-SOVEREIGNS OF EDWARD VI

No.	Descriptive comments	Rarity
H152	Tower I, EDWARD 6 legend, mm arrow, HR on rev. banner, lozenge stops	R3
H153	Southwark EDWARD 6 legend, mm E both sides, struck over arrow on obv.	R3
H154	Southwark EDWARD 6 legend, mm E both sides, struck over arrow on rev.	R3
H155	Southwark EDWARD 6 legend, mm E with gothic or Roman E below shield	R2
H156	Southwark EDWARD 6 legend, mm E, E below shield struck over reversed E	R4

HALF-SOVEREIGN OF EDWARD VI, 1547–53

Description and details of Edward VI half-sovereign, Bare head cuirassed bust, Second Period January 1549–April 1550 struck in 22 carat gold

Obverse: Bare head cuirassed facing right, obverse legend surrounding SCVTVM FIDEI PROTEGET EVM.

Reverse: quartered arms in crowned frame, E to left R to right, reverse legend EDWARD VI D G AGL FRA Z HIB REX.

Dated Tower I issue has TIMOR DOMINI FONS VITE obverse legend.
Bare head Durham House issue has LVCERNA PEDIBVS MEIS VERBUM EST obverse legend.
Tower mint issue see H157–H159 in tabulation with mint mark arrow or 6.
Southwark mint issue see H160 in tabulation with mint mark Y.
Durham House issue see H161–H164 in tabulation with mint mark bow.

The abbreviated Latin reverse legends translate as: TIMOR DOMINI FONS VITE MDXLIX, "The fear of the Lord is a fountain of life, 1549" (Proverbs, 14, 27).
  SCVTVM FIDEI PROTEGET EVM, "The shield of faith shall protect him"
  LVCERNA PEDIBVS MEIS VERBUM EST, "Thy word is a lamp unto my feet" (Psalm 119, 015 from the Bible). This legend only used at Durham House mint.

Bare head mm arrow.

SECOND PERIOD BARE HEAD HALF-SOVEREIGNS OF EDWARD VI

No.	Descriptive comments	Rarity
H157	Tower I, 1549 in Roman numerals, bare head cuirassed right, mm arrow, obv. legend reads TIMOR DOMINI FONS VITE MDXLIX, square pellet stops	R6
H158	Tower I, undated, bare head cuirassed right, mm arrow, legend reads SCVTVM FEIDEI PROTEGET EVM, rosette stops obv. / square pellets rev	R2
H159	Tower I, undated, bare head cuirassed right, mm 6 similar legend	R6
H160	Southwark mint, undated, bare head cuirassed right, mm Y similar legend and stops	R
H161	Durham House*, 1548 in Roman numerals, half-length armoured bare head King right, SCVTUM legend with date, mm bow, incurved saltire stops, beaded circles	R7
H162	Durham House, bare head cuirassed, LVCERNA legend, mm bow, crescent stops, beaded circles	R6
H163	Durham House, bare head cuirassed, similar to above but rev. legend spells King's name as EDOVARD	R7
H164	Durham House, bare head cuirassed, SCVTVM legend, mm bow, beaded circles	R6

* Durham House Mint just south of the Strand in London, by todays Durham House Street, had Sir Martin Bowes as Under Treasurer hence the mint mark bow. The mint was only open from January to December of 1549 and no records of its activity survive apart from a contemporary estimate of production citing £80,000 worth of output for both gold and silver in one year of operation. The series has its own style in comparison to other gold coinage at that time, with half-length busts and the reverse shields and frames with frosted decoration, all are of extreme rarity.

THE GOLD SOVEREIGN SERIES

Description and details of Edward VI half-sovereign, Second Period, Latter issue

Obverse: Crowned cuirassed bust right, breastplate can be decorated or plain, legend surrounding reads EDWARD VI D G AGL FRA Z HIB REX.

Reverse: Quartered arms in crowned frame, E to left R to right, reverse legend SCVTVM FIDEI PROTEGET EVM.

Tower I issue see H165–H168 in tabulation with mint mark arrow or swan.
Tower II issue see H169–H171 in tabulation with mint mark grapple or martlet.
Southwark mint issue see H172–H173 in tabulation with mint mark Y.
Durham House issue see H174–H175 in tabulation with mint mark bow.

Crowned head mm swan.

Crowned head mm Y.

CROWNED BUST HALF-SOVEREIGNS OF EDWARD VI

No.	Descriptive comments	Rarity
H165	Tower I, crowned bust, mm arrow, plain breastplate, square stops obv. / rosette stops rev.	R2
H166	Tower I, crowned bust, mm swan, decorated breastplate, square stops obv. / rosette stops rev.	N
H167	Tower I, crowned bust, mm swan, decorated breastplate, square stops both sides	R2
H168	Tower I, crowned bust, mm swan obv. square stops / mm arrow rev. rosette stops	R5
H169	Tower II, crowned bust, mm grapple, plain breastplate, square stops obv. / rosette stops rev.	R2
H170	Tower II, crowned bust, mm grapple, plain breastplate, rosette stops obv.	R3
H171	Tower II, crowned bust, mm martlet, decorated breastplate, square stops both sides	R3
H172	Southwark mint, crowned bust, mm Y, plain breastplate, square stops obv. / rosette stops rev.	R3
H173	Southwark mint, crowned bust, mm Y, similar with decorated breastplate	R5
H174	Durham House, crowned armoured half-length bust right, mm bow, EDWARD VI legend both sides, incurved saltire stops, wire line circles	R6
H175	Durham House, crowned bust, mm bow, SCVTVM rev. legend, similar	R6

Description and details of Edward VI half-sovereign, Third Period

Obverse: Half-length armoured crowned King facing right, holding orb and sword upright with blade resting on shoulder, all within linear and beaded circle with legend surrounding, mint mark y or tun at top with legend reading EDWARD VI D G AGL FRAN Z HIB REX.

Reverse: Crowned quartered shield of arms with alternating English lions and fleur de lis, crowned lion supporter to left, dragon supporter to right, ER ligatured on banner below, roped circle and legend surrounding with mint mark Y or tun reads IHS AVTEM TRANCI PER MEDI ILLOR IBAT or similar.

Description and details of Edward VI half-sovereign, Third Period 1550–53 Crown gold fineness 22 carat

Obverse: Half-length armoured King with sword and orb right, legend surrounding reads EDWARD VI D G AGL FRA Z HIB REX.

Reverse: Crowned quartered shield of arms, E to left, R to right, legend reads HIS AVTE TRANCI PER MED ILLOR IBAT or similar abbreviated combination of letters, pellet punctuation both sides.

Now all Tower of London Mint only with mint mark Y or tun. See H176–178 in tabulation.

3rd Period mm Y.

3rd Period mm tun.

THIRD PERIOD HALF-SOVEREIGNS OF EDWARD VI

No.	Descriptive comments	Rarity
H176	Tower Mint mm Y	R3
H177	Tower Mint mm tun	N
H178	Tower Mint mm tun with frosted horizontal band and interior to crown on rev.*	S

* The frosted crown band can sometime be jewelled.

There exists a series of gold pattern coins of Edward VI of the same modular size (Half-Sovereign diameter) but of varying weights that equate with denominations of Sovereign, Half-Sovereign and Crown. They all feature designs with the bare head cuirassed similar to that in the second period of his coinage coupled with a reverse of a crowned Tudor rose with stem and leaves. The Half-Sovereign weight designs along with all the others are listed in Wilson and Rasmussen, and the Half-Sovereigns are numbers 5, 6 and 7 as well as number 4 which has been linked to his coronation with a dated inscription on what would be the bust side illustrated herewith.

The *Standard Catalogue* goes on to list the smaller fractional denominations as Crowns and Halfcrowns, whereas in North's *English Hammered Coinage Volume 2* they are listed as Quarter Sovereigns and Half-Quarter Sovereigns. We have chosen to stay with the modern *Standard Catalogue* definitions and therefore have not included such coins for this new section.

The Half denomination of the fine Sovereigns of Mary and Elizabeth I are denominated as 15 Shilling Ryals like the earlier issues of Henry VII and VIII and therefore are not listed.

Pattern Half-Sovereign dated 1547 (W. R. 4).

JAMES I (1603–25)

After a hiatus of 50 years, there is one last Half-Sovereign issue under the Stuart King James I in his first coinage only to accompany the Sovereign, its surviving examples are of extreme rarity today.

Description and details of James I half-sovereign, First Coinage 1603–04— 22 carat gold fineness

Obverse: First Crowned bust right, legend reads IACOBVS D G ANGL SCO FRA ET HIBER REX.

Reverse: Crowned shield of quartered arms, I to left and R to right, legend reads EXVRGAT DEVS DISSIPENTVR INIMICI. See H179 in tabulation.Now all Tower of London Mint only with mint mark Y or tun.
See H179 in tabulation.

(Images courtesy of Spink.)

HALF-SOVEREIGNS OF JAMES I

No.	Descriptive comments	Rarity
H179	First bust, mm thistle	R5

The denomination effectively continues as the fine gold Spur Ryal through the succeeding coinages as the half denomination of the Rose Ryal pegged at 15 Shillings. The second coinage issue of the denomination sometimes called a "Ship" Ryal is the last coin issued in the old medieval style like the earlier gold Noble with the King in ship. The following Spur Ryal of the third coinage changes design completely with a crowned British lion obverse with shield sceptre and quartered shield, the reverse with a rose on sunburst design reminiscent of the Edward IV Ryals of the medieval period. Meanwhile 20 Shilling Unites and Laurels and their half denominations coexist through the second and third coinages of James. This leads into the Half-Unites of Charles I which carry on through the Commonwealth period, then into the last hammered coinages of Charles II upon his Restoration. The Half-Guinea denomination then exists for 145 years from Charles II to George III taking us through to the Recoinage of 1817 and reintroduction of the Half-Sovereign at Ten Shillings.

THE "MODERN" SOVEREIGN SERIES

The sovereign series of coins which was originally introduced to replace the guinea. The quarter sovereign is a modern addition (shown actual size).
Note that throughout this publication all illustrations of coins are enlarged (not to scale) unless stated otherwise.

The death of George II on October 25, 1760 saw his grandson succeed to the throne as George III. At the time the gold coins in use were the guineas, half guineas, and later on the third guineas, although in 1762 a quarter guinea coin was issued.

The guinea was undoubtedly the major coin of the 18th century but far more often than not it encountered long periods of troubled times;[1] these included the withdrawal of huge quantities of guineas that had been in circulation far too long and so were very light in weight through simple wear. In 1793 war broke out with revolutionary France resulting in large quantities of gold leaving the country during this long war, and also during this time a similar situation arose with Spain that yet again caused revenue problems. Inevitably, gold was hoarded and its place was taken by banknotes of one pound and two pounds.

However, the guinea was to soldier on and so we move to probably one of the most important dates in the Royal Mint's history:[2] July 6, 1812. On this day William Wellesley Pole was appointed Master of the Mint. He came from a remarkable Irish family of which the great Duke of Wellington was the third of four brothers. The eldest of these being the Marquis of Wellesley, and the second was William Wellesley who later became Wellesley Pole in acknowledgement of a legacy. Pole had previously held the position of Clerk to the Ordnance, Secretary to the Admiralty, and Secretary for Ireland. He was given the appointment with specific orders to completely re-organise the Mint, and later he was to be responsible for the introduction of the new coinage.

Pole very soon discovered just how bad the present situation was, and in fact it had become almost impossible to maintain the existing currency system. It was quite obvious that something must be done, and a Privy Council Committee on Coin recommended a new gold coinage of ten shillings, 20 shillings, 40 shillings and five pound pieces, and this was approved by the Prince Regent on August 3, 1816.

The new sovereigns, given currency by a Royal Proclamation of July 1, 1817, were struck for the first time later that year, so the modern sovereign as we know it today was born. The sovereign and half sovereign replaced the guinea and third guinea. In addition the five pound and two pound coins came into being, albeit in a strictly limited capacity.

In the meantime important changes were happening at the Mint in respect of the engraving staff. Lewis Pingo,[3] the English Chief Engraver, who had been Chief Engraver since 1779, was retired. Nathaniel Marchant the Frenchman who was Second Engraver had reached the age of 76, and because of failing health he too was retired. Thomas Wyon was given the post of Chief Engraver and William Wyon became Second Engraver. At this point we must mention another person who was to be appointed to the engraving staff: Benedetto Pistrucci, a fiery Italian, but without doubt a unique engraver.

Pole wrote a letter to the Treasury on June 19, 1816[4]: "*I have thought it desirable to employ Mr Pistrucci, an artist of the greatest celebrity and whose work places him above all competition as a gem engraver, to make models for the dies of the new coinage and I request your lordships authority to pay Mr Pistrucci such remuneration as may be necessary for his works. It is my intention that the models of Mr Pistrucci should be engraved in Jasper from which our engravers will work in Steel and the models will be deposited in the Royal Mint and remain with the Dies and Proof Impressions of the several coins*".

Pistrucci had been introduced to Pole by Sir Joseph Banks, the influential President of the Royal Society. The appointment of Pistrucci was confirmed on June 26, 1816, and although Pole had wanted to employ him as the Chief Engraver he could not do so because Pistrucci, being Italian, was in fact classified as an alien, therefore he could not officially be given the top position. To overcome this he was employed as an outside assistant and Thomas Wyon continued as Chief Engraver.

Thomas Wyon died on September 22, 1817 and Pole wanted Pistrucci to occupy Wyon's position. However, due to circumstances already described this was not possible, but a loophole was found that allowed Pistrucci to take over all of Wyon's duties, although not that of his official position. In this area the Mint official records were in fact left blank, and remained so until 1828 when William Wyon became Chief Engraver. So Pistrucci was to carry out all the duties of Chief Engraver, provide all models and engrave all dies, at a salary of £500 a year. William Wyon remained as assistant to Pistrucci.

Before the death of Thomas Wyon, Pistrucci had already been involved in the preparation of the new coinage: he had engraved a cameo of the King's head in Jasper, to serve as a model for the sovereign, shilling and sixpence. The second Jasper cameo was a similar piece, and he then cut a third Jasper cameo of the King's head to serve as a model for the half-crown. Finally he produced a model in wax of St George slaying the dragon to serve as a model for the reverse of the crown. For these four works Pistrucci was paid £312 8*s*.

Pistrucci himself suggested that his wax model of St George should be used for the new gold coinage, and as a result of this he was asked to produce a model; for this work he was paid the sum of 100 guineas. He was eventually asked to engrave both obverse and reverse dies of the new coinage, because the Mint engravers had been unable to successfully copy Pistrucci's models. However, the five and two pound coins issued for George IV did not feature Pistrucci's work as the obverse by William Wyon, after a model produced by Chantrey, and the reverse by Jean Merlen was used.

Since its introduction in 1817 the weight and fineness of the "modern" sovereign and its multiples and fractions has not altered and has remained constant right through to the present day. However, its design has changed a number of times and, of course, the obverse effigy of the reigning monarch changes. The most commonly used reverse is Pistrucci's iconic design, although even that has undergone minor changes at times, for example the original design portrayed St George armed with a lance, a broken piece of which lays on the ground beneath his horse's feet; the lance was later changed to a sword. Also many coins have St George with a streamer flowing from his helmet whilst others show him without the streamer.

Most of the sovereign series have been produced at the Royal Mint—first at its base at Tower Hill in London and more recently at the modern purpose-built premises in Llantrisant where production continues today. For a short period a small number of Branch Mints, effectively extensions of the British Royal Mint, were striking local gold into sovereigns. In addition, during the reign of Elizabeth II a number of "special" issues have also been produced.

All this and more is explained in the following pages and every type of sovereign struck, including collectable errors and varieties, as well as its multiples and fractions, has been given a reference number, however, unremarkable striking flaws have been excluded. It should be noted that gold coins can vary in their final colour according to the metal with which the gold is alloyed, for example, if silver is used then the resultant coin is yellow, but if copper is used the coin will have a more reddish hue.

The purpose-built Mint on Tower Hill which replaced the cramped conditions in
the Tower of London by the second decade of the 19th century
(image courtesy of the Royal Mint Museum).

Notes/References
1. G. P. Dyer, "The Modern Sovereign", *Royal Sovereign 1489–1989*, Royal Mint, 1989, pp. 41–43.
2. Sir John Craig, KCVO, LLD, "William Wellesley Pole", *The Mint,* Cambridge, 1953, pp. 278–89.
3. C. Eimer, *The Pingo Family & Medal Making in 18th Century Britain*, London, 1998.
4. M. A. Marsh, *Benedetto Pistrucci Principal Engraver & Chief Medallist of The Royal Mint 1783–1855*, Cambridge, 1996, pp. 16–17.

Pistrucci's original sketch for the reverse of the sovereign (courtesy of the Royal Mint Museum).

THE FIVE POUNDS

(FIVE SOVEREIGNS)

Considered by many to be the most exquisite example of the coin designers' art, the reverse of the first £5 coins produced during Victoria's reign depicts Una and the Lion by William Wyon, inspired by the poem "The Faerie Queene" by Edmund Spenser.

Specifications of the five pounds:
Weight: 39.94 gram.
Fineness, 22 carat: 11/12 fine gold, 1/12 alloy (this means that each Five Pound coin contains 36.61 grams of pure gold).
Millesimal fineness: 916.66.
Thickness: 3mm.
Diameter: 36.00mm.

GEORGE III, 1760–1820

The first five pound coins were classified as patterns, all dated 1820 with the edge inscribed DECUS ET TUTAMEN. ANNO REGNI LX, being the 60th year of the King's reign. The obverse carries the royal effigy and legend by Benedetto Pistrucci whilst the reverse portrays Pistrucci's iconic St George slaying the dragon on a plain field with no legend. Only 25 were struck, thus they are of the highest rarity. Just three other examples are known as proofs, all with plain uninscribed edges. There is also one struck in silver which is believed to have been the personal property of Pistrucci himself at one time.

An article about "English Gold Coins" by Edward Hawkins, relating to these pattern pieces appears in the *Numismatic Chronicle*, Volume 13, of 1850, page 170—only 30 years after the event. In it the author reveals that the coins were not complete at the time of the King's death, which occurred at 8.38pm on January 29, 1820 at Windsor, and that mint workers laboured through that night to finish off the work. Just 25 pieces were struck of the five pounds (£5), but by an error of communication a larger quantity of 60 pieces of the two pounds (£2) were struck. The list of recipients of the 25 £5 pieces appears in the article and is reproduced opposite.

Description and details of the George III five pounds

Obverse: The King's head right, laureate with short hair; the tie has a loop with two ends, neck bare. Legend: GEORGIUS III D: G: BRITANNIAR: REX F: D:. The top of the bust divides the legend. The date is at the bottom of the legend. The name PISTRUCCI appears below the truncation.

Reverse: St George with streamer flowing from helmet, mounted and slaying the dragon with a broken spear, the shaft of which lays on the ground. W.W.P. on ground. The name PISTRUCCI appears below and to the left of the ground line. No legend.

Edge: Plain, inscribed DECUS ET TUTAMEN. ANNO REGNI LX.

The coin is struck with a reverse die axis ↑↓

FIVE POUNDS OF GEORGE III

No.	Date	Type/Variety	Mintage	Rating
F1	1820	Weight 39.94g, LX on edge (WR177, L&S207)	25	R4
F2	1820	£5 plain edge, weight 39.81g (WR178, L&S209)	3	R6
F3	1820	Example struck in silver (ex Pistrucci, L&S208)	Probably unique	R7

Recipients of the original 25 five pound coins were:

Six for institutions:
  The Mint Cabinet
  The Bank of England
  The British Museum
  Glasgow University
  Dublin College
  The Bodleian Library

Eight for Royal Mint officials:
  Mr Jasper Atkinson (1790–1856), Provost
  Mr Robert Bingley (1766–1847), Assay Master
  Mr Henry Bingley (1801–84), Assay Master
  Mr Henry Field (1803–88), Assayer
  Mr Robert Finch, Moneyer and gentleman of Dollis Hill
  Mr James Morrison (1774–1856), Deputy Master
  Mr Robert Mushet (1782–1828), Master's first clerk and melter
  Mr William Wyon (1795–1851), second engraver

Eleven for other "Important Persons":
  Marquis of Salisbury (1748–1823)
  Mr Robert Barclay (1751–1830), brewer and coin collector of Southwark
  Mr Thomas Dimsdale (1758–1823), banker and coin collector of Cornhill
  Mr William Durant (1779–1856), coin collector of Lowestoft and London W
  Mr Abraham Edmonds, surveyor and coin collector of Southwark
  Mr Christopher Edmonds (1774–1853), brother of Abraham, architect and coin collector of Southwark
  Sir Francis Freeling Bt (1763–1836), Secretary of the General Post Office and collector of gems, London W
  Mr Edward Hawkins (1780–1867), museum curator and coin collector of London W (author of the article)
  Mr John Henderson (1757–1829) coin collector of London W
  Rev. Joseph Martin (1776–1858), Church of England clergyman and coin collector of Bromley, Kent
  Mr Marmaduke Trattle (1752–1831), West Indian merchant and coin collector of London Wall

GEORGE IV, 1820–30

Following the death of George III William Wellesley Pole continued as Master of the Mint, and the engraving staff consisted of only Benedetto Pistrucci and William Wyon. However, Pistrucci made a strong appeal to Pole that the engraving staff should be brought more up to strength, and recommended the appointment of Jean Baptiste Merlen, a Frenchman. Thus on February 11, 1820 Merlen was made Assistant Engraver to Pistrucci.

During the reign of George IV the recoinage started under George III continued apace, and compared to later, few five pounds were struck, in fact almost all of those that are known carry the date 1826. That year a limited number of about 400 proof sets of all the current coins were issued and the only five pounds available were those contained within these sets. Interestingly these coins weighed 40 grams and have the words DECUS ET TUTAMEN ANNO REGNI SEPTIMO on the edge, however, a very small number are also known struck on a thicker flan of 46.52 grams, these have a plain edge. In addition a single unique plain edge example also exists with a lighter weight of 39.88 grams.

The five pound coins all bear the King's effigy by William Wyon after the model produced by Francis Leggatt Chantrey, with the reverse depicting an elaborate crowned shield designed by Johann Merlen, as explained in the chapter on the two pound coin on pages 40–41.

There are a number of pattern uniface obverses known, struck in gold and dated 1825, which could be trials for the crown coin as the obverse is the same for both. In 1829 a slightly larger head was used for the crown and examples of these gold obverse strikes also exist bearing that bust and date, which gives credence to the suggestion that they could be trials (WR216 and 217 respectively).

Description and details of the George IV five pounds

Obverse: The King's bare head left, with short hair; Legend: - GEORGIUS IV DEI GRATIA -. The date is at the bottom of the legend.

Reverse: A crowned and mantled Ensigns Armorial of the United Kingdom. The centre of the shield features a smaller crowned shield depicting the Hanoverian arms. Legend: BRITANNIARUM REX FID: DEF.

Edge: Plain or inscribed DECUS ET TUTAMEN ANNO REGNI SEPTIMO (1826).
The coin is struck with a reverse die axis ↑↓

FIVE POUNDS OF GEORGE IV

No.	Date	Type/Variety	Mintage	Rating
F6	1826	Weight 40.00g, lettered edge (WR213, L&S27)	c. 400	S
F7	1826	Weight 39.88g, plain edge (WR214, L&S26)	Possibly unique	R7
F8	1826	Thicker flan, plain edge, weight 46.52g (WR214, L&S25)	Very few	R6
F9	1829	Larger bare head, plain edge, weight 38.74g (WR215, L&S36)	Very few	R7

WILLIAM IV, 1830–37

Officially the Royal Mint records show that no five pound coins were struck during the reign of William IV. However, the silver crown dies were used to make a gold version of the same weight as five sovereigns at c. 40 grams. The records name these coins as "Crowns struck in gold", therefore they are considered to be outside the scope of this publication. However, they are listed in Wilson & Rasmussen and Linecar & Stone as WR270 and L&S2 respectively (see Bibliography).

VICTORIA, 1837–1901

TYPE 1: UNA AND THE LION

Queen Victoria began her reign upon the death of her uncle, William IV, on June 20, 1837. An Order in Council was issued on June 8, 1838, followed by a proclamation on July 5 ordering the striking of five pound pieces, sovereigns and half-sovereigns. Patterns of a different design of the five pound piece were also produced, and these were the well known "Una and the Lion" type.

The gold Una and the lion five pounds of 1839 represents the pinnacle of the modern milled British gold coin series. Amongst the most classic of the coin designs in the entire British series, engraver William Wyon's masterwork at the height of his career, was produced as the key coin for the anticipated proof set of all the Young Head denominations that are dated 1839. Royal Mint records shows that some 400 sets were issued, which were sold gradually over the following decade or more, though likely single coins were available too.

The obverse design depicts the young Queen then only around 20 years of age with her hair bound and filleted, the leading front fillet ornamented with six full scrolls like cresting waves, passing to the right; the rear fillet with ten pairs of leaves pointing upwards along a stem, with an extra one at the lower extreme and a partial extra pair at top. The Wyon name is displayed prominently raised on the truncation of the neck, with his credentials as a member of the Royal Academy of Art.

The Latin legend on the obverse of this coin reads VICTORIA D: G: REGINA F: D: which translates as "Victoria, by the grace of God, Queen of the Britons, Defender of the Faith". That on the reverse reads DIRIGIT DEUS GRESSUS MEOS, which translates as "May God direct my steps", from Psalm 119. The edge inscription translates as "An ornament and a safeguard, in the third year of the reign", a reference to safeguarding the coin from the by then defunct illegal practice of edge clipping gold coins.

The depiction of the Queen as Una leading the British lion was inspired by the first book of the epic poem "The Faerie Queene" by Edmund Spenser (1553–99) as listed in Brewer's *Dictionary of Phrase and Fable*. Una being Truth, as truth is one. Briefly, the story of Una starts with her accompanying St George on his adventures and driven by a storm into the "Wandering Wood" retires for the night into Hipocrisy's cell. St George leaves Una behind and in her search for him is caressed by a lion who afterwards attends her—as depicted on the coin. She next sleeps in the hut of Superstition and next morning meets Hipocrisy dressed as St George. They journey together and meet Sansloy (Lawless) who exposes Hipocrisy and kills the lion and carries off Una on his steed to a wild forest. Una is rescued by fauns and satyrs who attempt to worship her, but being restrained pay adoration to her donkey. She is delivered from the satyrs and fauns by Sir Satyrane and is told by Archimago that St George is dead, but later hears he is alive and captive of Orgoglio. She goes to King Arthur for aid who then slays Orgoglio and rescues St George. Una takes him to the house of Holiness to nurse St George then leads him to Eden where their union is consummated.

It is interesting to note that the Una and the Lion design has been revived in modern times by the Royal Mint from the original dies, for a 2019-dated issue of two ounce silver and gold coins.

Description and details of the Victoria Una and the Lion five pounds

Obverse: The Queen's truncated bust facing left, with her hair tied back into a chignon and held with two fillets. Legend: VICTORIA D:G: BRITANNIARUM REGINA F: D:

Reverse: A depiction of the Queen as Una holding sceptre in her right hand and orb in her left, a lion standing behind her, facing left. Legend: DIRIGIT DEUS GRESSUS MEOS. The date MDCCCXXXIX. in exergue. W. WYON, R.A. below

Edge: DECUS ET TUTAMEN * ANNO REGNIO TERTIO * in raised letters.

The coin is normally struck with straight upright die axis ↑↑ but a few have an inverted reverse axis ↑↓.

Of the approximately 400 known examples there are nine different variations of the basic design including the number of leaves and scrolls in the Queen's headdress on the obverse and the spelling of DIRIGE or DIRIGIT in the reverse legend.

There are also silver, copper and white metal versions of the Una and the lion five pounds of the varying obverse, reverse and edge designs.

F20. DIRIGIT, front fillet 5 scrolls, rear plain

F21. As above but plain edge

F22. DIRIGIT, front fillet 5 scrolls, rear plain, heavy flan 53.50g

F23. DIRIGE, front fillet 6 scrolls, rear 11 leaves

F24. DIRIGE, front fillet 6 scrolls, rear 11 leaves, plain edge

F25. DIRIGE, front fillet 6 scrolls, rear 11 leaves, plain edge, rim flaw

F26. DIRIGE, front fillet 5 scrolls, rear 9 leaves

F27. DIRIGE, front fillet 5 scrolls, rear 9 leaves, plain edge

F28. 1839 Young head crown obverse with Una reverse, in gold, DIRIGE type

UNA & THE LION FIVE POUNDS OF QUEEN VICTORIA

No.	Date	Type/Variety	Mintage	Rating
F20	1839	Front fillet 5 scrolls, rear plain; DIRIGIT (WR276, L&S15) ↑↑	ca. 400	R6
F21	1839	Front fillet 5 scrolls, rear plain; DIRIGIT; plain edge (WR277, L&S16) ↑↑	Incl. in above	R5
F22	1839	Front fillet 5 scrolls, rear plain; DIRIGIT; heavy flan 53.50g (WR281, L&S28)	Incl. in above	R7
F23	1839	Front fillet 6 scrolls, rear 11 leaves; DIRIGE (WR278, L&S17)	Incl. in above	R3
F24	1839	Front fillet 6 scrolls, rear 11 leaves; DIRIGE; plain edge (WR280, L&S2AU)	Incl. in above	R6
F25	1839	Front fillet 6 scrolls, rear 11 leaves; DIRIGIT; plain edge; rim flaw (WR282, L&S2BU)	Incl. in above	R7
F26	1839	Front fillet 5 scrolls, rear 9 leaves; DIRIGE (WR279, L&S18)	Incl. in above	R2
F27	1839	Front fillet 5 scrolls, rear 9 leaves; DIRIGE; plain edge (WR283, L&S32)	Incl. in above	R5
F28	1839	Crown obverse; DIRIGE (WR284, L&S35)	Incl. in above	R7

Una and the Lion by Briton Rivière.

TYPE 2: JUBILEE HEAD

After the issue of the Una and the lion five pounds of 1839 no more five or two pound coins were struck until 1887, which was the fiftieth anniversary of the Queen's accession. The Queen herself agreed to a change of coinage design and Mr J. E. Boehm, RA, was asked to prepare a portrait, and this was accepted by the Queen. Boehm modelled the portrait from life.[1]

Joseph Edgar Boehm (Bohm) was born in Vienna in 1834, the son of J. D. Boehm the medallist and gem-engraver. He settled in England some time after 1862 and, like his father before him, he was a gifted medallist and sculptor. Queen Victoria appointed him Sculptor in Ordinary in 1881 and he was made a Royal Academician in 1882. In 1889 he was granted a Baronetcy. He died in 1890.

Boehm's effigy of the Queen was adopted for the obverses of all the "Jubilee" coinage including the five pounds, and his initials appear below the monarch's shoulder. Pistrucci's popular St George and dragon, which was already widely used on the full and half sovereign (*qv*), appears on the reverse with his initials below and to the right of the ground line. However, a rare pattern piece omits these initials. Like the five pounds of George III, no legend appears on the reverse, although the date 1887 is centred in the reverse exergue and the rim is straight grained.

Interestingly in 1871 Branch Mints had been opened in Australia (see page 84 *et seq*) and it was proposed that in addition to the lower denomination gold coins being struck in Sydney, a small number of five pound pieces should be produced. As a result an unrecorded but obviously miniscule number were struck as proofs dated 1887. They can be identified by the addition of a letter "S" on the ground line of the reverse. These coins are extremely rare today and are rated R7. In addition there are official records of £5 dies dated 1888 being produced for Sydney but it seems they were never used.

FIVE POUNDS OF VICTORIA, 1837–1901

Description and details of the Victoria Jubilee Head five pounds

Obverse: Boehm's effigy of the Queen facing left wearing a small crown from which hangs a shoulder-length veil. Legend: VICTORIA D:G: BRITT: REG: F:D:. Initials J.E.B. below shoulder line.

Reverse: Pistrucci's St George armed with a sword slaying the dragon. The date 1887 appears below the exergue ground line with the letters B.P. to right.

Edge: Milled.

The coin is struck with a straight die axis ↑↑.

JUBILEE HEAD FIVE POUNDS OF QUEEN VICTORIA

No.	Date	Type/Variety	Mintage	Rating
F30	1887	Normal	53,844	C
F31	1887	Proof (WR285, L&S72)	797	S
F32	1887	£5, no B.P. in exergue (WR286, L&S73)	Small number	R4
F32A	1887	Proof, Sydney striking with S mint mark	Very few	R7

Notes/References
[1] L. Forrer, *Biographical Dictionary of Medallists, Vol. 1*, Spink & Son, London, 1902, pp. 97–98.

TYPE 3: OLD OR VEILED HEAD

The final type of Queen Victoria's coins are known as the "Old Head" or occasionally the "Veiled Head" series, from the style of the veiled image of the Queen on the obverse.

In February 1891 the Chancellor of the Exchequer requested that a committee be formed to meet and propose a design for a new coinage.[1] The committee comprised many important dignitaries including the Deputy Master of the Mint, Mr C. W. Fremantle, and interestingly Mr John Evans, FRS, President of the Numismatic Society.

Following the recommendations of this committee, the Queen accepted the design of an effigy by Thomas Brock, RA, which would be used on the obverse of all coins of the realm including a five pound piece struck in 1893 only. His initials appear below the Queen's couped shoulder. Once again Pistrucci's St George slaying the dragon was retained for the reverse of the gold coins and his initials appear above and to the right of the date. Like the Jubilee five pounds, the edge is straight grained.

Description and details of the Victoria Old Head five pounds

Obverse: Thomas Brock's effigy of the Queen's veiled head facing left, with initials T.B. below. Legend: VICTORIA · DEI · GRA · BRITT · REGINA · FID · DEF IND · IMP · .
Reverse: Pistrucci's St George armed with a sword slaying the dragon. The date 1887 appears below the exergue ground line with the letters B.P. to right.
Edge: Milled.
The coin is struck with a straight die axis ↑↑.

No.	Date	Type/Variety	Mintage	Rating
\multicolumn{5}{c}{**OLD HEAD FIVE POUNDS OF QUEEN VICTORIA**}			
F33	1893	Normal	20,405	N
F34	1893	Proof (WR287, L&S108)	773	S

Notes/References
[1] L. Forrer, *Biographical Dictionary of Medallists, Vol. 1,* Spink & Son, London, 1902, pp. 165–166.

EDWARD VII, 1901–10

Though Edward VII began his reign in 1901 the new coinage was not introduced until 1902: the gold and silver coins were in fact authorised by Royal Proclamation on December 10, 1901. The five pound piece was only struck in 1902.

The Mint Engraver, George William de Saulles, had been introduced to the Mint at the end of 1892 in succession to Leonard Wyon.[1] He had been apprenticed to Joseph Moore of Birmingham and later worked at Pinches from where he was in fact called to the Mint by the Deputy Master, Sir Charles Fremantle. He modelled and engraved the obverse for the new coinage and once more Pistrucci's St George was retained for the reverse of the gold coins. De Saulles died in July 1903. His initials DeS. appear below the truncation on the obverse. The edge is straight grained. As the 1887 £5, a miniscule number were struck at the Sydney Branch Mint and are rated R7.

Description and details of the Edward VII five pounds

Obverse: de Saulles' effigy of the King facing right, with initials DeS. on truncation. Legend: EDWARDVS VII DEI GRA: BRITT: OMN: REX: FID: DEF: IND: IMP:
Reverse: Pistrucci's St George armed with a sword slaying the dragon. The date 1902 appears below the exergue ground line with the letters B.P. to right.
Edge: Milled.
The coin is struck with a straight die axis ↑↑.

FIVE POUNDS OF EDWARD VII

No.	Date	Type/Variety	Mintage	Rating
F35	1902	Normal	34,910	N
F36	1902	Matt Proof (WR404, L&S1)	8,066	N
F37	1902	Partial matt, grainy finish, bevelled rims (WR403)	Very few	R7
F37A	1902	Proof, Sydney striking with S mint mark	Very few	R7

Notes/References
[1] L. Forrer, *Biographical Dictionary of Medallists, Vol. 1*, Spink & Son, London, 1902, p. 385.

GEORGE V, 1910–36

The year 1911 saw the issue of the first gold coins for George V. The obverse effigy of the new king was the work of Edgar Bertram Mackennal, an Australian born in Melbourne in 1863. As the previous reign, Benedetto Pistrucci's St George slaying the dragon continued to appear on the reverse of the new gold coinage.

Mackennal, who later became Sir Edgar Bertram Mackennal, RA, was a sculptor of considerable talent in both marble and bronze, and he gained many commissions for his work that can be seen in England and Australia as well as Denmark, France and India. Among his most important works to be seen in the UK are the recumbent figures of Edward VII and Queen Alexandra at the Royal Mausoleum at Frogmore, Windsor, which he completed in 1911; a marble portrait of Queen Alexandra for the Sandringham Church in Norfolk, 1930; and a statue of Thomas Gainsborough which can be seen at Sudbury in Suffolk. He also designed and engraved the 1911 Coronation Medal. He came to England in 1891 and shortly after set up a studio in St John's Wood, London, then in 1914 he moved to Watcombe Hall near Torquay in Devon and lived there until his death in 1931. He is remembered as a truly great artist, especially in Australia. After being elected an Associate of the Royal Academy he later became the only Australian to become a full member of the Royal Academy.

For the coinage of George V, Mackennal first produced a model from photographs and was then granted a special sitting by the King. The five pound piece was only struck in 1911 as a proof coin with a grained edge and is relatively scarce. As standard practice, the engraver's initials, B.M., appear on the truncation and Pistrucci's familiar initials can be seen on the reverse, above and to the right of the date.

Description and details of the George V five pounds

Obverse: Bertram Mackennal's' effigy of the King facing left, with initials B.M. on truncation. Legend: GEORGIVS V DEI GRA: BRITT: OMN: REX: FID: DEF: IND: IMP:
Reverse: Pistrucci's St George armed with a sword slaying the dragon. The date 1911 appears below the exergue ground line with the letters B.P. to right.
Edge: Milled.
The coin is struck with a straight die axis ↑↑.

FIVE POUNDS OF GEORGE V

No.	Date	Type/Variety	Mintage	Rating
F38	1911	Proof (WR414, L&S1)	2,812	S

The Australian born Edgar Bertram Mackennal designer of the King George V obverse effigy on the sovereign issue of 1911. The classic St George and the dragon design by Benedetto Pistrucci was retained for the reverse.

EDWARD VIII (JANUARY–DECEMBER 1936)

Though Edward VIII abdicated in late 1936, coinage proposals were well advanced and only a tiny quantity of complete proof sets were ever struck from images by Thomas Humphrey Paget, thus making the sovereign series the greatest rarities. Paget was the only artist commissioned to produce designs for the new coinage and his success was such that he was later asked to supply images which were used on the coinage of George VI. His initials, HP appear on the truncation of the king's bust. Interestingly Edward insisted on his effigy facing left on the coinage just as his father before him. This effectively broke with the age-old tradition of succeeding monarchs facing opposite directions on the coins. Allegedly this was because he considered that his left side was more imposing than his right. The reverse of the gold coins carry the familiar figure of St George slaying the dragon by Pistrucci.

Description and details of the Edward VIII sovereign

Obverse: Paget's effigy of the King facing left, with initials HP on truncation. Legend: EDWARDVS VIII D: G: BR: OMN: REX: F: D: IND: IMP.
Reverse: Pistrucci's St George slaying the dragon. Date below exergue ground line and initials B.P. above right.
Edge: Milled.
The coin is struck with a straight upright die axis ↑↑.

FIVE POUNDS OF EDWARD VIII

No.	Date	Type/Variety	Mintage	Rating
F39	1937	Pattern (WR432)	6	R5

Note: At the time of writing, the Edward VIII gold Pattern Five Pounds is the most valuable British coin ever sold; it secured over £2 million.

GEORGE VI, 1936–52

After the abdication of Edward VIII his younger brother became king, as George VI. Following his success with Edward's coinage Paget was again requested to supply the image for the coins of the new king, and in keeping with tradition Pistrucci's St George was chosen for the reverse. The five pounds was struck in normal proof finish as part of a set to celebrate the Coronation, but a very small number are also known which have a Matt proof finish. Interestingly there are two known die varieties of the five pound coin where the first letter I of legend can point to either a border tooth or a space. Unusually it was decided to strike the gold coins for the sets with a plain edge instead of the by now familiar straight milling.

Building on his success with the UK coinage Paget went on to design coins and medals for a number of different countries, his most notable success being the medals for the 1970 Commonwealth Games which featured a portrait of the Duke of Edinburgh. He died in 1974.

Description and details of the George V five pounds

Obverse: Paget's effigy of the King facing left, with initials HP on truncation. Legend: GEORGIVS VI D:G: BR: OMN: REX F: D: IND: IMP:
Reverse: Pistrucci's St George armed with a sword slaying the dragon. The date 1937 appears below the exergue ground line with the letters B.P. to right.
Edge: Plain.
The coin is struck with a straight die axis ↑↑.

FIVE POUNDS OF GEORGE VI

No.	Date	Type/Variety	Mintage	Rating
F40	1937	Proof (WR435, L&S1)	5,501	N
F41	1937	Matt proof (WR436, L&S2)	Very few	R7

ELIZABETH II, 1952–2022

Queen Elizabeth II succeeded her father on February 6, 1952 and progressed through six different busts (if the 90th Birthday, one-off portrait by Butler is included) of this monarch who passed away on September 8, 2022, not long after her Platinum Jubilee celebration. The first bust type was the work of Mary Gillick who was granted personal sittings by the Queen. The second bust was by Arnold Machin and the third bust was the work of Raphael David Maklouf, who also was granted personal sittings by the Queen. The fourth bust was by the sculptor and medallist Ian Rank-Broadley who worked from photographs taken specially for coinage purposes by permission of Her Majesty. The final bust, the fifth, is by Jody Clark and it is the first to be totally designed on a computer. The reverses for the gold coins of these different issues all, except those issues produced for a special occasion, display Benedetto Pistrucci's St George armed with a sword slaying the dragon.

The decision to adopt a decimal currency system was announced in March 1966, and the introduction of the new coinage was scheduled for February 15, 1971. It was obvious that the Royal Mint facilities at Tower Hill would not enable them to cope with the demands of the new coinage, and indeed it brought to an end centuries of minting in London when the Government decided to build a new mint in Llantrisant, Wales.

The old Mint building at Tower Hill had been used by the Royal Mint for the past 150 years. It had been designed by the architect James Johnson who died in 1807 before its completion. After his death Sir Robert Smirke took over the work and this truly magnificent Georgian building was finished in 1811, the keys being formally handed to the Constable in August 1812. The very last coin to be struck at the Royal Mint, Tower Hill, was a gold sovereign bearing the date 1974 and was struck on November 10, 1975.

The Queen has always shown a keen interest in our coinage and its minting, and on December 17, 1968 the new Royal Mint at Llantrisant was officially opened by Her Majesty. In 1982 another great traditional occasion was honoured by her presence when she attended the Trial of the Pyx. The Trial is held annually and in 1982 it marked the 700th anniversary of this very ancient ceremony. Her Majesty's gracious presence at Goldsmith's Hall on February 25, 1982 for the ceremony was itself an historic occasion, being the very first time a reigning Queen had attended this ceremony.

The Trial of the Pyx is held every year and its purpose is to provide an independent check on the accuracy of composition, weight and fineness of the coins minted in the previous year. The law defines that the Mint must set aside for trial one in every 2,000 gold coins minted. The Pyx is the box in which the samples of coins are kept. Having been sworn in by the Queen's Remembrancer, the Trial jury, consisting of Freemen of the Goldsmith's Company, take from each packet whatever coins they deem necessary. These coins are then individually weighed and melted into an ingot to be later assayed. The remaining coins are weighed in bulk from which the jury selects as many coins as they think necessary. These are then weighed and assayed individually. The Trial is then adjourned for a few weeks while assaying is carried out and finally on a given date the jury re-assembles in Goldsmith's Hall and the verdicts are read out by the Clerk of the Company. Normally the Chancellor of the Exchequer is in attendance.

Since the five pounds bearing the portrait by Mary Gillick, struck at the time of the Coronation in 1953 for institutions but never issued to the public, there have been a number of gold five pound coins produced by the Royal Mint, commencing in 1980. But probably the most important issue was for the 500th anniversary of the sovereign, 1489–1989. These splendid proof coins, celebrating the remarkable history of the gold sovereign and portraying Her Majesty the Queen enthroned on the obverse and a crowned shield of arms imposed upon a double rose on the reverse is the work of Bernard Sindall. Following the success of that issue the Mint has capitalised on a buoyant market to produce coins of the sovereign series from the five pounds down virtually every year, mainly as part of their annual "Year Sets". Naturally many of these sets get split up and the individual coins can be readily found on the market.

In addition to the proof five pounds a normal or uncirculated edition has been produced most years, the first being in 1984. To differentiate these coins from the proofs a tiny U in a circle was added and can be found to the left of the date on the reverse, a practice which ended in 2001. However, in 2000, in addition to the five pounds with the U in circle, an unspecified number of bullion coins were also issued without it.

The numbers of the different five pound coins issued each year has varied dramatically from just six of the first type to over 15,000 of the 1984 normal uncirculated issue, with the more recent issues settling around 1,000 and sometimes less.

Further details of the designs and their designers can be found under the chapter on the sovereign as most of the coins in the sovereign series follow the same criteria and are relevant to the whole series.

Description and details of the Elizabeth II First bust type five pounds

Obverse: Mary Gillick's laureated effigy of the Queen facing right. Legend: + ELIZABETH II DEI GRA: BRITT: OMN: REGINA F: D:

Reverse: Pistrucci's St George armed with a sword slaying the dragon. The date 1953 appears below the exergue ground line with the letters B.P. to right.

Edge: Plain.

The coin is struck with a straight die axis ↑↑.

FIVE POUNDS OF ELIZABETH II, FIRST BUST

No.	Date	Type/Variety	Mintage	Rating
F42	1953	Proof (WR444, L&S1)	At least 6	R5
F43	1953	Pattern, TRIAL incuse on obverse field (WR445) Probably unique		R7

Description and details of the Elizabeth II Second bust type five pounds

Obverse: Effigy of the Queen facing right wearing a tiara and off-the shoulder dress, by Arnold Machin.
  Legend: ELIZABETH · II · DEI GRATIA · REGINA · F: D:
Reverse: Pistrucci's St George armed with a sword slaying the dragon. The date appears below the exergue ground line with the letters B.P. to right. The Normal (Unc) edition has a small U in a circle in the reverse exergue.
Edge: Milled.
The coin is struck with a straight die axis ↑↑.

FIVE POUNDS OF ELIZABETH II, SECOND BUST

No.	Date	Type/Variety	Mintage	Rating
F44	1980	Proof	10,000	C
F45	1981	Proof	5,400	C
F46	1982	Proof	2,500	N
F47	1984	Proof	8,000	S
F48	1984	Normal, with U in circle to left of date (Spink SE2)	15,104	C

Description and details of the Elizabeth II Third bust type five pounds

Obverse: Effigy of the Queen facing right wearing a coronet, couped (1987 and 1988 issues have an uncouped draped portrait), by Raphael Maklouf, with designer's initials, RM, at base of truncation. Legend: ELIZABETH II · DEI · GRA · REG · F · D.

Reverse: Pistrucci's St George armed with a sword slaying the dragon. The date appears below the exergue ground line with the letters B.P. to right. The Normal (Unc) edition has a small U in a circle in the reverse exergue.

Edge: Milled.

The coin is struck with a straight die axis ↑↑.

FIVE POUNDS OF ELIZABETH II, THIRD BUST

No.	Date	Type/Variety	Mintage	Rating
F49	1985	Proof	6,130	N
F50	1985	Normal, with U in circle to left of date	13,626	C
F51	1986	Normal, with U in circle to left of date	7,723	C
F52	1987	Normal but with uncouped bust*	5,694	C
F53	1988	Normal but with uncouped bust*	3,315	N
F54 & F55	1989	See special issues for details*		
F56	1990	Proof	1,721	N
F57	1990	Normal, with U in circle to left of date	1,226	N
F58	1991	Proof	1,336	N
F59	1991	Normal, with U in circle to left of date	976	S
F60	1992	Proof	1,165	N
F61	1992	Normal, with U in circle to left of date	797	S
F62	1993	Proof	1,078	N
F63	1993	Normal, with U in circle to left of date	906	S
F64	1994	Proof	918	N
F65	1994	Normal, with U in circle to left of date	1,000	S
F66	1995	Proof	718	N
F67	1995	Normal, with U in circle to left of date	1,000	S
F68	1996	Proof	742	N
F69	1996	Normal, with U in circle to left of date	901	S
F70	1997	Proof	860	N
F71	1997	Normal, with U in circle to left of date	802	S

* These designs carry a variant of the obverse and strictly speaking should not be included with the third bust type.

THE GOLD SOVEREIGN SERIES

Description and details of the Elizabeth II Fourth bust type five pounds

Obverse: Effigy of the Queen facing right wearing a tiara by Ian Rank-Broadley, with designer's initials, IRB, at base of truncation. Legend: ELIZABETH · II · DEI · GRA REGINA · FID · DEF .

Reverse: Pistrucci's St George armed with a sword slaying the dragon. The date appears below the exergue ground line with the letters B.P. to right. Until and including the 2001 issue the Normal (Unc) edition has a small U in a circle in the reverse exergue.

Edge: Milled.

The coin is struck with a straight die axis ↑↑.

FIVE POUNDS OF ELIZABETH II, FOURTH BUST

No.	Date	Type/Variety	Mintage	Rating
F72	1998	Proof	789	N
F73	1998	Normal, with U in circle to left of date	825	S
F74	1999	Proof	991	C
F75	1999	Normal, with U in circle to left of date	970	S
F76	2000	Proof	1,000	N
F77	2000	Brilliant uncirculated issue, with U in circle to left of date	994	S
F77A	2000	Bullion issue	4,177	C
F78	2001	Proof	1,000	N
F79	2001	Normal, with U in circle to left of date	1,000	S
F80	2002	See special issues for details		
F81	2002	See special issues for details		
F82	2003	Proof	2,050	N
F83	2003	Normal	812	S
F84	2004	Proof	1,749	N
F85	2004	Normal	1,000	S
F86	2005	See special issues for details		
F87	2005	See special issues for details		
F88	2006	Proof	1,750	N
F89	2006	Normal	731	S
F90	2007	Proof	1,750	N
F91	2007	Normal	768	S

FIVE POUNDS OF ELIZABETH II, FOURTH BUST *continued*

No.	Date	Type/Variety	Mintage	Rating
F92	2008	Proof	1,750	N
F93	2008	Normal	750	S
F94	2009	Proof	1,750	N
F95	2009	Normal	1,000	S
F96	2010	Proof	1,461	N
F97	2010	Normal	1,000	S
F98	2011	Proof	1,028	N
F99	2011	Normal	657	S
F100	2012	See special issues for details		
F101	2012	See special issues for details		
F102	2013	Proof	388	S
F103	2013	Normal	262	R
F104	2014	Proof	375	S
F105	2014	Normal	605	S
F106	2015	Proof	507	S

A GUIDE TO THE GUINEA

THE DEFINITIVE GUIDE TO ONE OF BRITAIN'S MOST FAMOUS COINS!

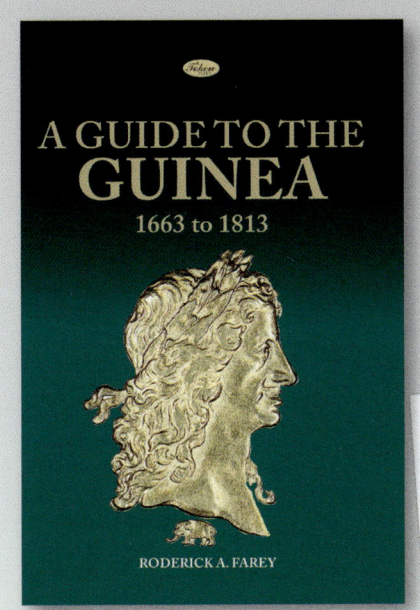

Covering the history of the Guinea from its beginnings in the reign of the newly restored monarch Charles II to its demise as a circulating coin and replacement by the modern sovereign in the time of George III, this book will tell you all you need to know about the "golden guinea" and all its varieties. A separate eight-page Price Guide to the Guinea is also included with the book.

Telephone 01404 46972 or log onto www.tokenpublishing.com for your copy.

THE GOLD SOVEREIGN SERIES

Description and details of the Elizabeth II Fifth bust type five pounds

Obverse: Effigy of the Queen facing right wearing a tiara by Jody Clark, with designer's initials, JC, at base of truncation. Legend: ELIZABETH · II · DEI · GRA REGINA · FID · DEF .
Reverse: Pistrucci's St George armed with a sword slaying the dragon. The date appears below the exergue ground line with the letters B.P. to right.
Edge: Milled.
The coin is struck with a straight die axis ↑↑.

FIVE POUNDS OF ELIZABETH II, FIFTH BUST

No.	Date	Type/Variety	Mintage	Rating
F110	2015	Proof	598	S
F111	2015	Normal	609	S
F112	2016	Normal	498	R
F113	2016	See special issues for details*		
F114	2017	See special issues for details		
F115	2017	See special issues for details		
F116	2018	Proof, with 65 privy mark	849	N
F117	2018	Normal, with 65 privy mark	459	S
F118	2019	Proof	618	N
F118A	2019	With BU matt finish	400	S
F119	2020	See special issues for details		
F121	2021	Proof, with 95 in crown privy mark	500	N
F122	2021	With BU matt finish	347	S

* As this issue carries a portrait by James Butler, strictly speaking it should not be included with the fifth bust type.

65 privy mark

95 in crown privy mark

ELIZABETH II FIVE POUNDS —SPECIAL ISSUES

All special issues are listed sequentially with the standard coins but in addition are listed separately here for identification purposes.

500th ANNIVERSARY OF THE SOVEREIGN 1489–1989. Obverse and reverse by Bernard Sindall

No.	Date	Type/Variety	Mintage	Rating
F54	1989	Proof	5,000	C
F55	1989	Normal, U added under throne on obverse	2,937	N

GOLDEN JUBILEE OF HER MAJESTY QUEEN ELIZABETH II. Obverse by Ian Rank-Broadley, Shield reverse by Timothy Noad

No.	Date	Type/Variety	Mintage	Rating
F80	2002	Proof	3,000	N
F81	2002	Normal	1,370	N

MODERN INTERPRETATION OF ST GEORGE. New reverse for 2005 by Timothy Noad

No.	Date	Type/Variety	Mintage	Rating
F86	2005	Proof	2,161	N
F87	2005	Normal	936	S

FIVE POUNDS OF ELIZABETH II, 1952–2022

DIAMOND JUBILEE OF HER MAJESTY QUEEN ELIZABETH II. Stylised reverse by Paul Day

No.	Date	Type/Variety	Mintage	Rating
F100	2012	Proof	956	N
F101	2012	Normal	496	R

90th BIRTHDAY OF HER MAJESTY THE QUEEN. Obverse portrait by James Butler

No.	Date	Type/Variety	Mintage	Rating
F113	2016	Proof	573	R

75

200th ANNIVERSARY OF THE SOVEREIGN. Jody Clark obverse. Reverse as 1817–20 sovereign

No.	Date	Type/Variety	Mintage	Rating
F114	2017	Proof	749	R
F115	2017	Normal	992	N

200th ANNIVERSARY OF THE DEATH OF GEORGE III. Jody Clark obverse. Reverse with Royal cypher mint mark

No.	Date	Type/Variety	Mintage	Rating
F119	2020	Proof	549	N
F120	2020	With BU matt finish	355	S

FIVE POUNDS OF ELIZABETH II, 1952–2022

**PLATINUM JUBILEE OF HER MAJESTY QUEEN ELIZABTH II. Jody Clark obverse.
Timothy Noad Reverse**

No.	Date	Type/Variety	Mintage	Rating
F123	2022	Proof	700	N
F124	2022	With BU matt finish	810	N
F125	2022	Piedfort Proof	70	R

CHARLES III, 2022–

The new reign dawned for King Charles III on accession to the throne from the Late Queen on September 8, 2022. The 73-year-old King had been the longest ever Monarch-in-waiting as the Prince of Wales in British history, though preparations for his new coinage, as well as banknotes and stamps, had been in gestation for some time beforehand. Martin Jennings was the sculptor charged with the new coinage design which has also been applied as the new stamp effigy. Totally designed on computers, the effigy has so far been produced with a bare head design like that of the earlier 20th century kings and for the special Coronation issues with a crowned head design. Special edition reverse designs for Sovereign series gold has so far been produced for a Memorial design to the Late Queen as well as the Coronation Sovereign. The familiar St George and dragon design by Benedetto Pistrucci has since returned to the series for the 2024-dated issues. We await with interest to see what other designs will appear in the future.

Description and details of the Charles III bare head five pounds Memorial reverse

Obverse: Bare head effigy of King Charles III left by Martin Jennings, raised initials below neck MJ. Legend CHARLES III. DEI. GRA. REX. FID. DEF.
Reverse: Royal heraldic coat of arms with crowned lion and unicorn supporters, crowned helm above, banner motto below DIEU ET MON DROIT with date.
Edge: Milled.
The coin is struck with a straight upright die axis ↑↑

FIVE POUNDS OF CHARLES III, 2022–

MEMORIAL ISSUE FOR THE LATE QUEEN ELIZABETH II.

No.	Date	Type/Variety	Mintage	Rating
F126	2022	Proof	1,113	N
F127	2022	With BU matt finish	661	N

Description and details of the Charles III crowned head
Five Pounds reverse

Obverse: Crowned head effigy of King Charles III left by Martin Jennings, raised initials below neck MJ. Legend CHARLES III. DEI. GRA. REX. FID. DEF.
Reverse: Pistrucci's St George armed with sword slaying the dragon. The date in the exergue below the ground line with PISTRUCCI. in small raised letters to upper left.
Edge: Milled.
The coin is struck with a straight upright die axis ↑↑

CORONATION WITH CROWNED HEAD AND ST GEORGE & DRAGON REVERSE.

No.	Date	Type/Variety	Mintage	Rating
F128	2023	Proof	1,785	N
F129	2023	Matt Proof edition as a set	23	R3
F130	2023	With BU matt finish	450	S

Description and details of the Charles III bare head Five Pounds

Obverse: Bare head effigy of King Charles III left by Martin Jennings, raised initials below neck MJ. Legend CHARLES III. DEI. GRA. REX. FID. DEF.
Reverse: Pistrucci's St George armed with sword slaying the dragon. The date in the exergue below the ground line with PISTRUCCI. in small raised letters to upper left.
Edge: Milled.
The coin is struck with a straight upright die axis ↑↑

REGULAR FORMAT WITH BARE HEAD LEFT AND ST GEORGE & DRAGON REVERSE.

No.	Date	Type/Variety	Mintage	Rating
F131	2024	Proof	9,260	C

TWO POUNDS

(DOUBLE SOVEREIGN)

Obverse of the two pound coin by Bernard Sindall struck in 1989 to
commemorate the 500th anniversary of the original sovereign.

Specifications of the two pounds:

Weight: 15.98 grams.

Fineness, 22 carat: 11/12 fine gold, 1/12 alloy (this means that each TWO pound coin contains 14.644 grams of pure gold).

Millesimal fineness: 916.66.

Thickness: 2mm.

Diameter: 28.40mm.

GEORGE III, 1760–1820

When it was initially decided to replace the guinea series it was expected that the two pounds would be a popular coin with the public, but this was not to be, thus even today this denomination is not collected so avidly as its larger or even its smaller cousins in the series. Just as the five pounds, the very first two pound coins were dated 1820 with the edge inscribed DECUS ET TUTAMEN. ANNO REGNI LX, being the 60th year of the King's reign. The obverse carries the royal effigy and legend by Benedetto Pistrucci whilst the reverse portrays Pistrucci's enigmatic St George armed with a broken spear slaying the dragon, on a plain field with no legend. Interestingly it was proposed to strike the same small number of coins as the five pounds but due to a communication error at the mint a total of 60 were produced, albeit in a great hurry owing to the King's untimely death. These remain of the highest rarity. An unknown but assumed minute number were struck as plain edge proofs and a single example exists in silver which is believed to have been in the personal possession of Pistrucci. In addition a unique piece exists which is a uniface trial striking of the reverse only.

Description and details of the George III two pounds

Obverse: The King's head right, laureate with short hair; the tie has a loop with two ends, neck bare. Legend: GEORGIUS III D:G:BRITANNIARUM REX F: D: The King's bust does not interrupt the legend. The date is at the bottom of the legend.

Reverse: St George with streamer flowing from helmet, mounted and slaying the dragon armed with a broken spear, the shaft of which lays on the ground. No legend. The designer's initials B.P. appear in the exergue to the right below the ground line.

Edge: Plain, inscribed DECUS ET TUTAMEN. ANNO REGNI LX.

The coin is struck with a reverse die axis ↑↓

TWO POUNDS OF GEORGE III

No.	Date	Type/Variety	Mintage	Rating
T1	1820	Pattern, LX on edge, weight 18.87g (WR179)	60	R3
T2	1820	Pattern, plain edge, weight 16.00g (WR180)	Very few	R6
T3	1820	Example struck in silver (ex Pistrucci)	Probably unique	R7
T4	1820	Uniface trial of reverse, probably unique	Probably unique	R7

GEORGE IV, 1820–30

During the reign of George IV there were to be two different designs of the sovereign series except the five pounds. The first was authorised by Order in Council dated May 5, 1821 in accordance with the following submission bearing the date April 10, 1821 by William Wellesley Pole, Master of the Mint: "*In further pursuance of your Majesty's Commands that Dies should be prepared for the Coining of Your Majesty's Monies I humbly beg leave to lay before Your Majesty a Design for the Gold Sovereign or Twenty Shilling piece having for the Obverse Impression the effigy of Your Majesty with the Inscription 'Georgius IIII D.G.Britanniar Rex F:D:' and for the Reverse the Image of St George, armed, sitting on horseback attacking the Dragon with a Sword having broken his Spear in the Encounter, and the date of the Year. The edge of the piece is intended to be marked with the new invented Graining used on Coins of His late Majesty.*"

The new coinage was by now becoming an urgent requirement and Pistrucci began his work, and all the obverses for the entire coinage were modelled and cut by him using the same laureate head bust that he had used for the Coronation Medal. However, subsequent events overtook production of the coinage.

Before going into details of the "new bare head" series that followed, it is necessary to record a chapter of events that occurred during 1823 and 1824, events that were to have a considerable effect on the proposed new coinage. Pole had become upset at a Cabinet reconstruction in 1823 and resigned as Master in the August of that year, and he was replaced by Thomas Wallace in October 1823. Wallace was considered a good replacement, and he was in fact particularly keen on the design of coins.

During 1823 the English sculptor Francis

Legatt Chantrey (1781–1841) was asked to prepare a bust of the King simply because His Majesty fancied a new image. Chantrey was a sculptor of the highest merit who had studied art at the Royal Academy of which he was elected a member in 1818. He was knighted by William IV in 1830. He earned the distinction of being the finest bust sculptor of his time, so it was inevitable that the King should decide to accept the Chantrey bust for the proposed new coinage of 1825. His Majesty also requested that it should be used for the effigy on the obverse of the new double-sovereign to be struck in 1823.

Pistrucci was instructed to use Chantrey's model and to proceed with the engraving of the new coin, but this he promptly refused to do. Throughout his career Pistrucci had often been difficult to please and he declared that he could only work from life and felt it degrading to copy another artist's work. But this time the King insisted that the Chantrey bust should be used. Wallace, the new Master, reported that Pistrucci had refused to carry out his orders and as a result he was relieved of his coinage duties. It was in fact Merlen, the Assistant Engraver, who eventually engraved the obverse die for the double-sovereign.

On June 23, 1824, the Master of the Mint recommended that Merlen be employed to prepare the design and engrave dies for the new series of gold and silver coins. At the same time William Wyon, the Second Engraver, was called to prepare designs and engrave the head dies for the proposed new coinage which he did using Chantrey's work as his model. Later, on January 15, 1828, with Pistrucci already having lost his position, William Wyon was given the post of Chief Engraver and Pistrucci the somewhat lower position of Chief Medallist, though both were given the same salary of £350 a year.

The two pound coins all have a bare headed bust of the King. Those dated 1823 carry that by Merlen paired with Pistrucci's reverse with St George now armed with a sword, whereas the later issues use the Willam Wyon bust obverse with the crowned and mantled ensigns armorial reverse by Merlen.

The only year that currency two pounds were struck was 1823 although, even today it is not known just how many were produced, although they remain quite scarce. These all have an inscribed edge. The later "shield reverse" types are all rare except the 1826 which were issued with the year sets and these are scarce.

Description and details of the George IV two pounds type I

Obverse: The King's bare head left, with short hair. Legend: GEORGIUS IIII D: G: BRITANNIAR: REX F: D: . Designer's initials J.B.M. below truncation.

Reverse: St George slaying the dragon armed with a sword. The date is shown below the exergue line with the letters B.P. to the right, for Benedetto Pistrucci. Raised W.W.P. William Wellesley Pole) on ground line below broken lance.

Edge: Inscribed DECUS ET TUTAMEN ANNO REGNI IV or plain.
The coin is struck with a reverse die axis ↑↓

TYPE I TWO POUNDS OF GEORGE IV

No.	Date	Type/Variety	Mintage	Rating
T6	1823	Normal	Maximum 15,419	N
T7	1823	Proof (WR218)	Small number	R5
T8	1823	Pattern, no J.B.M. on obverse (WR219)	Probably unique	R7

Description and details of the George IV two pounds type II

Obverse: The King's bare head left, with short hair. Legend: - GEORGIUS IV DEI GRATIA. The date is at the bottom of the legend.

Reverse: A crowned and mantled Ensigns Armorial of the United Kingdom. The centre of the shield features a smaller crowned shield depicting the Hanoverian arms. Legend: BRITANNIARUM REX FID: DEF: .

Edge: Inscribed DECUS ET TUTAMEN ANNO REGNI ... or plain.

The coin is struck with a reverse die axis ↑↓

TYPE II TWO POUNDS OF GEORGE IV

No.	Date	Type/Variety	Mintage	Rating
T9	1824	Pattern, lettered edge (WR220)	Very few	R6
T10	1824	Pattern, plain edge (WR221)	Very few	R7
T11	1824	Uniface obverse only (WR222)	Probably unique	R7
T11A	1824	Struck in copper	Very few	R6
T12	1825	Pattern, lettered edge (WR223)	Small number	R5
T13	1825	Pattern, plain edge, larger flan plain rim to toothed border (WR224)	Probably unique	R7
T14	1825	Pattern, plain edge (WR225)	Very few	R6
T15	1825	Pattern, incuse edge lettering error no A in ANNO (WR226)	Very few	R6
T16	1826	Proof, lettered edge as issued in sets (WR228)	c. 400	S
T17	1826	Proof but struck on thicker 21.05g flan, plain edge (WR227)	Not known	R6

WILLIAM IV, 1830–37

William IV succeeded his brother on June 26, 1830, and for some time it appeared that little or nothing was being done about the new coinage. On November 15, 1830, John Charles Herries, MP, who was then Master of the Mint, felt it was necessary to explain why there was a delay in the preparation of the new dies.

He said: *"The delay which has occurred in presenting the Memorial since His Majesty's commands were issued, although not beyond the usual period, has arisen in consequence of the difficult and anxious desire to obtain an accurate and approved resemblance of His Majesty, who was pleased to command that the effigy on his coins should be taken from the Bust which was executed at the time by Mr Chantrey. For this purpose it was desirable that a model should be prepared by Mr Chantrey adapted to the style used on the Coinage before Mr Wyon could be set to work; this of course occupied some time in addition to the time required by Mr Wyon for engraving the Dies on Steel (always a work of much labour) and the more so on this occasion when it was necessary to be done under the immediate personal superintendence and instruction of Mr Chantrey."*

Shortly after this statement Herries resigned and in December of that year was replaced by George Eden, 2nd Earl of Auckland, who remained Master until 1834. However, the dies for the new coinage had in fact been prepared before the Herries statement, because on October 28, 1830 the Master had written to the Mint Board as follows: *"Mr Herries communicates to the Mint Board His Majesty's entire approbation of the Engraving of the Head of His Majesty for the New coin executed by Mr Wyon, from the model prepared by Mr Chantrey, to whom His Majesty was graciously pleased to sit for the purpose.*

Mr Herries further acquaints the Board that it is His Majesty's pleasure that Engraving from the same model, and from no other, shall be used for all coins, whether in Gold, Silver or Copper that are to bear the effigys (sic) of His Majesty in order that there may be a perfect uniformity throughout the Coinage of His Majesty's Reign in that respect."

The design of the new gold coinage, which included the two pounds as well as the sovereign, was approved by an Order in Council dated November 22, 1830, according to the following description: *"The Sovereign having for the Obverse Impression the Effigy of Your Majesty with the inscription GULIELMUS IIII D.G.BRITANNIAR.REX F.D. and for the reverse the Ensigns Armorial of the United Kingdom contained in a Shield—plain—with the date of the year and a graining on the edge of the piece."* William Wyon, the Chief Engraver, engraved the dies from the model once again prepared by Francis Legatt Chantrey. The reverse was both designed and engraved by Jean Baptiste Merlen.

About 225 proof sets were issued in 1831 containing all the coins, including the two pounds, but not five pounds.

Description and details of the William IV two pounds

Obverse: The King's bare head to right. At the base of the truncation the letters W.W. incuse, with stops, initials of William Wyon. Legend: GULIELMUS IIII D: G: BRITANNIAR: REX F: D:.
Reverse: The Ensigns Armorial of the United Kingdom within a shield surmounted by a crown, in the centre a smaller shield containing the Hanoverian arms surmounted by a small crown. The word ANNO appears in the field at the bottom of the left side and the date appears in a similar position on the right side.
Edge: Plain.
The coin is struck with a reverse die axis ↑↓.

TWO POUNDS OF WILLIAM IV

No.	Date	Type/Variety	Mintage	Rating
T20	1831	Proof, as issued in sets (WR258)	c. 225	R

VICTORIA, 1837–1901

The reign of Queen Victoria is interesting in that no two pound coins were struck until the Jubilee of 1887, although two intriguing uniface patterns or trial pieces are known: one from 1838 and the other 1841. The earlier one is actually an undated striking of a crowned shield type reverse by Merlen, similar to that used on the sovereign of that year. Very little is known about this piece other than it was first recorded by Hocking as being in the Royal Mint collection in 1906[1] and is believed to be unique. The other item is also believed to be unique and it too resides in the Royal Mint collection. The design has been credited to James Wyon (1804–68) who at the time was assistant engraver to his cousin William. On William's death in 1851 he became Resident Engraver at the Mint on probation, a position that was made official in 1854. The piece features an ornamental trident between two dolphins. The date appears at the bottom divided by the trident's shaft.

UNIFACE PATTERN TWO POUNDS OF QUEEN VICTORIA

No.	Date	Type/Variety	Mintage	Rating
T21	1838	Crowned shield design, undated (WR288)	Probably unique	R7
T22	1841	Trident and dolphins design (WR289)	Probably unique	R7

TYPE 1: JUBILEE HEAD

The first type to be issued was struck as part of the proof sets for Her Majesty's Golden Jubilee. Like the rest of the gold coins that year it featured the Jubilee head by Joseph Edgar Boehm on the obverse, with the iconic St George and the dragon reverse by Pistrucci. The sets sold well with the Royal Mint producing around 800 sets, many of which have been split up over time but the complete sets still command high prices. There are a number of known varieties of the two pounds and all of the major types have been listed, but probably the most well known are the different sizes of the dates and the designer's initials, B.P., on the reverse. A scarce type is that with the B.P. omitted. Another interesting type is the normal currency coin for which the proof obverse die was used, giving a noticeable variety. For the relatively common currency coin the B of BRITT: in the legend is well clear of the Queen's crown, whereas for the proof coin it appears to be sitting over the crown. It seems that a small number of currency coins were struck using the proof die. In addition a very small quantity of proof coins were struck at the Sydney branch mint and can be identified by the small S in the centre of the reverse groundline. However, it is thought that some of these were struck as late as 1927.

Description and details of the Victoria Jubilee Head two pounds

Obverse: Boehm's effigy of the Queen facing left wearing a small crown from which hangs a shoulder-length veil. Legend: VICTORIA D:G: BRITT: REG: F:D:. Initials J.E.B. below shoulder line.
Reverse: Pistrucci's St George armed with a sword slaying the dragon. The date 1887 appears below the exergue ground line with the letters B.P. to right.
Edge: Milled.
The coin is struck with a straight die axis ↑↑.

THE GOLD SOVEREIGN SERIES

Normal type, small date and small B.P.

Normal type, large date and large B.P.

The proof obverse and the currency obverse,
illustrating the position of the B in BRITT:

JUBILEE HEAD TWO POUNDS OF QUEEN VICTORIA

No.	Date	Type/Variety	Mintage	Rating
T24	1887	Normal but with proof coin obverse die B of BRITT above right side of crown, quantity struck unknown (DISH C205)	Incl. below	R5
T25	1887	Normal, B of BRITT to right of crown smaller date, small B.P. (DISH C206)	Incl. below	N
		A sub-variety of T25 has vertical die break commencing at the Queen's eye		
T26	1887	Normal, larger date, large B.P. (DISH C207)	91,345	C
		A sub-variety of T26 has a break in the streamer flowing from St George's helmet		
T27	1887	Proof, with small B.P. and date (WR290) (DISH P203)	797	S
T27A	1887	Proof (WR290) with large B.P. and date (DISH P204)	Incl. above	R5
T28	1887	Proof, B.P. omitted in reverse exergue (WR291) (DISH P201)	Incl. above	R5
T29	1887	Uniface reverse only	Very few	R7
T30	1887	Uniface reverse only, B.P. omitted	Very few	R7
T31	1887	Proof, with small S in centre of groundline on reverse (some of these were struck as late as 1927) (DISH P208)	Small number	R4

TYPE 2: OLD OR VEILED HEAD

As mentioned earlier, the final type of Queen Victoria's coins are known as the "Old Head" or occasionally the "Veiled Head" series, from the style of the veiled image of the Queen on the obverse.

Following the recommendations of the committee set up in 1891, the Queen formally accepted the design of an effigy by Thomas Brock, RA, which would be used on the obverse of all coins of the realm including the gold five and two pound coins which were struck in 1893 only. His initials appear below the Queen's couped shoulder. As the five pounds, Pistrucci's St George was used for the reverse of the two pounds and his initials appear above and to the right of the date. In keeping with the other gold coins of the series, the edge is straight grained. There are no known varieties and the coins were only struck in currency grade and proof.

Description and details of the Victoria Old Head two pounds

Obverse: Thomas Brock's effigy of the Queen's veiled head facing left, with initials T.B. below. Legend: VICTORIA · DEI · GRA · BRITT · REGINA · FID · DEF IND · IMP · .
Reverse: Pistrucci's St George armed with a sword slaying the dragon. The date 1893 appears below the exergue ground line with the letters B.P. to right.
Edge: Milled.
The coin is struck with a straight die axis ↑↑.

OLD HEAD TWO POUNDS OF QUEEN VICTORIA

No.	Date	Type/Variety	Mintage	Rating
T35	1893	Normal	52,212	N
T36	1893	Proof (WR294)	773	R

EDWARD VII, 1901–10

Though Edward VII began his reign in 1901 the new coinage was not introduced until 1902: the gold and silver coins were in fact authorised by Royal Proclamation on December 10, 1901. In the same way as the five pound coin the two pound piece was only struck in 1902, using the King's effigy as engraved by Mint Engraver, George William de Saulles, who had succeeded Leonard Wyon in 1892. His initials DeS. appear below the truncation on the obverse. Once more Pistrucci's St George was retained for the reverse of the gold coins. The edge is straight grained. Both the currency and the proof coins are often seen but what is less well known is the issue of a proof coin with a bevelled rim and with a grainy finish to the incomplete matt surface. A very small number of Matt proofs were also struck at the Sydney branch mint.

Description and details of the Edward VII two pounds

Obverse: de Saulles' effigy of the King facing right, with initials DeS. on truncation. Legend: EDWARDVS VII DEI GRA: BRITT: OMN: REX: FID: DEF: IND: IMP:

Reverse: Pistrucci's St George armed with a sword slaying the dragon. The date 1902 appears below the exergue ground line with the letters B.P. to right.

Edge: Milled.

The coin is struck with a straight die axis ↑↑.

TWO POUNDS OF EDWARD VII

No.	Date	Type/Variety	Mintage	Rating
T40	1902	Normal	46,000	N
T41	1902	Matt Proof (WR406)	8,066	N
T42	1902	Partial matt, grainy finish, bevelled rims (WR405)	Very few	R7
T43	1902	Proof, S in centre of groundline on reverse	Very few	R7

GEORGE V, 1910–36

The two pound coin, like the five pounds, was only struck in 1911 as a proof coin with a grained edge and is relatively scarce. The obverse effigy of the new king was the work of Edgar Bertram Mackennal, an Australian born in Melbourne in 1863 who was later made a Knight Commander of the Royal Victorian Order. His initials B.M. appear on the truncation. As the previous reign, Pistrucci's St George continued to be used for the reverse of the new gold coinage and his familiar initials can be seen on the reverse, above and to the right of the date. There are no known varieties.

Description and details of the George V two pounds

Obverse: Bertram Mackennal's' effigy of the King facing left, with initials B.M. on truncation. Legend: GEORGIVS V DEI GRA: BRITT: OMN: REX: FID: DEF: IND: IMP:
Reverse: Pistrucci's St George armed with a sword slaying the dragon. The date 1911 appears below the exergue ground line with the letters B.P. to right.
Edge: Milled.
The coin is struck with a straight die axis ↑↑.

TWO POUNDS OF GEORGE V

No.	Date	Type/Variety	Mintage	Rating
T44	1911	Proof (WR415)	2,812	S

EDWARD VIII (JANUARY–DECEMBER 1936)

Only a tiny quantity of complete proof sets were struck dated 1937 as the King had abdicated in favour of his younger brother. The left-facing effigy of the King was engraved by Thomas Humphrey Paget, the only artist commissioned to produce designs for the new coinage and he was later asked to supply images which were used on the coinage of George VI. His initials, HP, appear on the truncation of the King's bust. The reverse of the gold coins carry the familiar figure of St George slaying the dragon by Pistrucci and his initials can be seen in the exergue to the right of the date.

Description and details of the Edward VIII two pounds

Obverse: Paget's effigy of the King facing left, with initials HP on truncation. Legend: EDWARDVS VIII D: G: BR: OMN: REX: F: D: IND: IMP.
Reverse: Pistrucci's St George slaying the dragon. Date below exergue ground line and initials B.P. above right.
Edge: Milled.
The coin is struck with a straight upright die axis ↑↑.

		TWO POUNDS OF EDWARD VIII		
No.	Date	Type/Variety	Mintage	Rating
T45	1937	Pattern (WR433)	6	R5

GEORGE VI, 1936–52

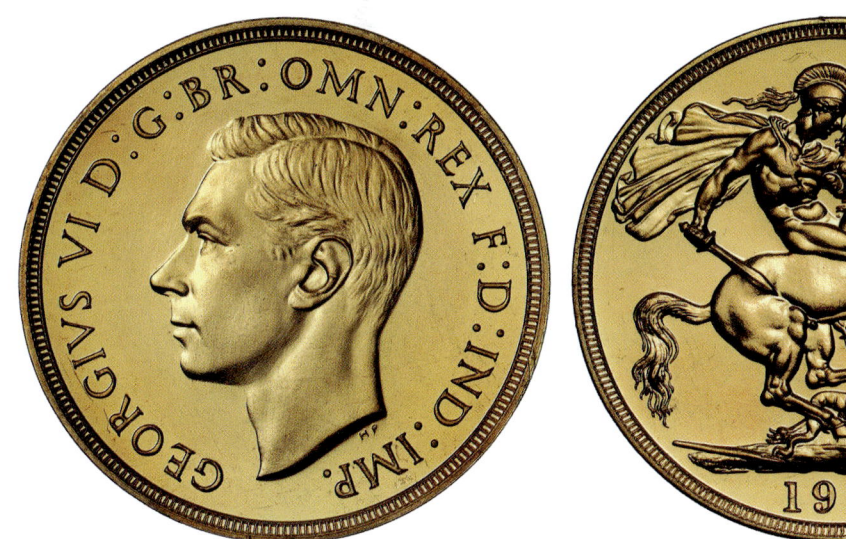

Following his success with Edward's coinage Thomas Humphrey Paget was again requested to supply the obverse image of the new king, and in keeping with tradition Pistrucci's St George was chosen for the reverse. The two pounds and the five pounds were struck in normal proof finish as part of a set to celebrate the Coronation, but a very small number are also known which have a matt proof finish. Paget's initials appear on the truncation and Pistrucci's can be seen in the reverse exergue. No varieties are known.

Description and details of the George V two pounds

Obverse: Paget's effigy of the King facing left, with initials HP on truncation. Legend: GEORGIVS VI D:G: BR: OMN: REX F: D: IND: IMP:
Reverse: Pistrucci's St George armed with a sword slaying the dragon. The date 1937 appears below the exergue ground line with the letters B.P. to right.
Edge: Plain.
The coin is struck with a straight die axis ↑↑.

TWO POUNDS OF GEORGE VI

No.	Date	TypeVariety	Mintage	Rating
T46	1937	Proof (WR437)	5,501	N
T47	1937	Matt proof (WR438, L&S2)	Very few	R7

ELIZABETH II, 1952–2022

As described earlier, to date we have seen five different effigies of Her Majesty the Queen on the coinage. The first type was the work of Mary Gillick, the second was by Arnold Machin and the third was the work of Raphael David Maklouf, the fourth was by the sculptor and medallist Ian Rank-Broadley, the fifth is by Jody Clark and a sixth, one-off bust was issued in 2016 for the Queen's 90th Birthday by James Butler. The reverses for the gold coins of these different issues all, except those issues produced for a special occasion, display Benedetto Pistrucci's St George slaying the dragon.

At the time of the Coronation in 1953 a two pound coin bearing the portrait by Mary Gillick was struck for institutions but never actually issued to the public. However, since 1980 there have been a number of gold two pound coins produced by the Royal Mint, including an issue for the 500th anniversary of the sovereign in 1989. This issue portrays Her Majesty the Queen enthroned on the obverse and a crowned shield of arms imposed upon a double rose on the reverse. Since then the complete sovereign series including the two pounds, has been struck virtually every year, mainly as part of the annual "Year Proof Sets" and other sets that are marketed from time to time. It is often the coins from these sets which are available to collectors.

Description and details of the Elizabeth II First bust type two pounds

Obverse: Mary Gillick's laureated effigy of the Queen facing right. Legend: + ELIZABETH II DEI GRA: BRITT: OMN: REGINA F: D:

Reverse: Pistrucci's St George armed with a sword slaying the dragon. The date 1953 appears below the exergue ground line with the letters B.P. to right.

Edge: Plain.

The coin is struck with a straight die axis ↑↑.

TWO POUNDS OF ELIZABETH II, FIRST BUST

No.	Date	Type/Variety	Mintage	Rating
T48	1953	Proof (WR446)	At least 6	R5
T49	1953	Pattern, TRIAL incuse on obverse field (WR447)	Prob. unique	R7

THE GOLD SOVEREIGN SERIES

Description and details of the Elizabeth II Second bust type two pounds

Obverse: Effigy of the Queen facing right wearing a tiara and off-the shoulder dress, by Arnold Machin.
Legend: ELIZABETH · II · DEI GRATIA · REGINA · F: D:

Reverse: Pistrucci's St George armed with a sword slaying the dragon. The date appears below the exergue ground line with the letters B.P. to right. The Normal (Unc) edition has a small U in a circle in the reverse exergue.

Edge: Milled.

The coin is struck with a straight die axis ↑↑.

TWO POUNDS OF ELIZABETH II, SECOND BUST

No.	Date	Type/Variety	Mintage	Rating
T50	1980	Proof	10,000	C
T51	1982	Proof	2,500	N
T52	1983	Proof	12,500	C

Description and details of the Elizabeth II Third bust type two pounds

Obverse: Effigy of the Queen facing right wearing a coronet, couped (1987 and 1988 issues have an uncouped draped portrait), by Raphael Maklouf, with designer's initials, RM, at base of truncation. Legend: ELIZABETH II · DEI · GRA · REG · F · D.

Reverse: Pistrucci's St George armed with a sword slaying the dragon. The date appears below the exergue ground line with the letters B.P. to right. The Normal (Unc) edition has a small U in a circle in the reverse exergue.

Edge: Milled.

The coin is struck with a straight die axis ↑↑.

TWO POUNDS OF ELIZABETH II, THIRD BUST

No.	Date	Type/Variety	Mintage	Rating
T53	1985	Proof	5,849	N
T54	1987	Proof	14,301	C
T55	1988	Proof	12,743	C
T56	1989	See special issues for details*		
T57	1990	Proof	4,374	N
T58	1991	Proof	3,108	N
T59	1992	Proof	2,608	N
T60	1993	Proof	2,155	N
T61	1996	Proof	1,610	N

Description and details of the Elizabeth II Fourth bust type two pounds

Obverse: Effigy of the Queen facing right wearing a tiara by Ian Rank-Broadley, with designer's initials, IRB, at base of truncation. Legend: ELIZABETH · II · DEI · GRA REGINA · FID · DEF .
Reverse: Pistrucci's St George armed with a sword slaying the dragon. The date appears below the exergue ground line with the letters B.P. to right. Until and including the 2001 issue the Normal (Unc) edition has a small U in a circle in the reverse exergue.
Edge: Milled.
The coin is struck with a straight die axis ↑↑.

TWO POUNDS OF ELIZABETH II, FOURTH BUST

No.	Date	Variety	Mintage	Rating
T62	1998	Proof	1,349	N
T63	2000	Proof	2,250	N
T64	2002	See special issues for details		
T65	2003	Proof	2,050	C
T66	2004	Proof	1,749	N
T67	2005	See special issues for details		
T68	2006	Proof	2,290	N
T69	2007	Proof	2,401	N
T70	2008	Proof	2,333	N
T71	2009	Proof	2,416	N
T72	2010	Proof	2,019	N
T73	2011	Proof	2,149	S
T74	2012	See special issues for details		
T75	2012	See special issues for details		
T78	2013	Proof	1,263	S
T77	2013	Normal	124	R
T78	2014	Proof	681	N
T79	2014	Normal	835	S
T79A	2014	Normal, obverse with frosted Proof reverse	Incl. above	R
T80	2015	Proof	835	N

Description and details of the Elizabeth II Fifth bust type two pounds

Obverse: Effigy of the Queen facing right wearing a tiara by Jody Clark, with designer's initials, JC, at base of truncation. Legend: ELIZABETH · II · DEI · GRA REGINA · FID · DEF .
Reverse: Pistrucci's St George armed with a sword slaying the dragon. The date appears below the exergue ground line with the letters B.P. to right.
Edge: Milled.
The coin is struck with a straight die axis ↑↑.

TWO POUNDS OF ELIZABETH II, FIFTH BUST

No.	Date	Variety	Mintage	Rating
T81	2015	Proof	1,046	N
T82	2016	See special issues for details*		
T83	2017	See special issues for details		
T84	2018	Proof, with 65 mint mark	1,580	N
T85	2019	Proof	1,263	S
T86	2020	See special issues for details		
T86A	2020	Normal	Not known	C
T87	2021	Proof, with 95 in crown privy mark	991	N
T88	2021	Normal	Not known	C

* As this issue carries a portrait by James Butler, strictly speaking, it should not be included with the fifth bust type.

THE GOLD SOVEREIGN SERIES

ELIZABETH II TWO POUNDS —SPECIAL ISSUES

All special issues are listed sequentially with the standard coins but in addition are listed separately here for identification purposes.

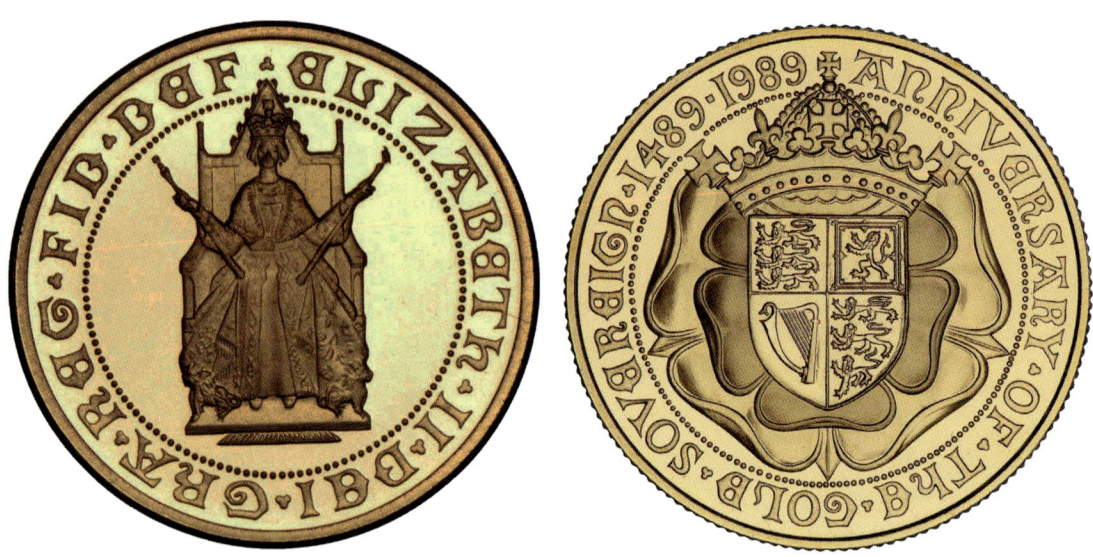

500th ANNIVERSARY OF THE SOVEREIGN 1489–1989. Obverse and reverse by Bernard Sindall

No.	Date	Type/Variety	Mintage	Rating
T56	1989	Proof	14,936	C

GOLDEN JUBILEE OF HER MAJESTY QUEEN ELIZABETH II. Obverse by Ian Rank-Broadley, Shield reverse by Timothy Noad

No.	Date	Type/Variety	Mintage	Rating
T64	2002	Proof	6,947	C
T64A	2002	Proof, finer miling	Incl. above	R

MODERN INTERPRETATION OF ST GEORGE. New reverse for 2005 by Timothy Noad

No.	Date	Type/Variety	Mintage	Rating
T67	2005	Proof	2,958	N

DIAMOND JUBILEE OF HER MAJESTY QUEEN ELIZABETH II.
Stylised reverse by Paul Day

No.	Date	Type/Variety	Mintage	Rating
T74	2012	Proof	1,956	N
T75	2012	Normal	119	R2

90th BIRTHDAY OF HER MAJESTY QUEEN ELIZABETH II.
Obverse portrait by James Butler

No.	Date	Type/Variety	Mintage	Rating
T82	2016	Proof	921	N

200th ANNIVERSARY OF THE SOVEREIGN. Jody Clark obverse.
Reverse as 1817 sovereign

No.	Date	Type/Variety	Mintage	Rating
T83	2017	Proof	1,198	N

200th ANNIVERSARY OF THE DEATH OF GEORGE III.
Jody Clark obverse. Reverse with Royal cypher mint mark

No.	Date	Type/Variety	Mintage	Rating
T86	2020	Proof	1,129	N

THE GOLD SOVEREIGN SERIES

PLATINUM JUBILEE OF HER MAJESTY QUEEN ELIZABETH II.
Jody Clark obverse.

No.	Date	Type/Variety	Mintage	Rating
T89	2022	Proof	700	N
T90	2022	Normal	Not known	C
T91	2022	Piedfort Proof	70	R

CHARLES III, 2022–

King Charles III ascended to the throne upon the death of his mother Queen Elizabeth II on September 8, 2022. The 73-year-old King was the oldest ascending Monarch in British history, the next closest being William IV who was nearly 65 when he succeeded his brother George IV in 1830. However, preparations for his new coinage, indeed anything official bearing his effigy, had been in preparation for some time. Sculptor Martin Jennings was charged with the new coinage design which has also been applied as the new stamp effigy. Designed digitally, there have so far been two coin portraits with a bare head design (similar to those of his grandfather, great-grandfather and great-great-grandfather) gracing most of the coinage, including the Sovereign series, and a crowned head design featuring on the special Coronation issues which also featured a special edition reverse. Another special reverse design for the Sovereign series was also produced as a Memorial design to the Late Queen. The familiar St George and dragon design by Benedetto Pistrucci has since returned to the series for the 2024-dated issues.

THE GOLD SOVEREIGN SERIES

Description and details of the Charles III bare head two pounds Memorial reverse

Obverse: re head effigy of King Charles III left by Martin Jennings, raised initials below neck MJ. Legend CHARLES III. DEI. GRA. REX. FID. DEF.
Reverse: Royal heraldic coat of arms with crowned lion and unicorn supporters, crowned helm above, banner motto below DIEU ET MON DROIT with date.
Edge: Milled.
The coin is struck with a straight upright die axis ↑↑

MEMORIAL EDITION.
Jody Clark obverse.

No.	Date	Type/Variety	Mintage	Rating
T92	2022	Proof	1,787	N
T93	2022	Normal	Not known	C

Description and details of the Charles III crowned head two pounds

Obverse: Crowned head effigy of King Charles III left by Martin Jennings, raised initials below neck MJ. Legend CHARLES III. DEI. GRA. REX. FID. DEF.
Reverse: Pistrucci's St George armed with sword slaying the dragon. The date in the exergue below the ground line with B.P. in small raised letters to upper right.
Edge: Milled.
The coin is struck with a straight upright die axis ↑↑

		CORONATION WITH CROWNED HEAD AND ST GEORGE & DRAGON REVERSE.		
No.	*Date*	*Type/Variety*	*Mintage*	*Rating*
T94	2023	Proof	1,785	N
T95	2023	Matt Proof, edition as a set	23	R3
T96	2023	Normal	Not known	C

THE GOLD SOVEREIGN SERIES

Description and details of the Charles III bare head two pounds

Obverse: Crowned head effigy of King Charles III left by Martin Jennings, raised initials below neck MJ. Legend CHARLES III. DEI. GRA. REX. FID. DEF.
Reverse: Pistrucci's St George armed with sword slaying the dragon. The date in the exergue below the ground line with B.P. in small raised letters to upper right.
Edge: Milled.
The coin is struck with a straight upright die axis ↑↑

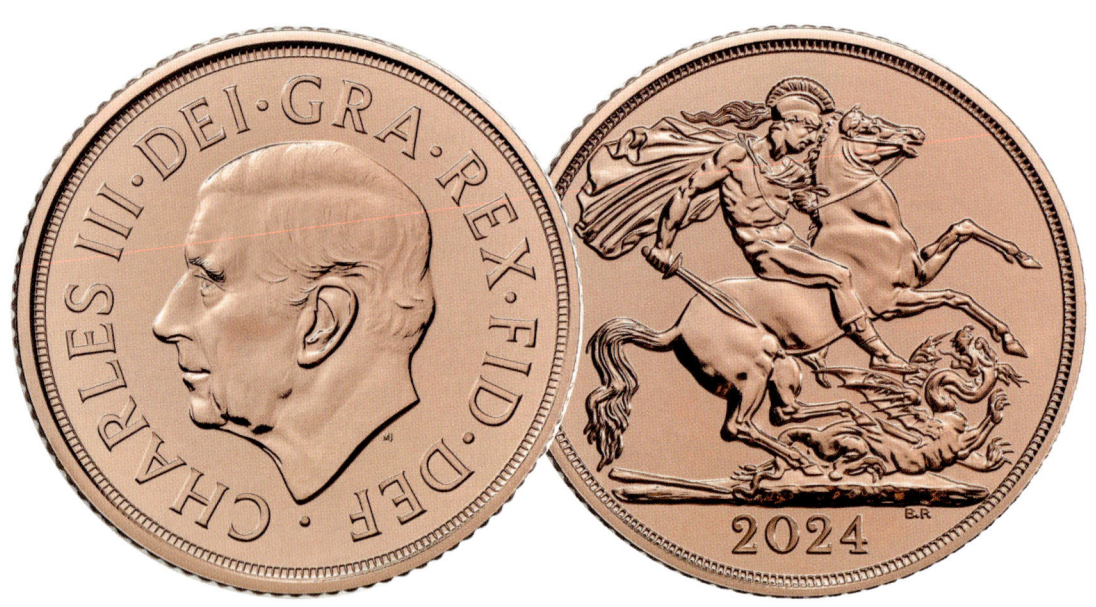

REGULAR FORMAT FIVE POUNDS OF CHARLES III WITH BARE HEAD LEFT AND ST GEORGE & DRAGON REVERSE

No.	Date	Type/Variety	Mintage	Rating
T97	2024	Proof	800	C
T98	2024	Normal	Not known	C

THE SOVEREIGN

The finest known example of the 1819 sovereign.

As explained in the chapter on the "Modern Sovereign Series", pp. 45–47, it was the master craftsman Benedetto Pistrucci who was responsible for our first gold coins that replaced the worn out guineas. However, even Pistrucci himself could not have foreseen the enduring impact his magnificent design was to have on our coinage throughout the years that followed. The Sovereign itself became so popular that it remained in circulation as a one pound coin right up to World War I. In 2017 the Royal Mint commemorated the 200th anniversary of Pistrucci's masterwork by producing coins of the series for that year bearing a reworked image of the very first sovereign reverse, even down to including the broken lance of Pistrucci's original drawings which was replaced by a sword in the later portrayals of St George.

Specifications of the Sovereign:
Weight: 7.988 grams.
Fineness, 22 carat: 11/12 fine gold, 1/12 alloy (this means that each Sovereign contains 7.322 grams of pure gold).
Millesimal fineness: 916.66.
Thickness: 1.52mm.
Diameter: 22.5mm.

THE GOLD SOVEREIGN SERIES

Pistrucci's original sketch for the obverse of the first sovereign (courtesy of the Royal Mint Museum).

GEORGE III, 1760–1820

From the numismatist's point of view sovereigns of George III are becoming more difficult to find in really nice condition, and even of the common dates any above the grade of EF are virtually impossible to find.

Without doubt the rarest coin in this series is that of 1819 (listed as Marsh No. 3), and as mentioned in the first edition of this book in 1980 the author could only recall having seen one poor example of this date after many years searching. Over the next 20 years it seemed that only two more came to light. The best of these appeared in October 1998, when Sotheby's held a fine Coins, Medals and Banknotes auction in London. Lot 286 featured a superb example of the 1819 sovereign—it was indeed a fine specimen and the best of the ten coins that are known to exist today. The hammer price was an incredible £50,000 then, but when the same coin sold at the auction of the Bentley Collection in 2012 it realised £186,000. This coin must be regarded as one of the rarest within the whole sovereign series.

Many of the pieces listed were struck in very small numbers but unfortunately no records remain to give the exact quantity. Where it is probable that only a few were produced or are known to exist today, this has been made clear in the accompanying tables under the "Mintage" heading by the entry "Very few" appearing.

Description and details of the George III sovereign

Obverse: The King's head right, laureate with short hair; the tie has a loop with two ends, neck bare.
   Legend: GEORGIUS III D:G:BRITANNIAR:REX F:D: The date is at the bottom of the legend.
Reverse: St George with streamer flowing from helmet, mounted and slaying the dragon with a spear, all within the garter inscribed HONI.SOIT.QUI.MAL.Y.PENSE. On the ground under the broken shaft of the spear are the tiny incuse letters B.P. for Benedetto Pistrucci, and below them on the buckle of the garter are the incuse initials W.W.P. for William Wellesley Pole.
Edge: Milled.
The coin is struck with a reverse die axis ↑↓

No. 1 enlarged x3.

SOVEREIGNS OF GEORGE III

No.	Date	Type/Variety	Mintage	Rating
1	1817	Normal	3,235,239	N
1A	1817	Milled edge proof (WR196–7)	Very few	R5
1B**	1817	Currency—struck en medaille ↑↑	Incl. in above	R4
2	1818	Normal	2,347,230	N
2A	1818	Ascending colon after BRITANNIAR. Clear space between REX and F:D:	Incl. in above	S
2B*	1818	Wiry curls, legend as normal	Incl. in above	—
2C*	1818	Wiry curls, legend as 2A	Incl. in above	—
2D	1818	Milled edge proof, ascending colon (WR198)	Very few	R6
3	1819	Normal †	3,574	R5
4	1820	Normal, date open 2	2,101,994 ‡	S
4A	1820	Short date figures	Incl. in above	R3
4B	1820	Compact date, closed 2 in date	Incl. in above	R
4C	1820	First digit in date a letter I	Incl. in above	R3
4D	1820	Larger date, 8 and 2 nearly touch	Incl. in above	R2
4E	1820	Date with open 2 and 0 tilted to right	Incl. in above	R2
4F	1820	Milled edge proof (WR200)	Very few	R4

* M.2B and 2C are currently unconfirmed.
** Beware of modern counterfeits of this unusual error die axis.
† There is believed to be an 1819 proof but it has not been recorded since World War II.
‡ This figure includes Mr Marsh's estimate of how many 1820 dated George III Sovereigns continued to be struck into 1821 until the new dies were ready for George IV. Calendar year mintage for 1820 actually = 931,994.
Note. There are various trials and patterns c. 1816 that led to the 1817 currency sovereign (see *English Pattern Trial and Proof Coins in Gold 1547–1968* by Alex Wilson and Mark Rasmussen).

SOVEREIGNS OF GEORGE III, 1760–1820

Descending colon.
Note: the normal types of 1817, 1818 and 1819 have this style of colon

No. 1 (actual size)

Ascending colon.
Note: the ascending colon is used on all 1820 issues

No. 1A. Milled edge proof

No. 2

No. 2A. Ascending colon

No. 3

No. 4

Normal date, open 2

117

No. 4A — Short date figures

No. 4B — Compact date, closed 2

No. 4C — First digit in date letter I

No. 4D — Larger date, 8 and 2 nearly touch

No. 4F — Open 2, 0 tilted to right

GEORGE IV, 1820–30

After the death of George III on January 29, 1820 it was decided that the Mint should continue to use the old sovereign dies, so in fact all the sovereigns struck in 1820 during the first part of the reign of George IV bore the bust of George III.

During the reign there were to be two different designs for the sovereign. The first was modelled and engraved by Benedetto Pistrucci, with a laureate head of the King on the obverse and featuring a slightly changed version of St George, on the reverse, now armed with a sword in place of the broken lance, and bearing the date in the exergue.

The "laureate head" sovereigns were in fact issued for every year of the reign from 1821 up to and including 1825, and low grade coins for the common years of 1821, 1822 or 1824 can easily be found. However, a word of caution is necessary in respect of the 1822 date, as counterfeits are to be found. Without doubt there are two very rare dates within the "laureate head" series, the 1823 and 1825. As an illustration, in the Bentley Collection (2012) the finest known example of the currency sovereign of 1823 sold for the hammer price of £18,000.

Following Pistrucci's refusal to use the effigy of the King designed by Francis Legatt Chantrey, the new "bare head" bust was engraved by William Wyon who later became Chief Engraver. Jean Baptiste Merlen Pistrucci's assistant engraved the attractive crowned shield reverse which was first issued in 1825—thus there are two different types of sovereign for this year. The bare head type continued to be struck until the end of the reign in 1830.

The "bare head" sovereigns are difficult to find and only those dated 1826 can be considered as easy to acquire in anything like EF. Those dated 1825, 1827, 1829 and 1830, are all rated scarce, and in better grades are difficult to find.

Those dated 1828 are without doubt the rarest sovereigns of the "bare head" series. The low mintage of this coin causes it to be rated R4. The explanation for this is because most of the coinage struck for 1828 was produced from old 1827 dies and it was only near the end of the year when the new 1828 dies came into use. Examples of the 1828 sovereign, even in VF condition now command five-figure sums.

Description and details of the George IV Laureate Head sovereign

Obverse: The King's bust to the left, laureate, tied with loop at two ends, hair short and bare neck. B.P. in small letters below truncation standing for Benedetto Pistrucci. Legend: GEORGIUS III D:G:BRITANNIAR:REX F:D:

Reverse: St George slaying the dragon now armed with a sword. The streamer is missing from the helmet and there is a difference in the arrangement of the cloak. The date is shown below the exergue line with the letters B.P. to the right, for Benedetto Pistrucci.

Edge: Milled.

The coin is struck with a reverse die axis ↑↓ which can sometimes be up to 45 degrees off-centre.

LAUREATE HEAD SOVEREIGNS OF GEORGE IV

No.	Date	Type/Variety	Mintage	Rating
5	1821	Normal	9,405,114	N
5A	1821	Milled edge proof (WR231)	Very few	R3
5B	1821	Plain edge proof (WR229–230)	Very few	R6
5C	1821	Copper proof with milled edge	Very few	R7
6	1822	Normal	5,356,787	N
6A	1822	Proof (WR232)	Very few	R7
7	1823	Normal	616,770	R3
8	1824	Normal	3,767,904	S
9*	1825	Normal	(See No. 10, 1825 "Bare Head" issue)	R3
9A	1825	Plain edge proof (WR234)	Very few	R6

*There is a trial piece struck in platinum dated 1825 which exists in connection with a request from the Colombian Government to supply platinum for a Sovereign-sized coinage. However, the Mint would not allow Sovereign dies to be used in the experimentation and the platinum proved too hard in its content to effectively strike a coinage. The few trial pieces known dated 1825 all have a George III obverse from the Irish ten pence bank token coupled with the 1825 copper farthing reverse, both coins being of a similar size in diameter to a Sovereign.

SOVEREIGNS OF GEORGE IV, 1820–30

No. 5

No. 5A. Milled edge proof

No. 5C. Copper proof, milled edge

No. 6

No. 9A. Plain edge proof

Description and details of the George IV Bare Head sovereign

Obverse: The King's bare head to the left. Legend: GEORGIUS IV DEI GRATIA. The date appears at the bottom of the coin below the truncation.

Reverse: The Ensigns Armorial of the United Kingdom contained in an ornate shield surmounted by the royal crown; the centre of the shield features a smaller shield surmounted by a small crown, and within this shield are displayed the Hanoverian arms. Legend: BRITANNIARUM REX FID: DEF:

Edge: Milled.

The coin is struck with a reverse die axis ↑↓ which can sometimes be up to 45 degrees off-centre.

Note. William Wyon engraved the King's head from Chantrey's bust and Jean Baptiste Merlen designed and engraved the reverse dies.

BARE HEAD SOVEREIGNS OF GEORGE IV

No.	Date	Type/Variety	Mintage	Rating
9B	1824	Pattern (WR233)	Very few	R7
10	1825	Normal	4,200,343*	S
10A	1825	Milled edge proof—8 heart semée	Very few	R4
10B	1825	Plain edge proof—7 heart semée	Very few	R5
10BB	1825	Proof, milled edge with 7 heart semee	Small number	R5
10C	1825	Copper proof	Very few	R6
10D	1825	"Barton's Metal" uniface obverse/reverse	Very few	R5
11	1826	Normal	5,724,046	N
11A	1826	Milled edge proof	c. 400	S
11B	1826	6 over small 6 and GEOR over small GEOR	Incl. in above	R5
12	1827	Normal	2,266,629	S
13	1828	Normal	386,182	R4
14	1829	Normal	2,444,652	S
15	1830	Normal	2,387,881	S
15A	1830	Milled edge proof	Very few	R7
15B	1830	Currency—struck en medaille↑↑	Inc. with M.15 above	R4

*This figure includes the 1825 laureate head mintage.

SOVEREIGNS OF GEORGE IV, 1820–30

No. 10

No. 10A. Milled edge proof

8 heart semée

7 heart semée

No. 10B. Plain edge proof

No. 10C. Copper proof

No. 10D. "Barton's metal" pattern with blank reverse

No. 11

THE GOLD SOVEREIGN SERIES

No. 11A. Milled edge proof

No. 11B. 6 over small 6 and GEOR over small GEOR

WILLIAM IV, 1830–37

William IV who was born on August 21, 1765, succeeded to the throne upon the death of his elder brother on June 26, 1830, and no currency gold coins were issued for that year. However, an Order in Council, dated November 22, 1830, specified that a double sovereign, sovereign and half-sovereign be struck in gold. These in fact became current by Proclamation on April 13, 1831. The gold coins of the reign of William IV carry an effigy of the King by William Wyon, who by this time had become the Chief Engraver. The reverse depicts the crowned and mantled ensigns armorial by Jean Baptiste Merlen.

With the sovereigns of this reign there have been a number of exciting discoveries in recent years. To establish new varieties, etc., it is of course essential for a large number of coins to be examined. During the early 1980s a quantity of William sovereigns were scrutinised, enabling a new bust type within the series to be identified.[1] As a result we have a first and second bust for the series (*see illustrations*).

Both first and second bust types are known to exist for 1831 and 1832 and in fact it is the second bust that appears on the 1831 proof and the 1830 prototype patterns.

Another variety of the first bust type is one that first appeared in the sale of the Captain K. J. Douglas-Morris, RN, collection in 1974,[2] lot 182. This is a currency sovereign dated 1831 of the first bust type but the WW on the truncation is without stops (M.16A). It is described as practically mint state and very rare, with less than ten examples known.

The next variety (M.21A)[3] is a sovereign bearing the date of 1837 with what appears at first to be a doubling of the 8, showing as two "tails" to the figure. It seems certain that when the engraver began this amazing series of errors the die included the figures 183 of the date and the engraver decided either to repair or reposition the figure 3. However, he did neither: in error he punched in the 3 over the 8. When he discovered this mistake he may well have become so distraught that his next effort became even more disastrous, and the 8 punch he then tried to use over the 3 was entered so low that it almost fouled the border heading. After a series of unsuccessful attempts he completed the job but the large lower half of his first 8 is still to be seen clearly hanging below the full figure 8 of the date. This particular die was such an atrocious and obvious piece of bad workmanship that it is unlikely to have escaped notice for very long, and then it would have been withdrawn and possibly destroyed. If this were the case we do not think many coins would have been struck from it, and so the variety must be considered as very rare.

The final new variety (M.20A) is in fact a much simpler piece to identify than the error date just described, and this sovereign[4] is a second bust type dated 1836. On the reverse side, at the bottom, another letter N has been entered into the lower garnishing directly above the last N in ANNO. It is very surprising that when one examines this error it looks as though no attempt has been made to correct it. This sovereign was examined by Mr G. P. Dyer of the Royal Mint and he has said that the letter N in question may have been deliberately placed, but at this time there is nothing to suggest what the letter N might be attributed to. However, we do of course know of sovereigns that have a special mark for identification purposes, the best known of these is the "Ansell" sovereign of 1859 (M.42A), so perhaps time again will provide an answer?

Description and details of the William IV sovereign

Obverse: The King's bare head to right. At the base of the truncation the letters W.W. incuse, with stops, standing for William Wyon. Legend: GULIELMUS IIII D:G:BRITANNIAR: REX F:D:

Reverse: The Ensigns Armorial of the United Kingdom within a shield surmounted by a crown, in the centre a smaller shield containing the Hanoverian arms surmounted by a small crown. The word ANNO appears in the field at the bottom of the left side and the date appears in a similar position on the right side.

Edge: Milled.

The coin is struck with a reverse die axis ↑↓. Can sometimes be up to 45 degrees off-centre.

Notes/References
1. M. A. Marsh, "William IV Sovereign. A Different Bust and a New Variety", *Spink Numismatic Circular*, May 1984, pp. 118–19.
2. Captain K. J. Douglas-Morris RN, "The Distinguished Collection of English Gold Coins 1700–1900", Sotheby and Co auction, November 1974, lot no. 182.
3. The variety was first identified by John Duggan of Blackburn and much assistance was given with its study by Mr G. P. Dyer and the engraving staff of the Royal Mint,
4. This sovereign was first noted on the list of Cheshire dealer Mr Roy Stirling in October 1995.

SOVEREIGNS OF WILLIAM IV, 1830–37

First bust
The bust is in general very slightly smaller and the hair is more finely engraved than the second.
The nose is sharper with nostril more pronounced and points directly at the second N in BRITANNIAR.
The hair arrangement at the top of the forehead is a single curl almost horizontal with a thin strand lying on its top pointed at each end, and there is a small gap between this and a small cluster of four curls that sit on the top of the head.
The hair at the bottom on the nape of the neck turns into the neck and is quite tight on it.
A curl of hair covers most of the top rear edge of the ear.
The initials W.W. incuse and with stops spaced widely.
The legend, on this bust, is generally more clearly spaced.

Second bust
Nose is smaller and points directly at the letter I next to the last N of BRITANNIAR.
The hair arrangement at the top of the forehead is now one single curl, again almost horizontal and bending back towards a cluster of four curls on the top of the head; a slightly different space separates the two.
The hair above the ear allows all of the top part of the ear to be seen and the hair at the bottom on the nape of the neck stands proud of the neck.
The obverse edge beading is noticeably coarser.
The initials W.W. incuse and with stops are closer together.
The legend is very poorly spaced and with several letters and figures touching.

No. 16 enlarged x3.

SOVEREIGNS OF WILLIAM IV

No.	Date	Type/Variety	Mintage	Rating
15C	1830	First bust. Nose points towards second N of BRITANNIAR; W.W. incuse with stops. Plain edge proof (WR259)	Very few	R6
15D	1830	Second bust. Nose points towards letter I next to last N of BRITANNIAR; W.W. incuse with stops. Plain edge proof (WR260)	Very few	R4
15E	1830	"Barton's Metal" uniface striking	Very few	R6
16	1831	First bust. W.W. incuse with stops	598,547	R2
16A	1831	First bust. WW incuse no stops	Incl. in above	R5
16B	1831	First bust proof. WW no stops (WR262)	Very few	R6
16C	1831	Second bust	Incl. in above for 1831	R5
16D	1831	Second bust. Plain edge proof	c. 225	S
17	1832	Second bust	3,737,065	S
17A	1832	First bust	Incl. in above	R3
17B	1832	First bust. Milled edge proof (WR263)	Very few	R6
18	1833	Second bust	1,225,269	S
18A	1833	Second bust. Proof (WR264)	Very few	R6
19	1835	Second bust	723,441	R
20	1836	Second bust	1,714,349	S
20A	1836	Second bust. Rev. additional letter N above ANNO	Incl. in above	R4
21	1837	Second bust	1,172,984	S
21A	1837	Second bust. Rev. error date 8	Incl. in above	R3
21B	1837	Second bust. Proof (WR265)	Very few	R7

Note. There are numerous other minor insignificant variations in small detail of legend and design in this issue.

SOVEREIGNS OF WILLIAM IV, 1830–37

W.W. incuse with stops

No. 16. Actual size

WW incuse no stops

No. 16A. WW no stops

No. 16C

No. 17

No. 17A

THE GOLD SOVEREIGN SERIES

No. 18

No. 19

No. 20

No. 20A

No. 21

No. 21A

VICTORIA, 1837–1901

When Queen Victoria began her reign upon the death of her uncle, William IV, on June 20, 1837, the first important change necessary was that of the royal arms, because they included the Hanoverian arms. The right to the Kingdom of Hanover was limited only to the male line, and they had been included in the royal arms since George I's accession to the throne. The change was in fact effected by an Order in Council dated July 26, 1837, which provided for the arms of Hanover to be omitted.

On August 22, 1837 the Chancellor of the Exchequer wrote to Henry Labouchere,[1] 1st Baron Taunton, who was now Master of the Mint: *"Her Majesty has commanded me to direct that the Chief Engraver and the Medallist of Her Majesty's Mint shall attend at Windsor Castle on Friday next for the purpose of having the advantage of study for their models in their respective departments. They should be at Windsor very early and should report their arrival to the Lord or Groom in waiting.*

Her Majesty will give the artists separate sittings on Friday."

William Wyon, the Chief Engraver, attended at Windsor and prepared a wax model of the Queen's effigy. It was interesting to note that Pistrucci, although Medallist at that time, did not attend and it is very likely that Jean Baptiste Merlen was involved with the reverse design. He certainly carried out the engraving. The new bust of the Queen that is known as the "Young head" is a fine example of design and engraving by William Wyon. The bust of the young Queen is shown turned to the left, head bound with a double fillet and the hair gracefully gathered up into a knot behind.

The designs for the sovereign were submitted to the Queen by Labouchere on February 15, 1838 as follows: *"In pursuance of Your Majesty's gracious Command that Dies for your Majesty's Coins should be prepared according to the Model of an Effigy of your Majesty, which I had the honour to submit for Your Majesty's approbation, and also new reverses for the Gold and Silver Coinage.*

I humbly beg leave to lay before your Majesty the annexed specimen of the Impression intended to be struck on the Sovereign or twenty shilling piece namely for the Obverse Impression the aforesaid Effigy of your Majesty with the inscription 'Victoria Dei Gratia' and the date of the Year. For the Reverse Impression the Ensigns Armorial of the United Kingdom according to the design approved by Your Majesty in Council dated 26 July 1837 contained in a plain shield, surmounted by the Royal Crown and encircled with a Laurel Wreath, with the inscription Britanniarum Regina Fid:Def: having the united Rose, Thistle and Shamrock placed under the Shield." The design of the obverse was engraved by William Wyon and the reverse by Jean Baptiste Merlen, and they were approved on February 26, 1838.

The first of the "shield" Type IA sovereigns issued bore the date of 1838 and so began what was to be another most interesting period in the history of our gold coinage.

During this first period of Victoria's coinage there were most important changes in the Mint. In 1841 Henry Labouchere, the Master, resigned and was replaced by William Ewart Gladstone, MP, who later became Prime Minister. Gladstone took much interest in his appointment, especially in the recoinage, and in his four-year spell as Master he made a valuable contribution to the running and efficiency of the Mint. He resigned in February 1845.

In July 1844 Jean Baptiste Merlen retired at the age of 75. He had been a member of the engraving staff since February 1820 when he was appointed Assistant to Pistrucci. So finally the Frenchman ended a long and valuable period of service to the Mint, and Leonard Charles Wyon, the son of William, was appointed Second Engraver to his father on July 23, 1844.

In 1845 Sir George Clerk, MP, who was Secretary of the Treasury, was appointed Master but he only held the post for a year. In July 1846 he was succeeded by Richard Lalor Shiel, MP, who continued as Master until December 1850, during which time he took a very active part in the running of the Mint and near the end of his time was instrumental in some important changes. Sir John Frederick William Herschel, Fellow and former Secretary of the Royal Society, was appointed the new Master in 1851, and it was at this time that other important events were happening in places far away from England that would have considerable effect on our gold coinage.

It was in May 1851 that gold was discovered in Australia, first in New South Wales and shortly afterwards in Victoria, and this led to heavy demands being made on the currency coinage of the colonies. These demands could not be met, and a petition by the Council of New South Wales was addressed to Her Majesty on December 19, 1851. It asked for a branch of the Royal Mint to be established at Sydney so that the people could convert their gold into money.

In South Australia the Adelaide Chamber of Commerce tried to help matters in 1852 by opening an Assay Office for assaying gold ingots, but they exceeded their powers by striking the Adelaide Token, or Pound as it became known. However, it was not to last long and the office was closed by Proclamation on February 17, 1853.

By Order of Council dated August 19, 1853, a branch mint for Sydney was authorised which opened on May 14, 1855.[2] The second branch mint, at Melbourne, opened on June 12, 1872.

An act passed in 1863 which, after stating that Queen Victoria had by Proclamation established the Sydney branch mint for making gold coins, the same as those issued by the Royal Mint in London, said it would be lawful for the Queen . . . to declare, gold coins made at the branch mint . . . to be legal tender within the United Kingdom of Great Britain and Ireland.

In 1866 the Colonial Branch Mint Act was passed. This gave a general power to the Queen, again by Proclamation, and so because of these two Acts the coins struck at the branch mints would be considered to be legal tender. However, the first series of Australian sovereigns struck at the Sydney branch mint in 1855 were not accepted as currency outside New South Wales. There had been problems over the design of these sovereigns, and also relating to their light colour caused by the use of silver instead of copper to form an alloy of the prescribed legal standard. They were in fact only recognised as legal tender sovereigns in the United Kingdom after 1866.

The Australian sovereign was first struck at the Sydney branch mint in 1855 and 1856, and the design of the first issue featured the bust of Victoria to the left, a very similar bust to the Type IA Shield sovereign, but certainly not of the same standard. The date appears below, and the legend surrounds the bust. However, the reverse of the coin is very different as it has AUSTRALIA across the centre of the field with a branch of laurel leaves on either side and the words ONE SOVEREIGN at the bottom. SYDNEY MINT is placed in a similar way at the top.

In 1851 James Wyon, a cousin of Leonard Charles Wyon, was appointed resident engraver at the Royal Mint, and it was he who engraved the first Australian Sydney branch mint sovereign. However, it failed to meet with approval and was replaced with a new bust and a slight change was made in the legend, but otherwise the coin is similar to the first issue. This new second bust is by L. C. Wyon and continues through until the series finished in 1870. Incidentally, all die work for the Australian branch mints was done in London, approved by the current Engraver of the Mint and then sent by ship to Australia. The branch mints did not have engraving staff, although some date alterations were made at the Melbourne branch mint as will be described later.

The new Sydney sovereign met with a certain amount of success when it was first issued and several countries adopted it as legal tender. However, one country, India, found it more useful as a bullion coin, and bearing in mind the circumstances of India at that time, when there was a suggestion of the introduction of a 10 rupee gold piece as legal tender, it seems the United Kingdom would have seen the Australian sovereign as a more suitable alternative. Indeed, Col. J. T. Smith, FRS, late Master of the Fort St George and Calcutta Mints,[3] was fully aware of the India situation and kept London well informed of progress.

Sovereigns from the shield series of Type IA, IB, IC and ID are, perhaps, the most attractive of Victoria's reign and they can present the collector with a great deal of difficulty, especially if he wants to acquire them in top condition—even many coins rated as common or normal will still be elusive. There are two important factors that contribute greatly to the difficulty mentioned, and one is that during Victoria's reign the sovereign was used very much for trading purposes, and being made of such soft gold, it took only a short period of time for wear to become very evident. The other big factor was the extensive recoinage that took place between 1842 and 1845 when more than £14,000,000 of light gold coinage, estimated to be one third of the total gold in circulation, was withdrawn. Around £500,000 more per year of gold coins below the legal weight limit continued to be taken out of circulation after 1845.

Shortly after *The Gold Sovereign* was first published in 1980, Mr Marsh discovered an overdate from the sovereign series of the London Mint that had never before been recorded and one indeed that many felt could not exist. The sovereign bearing the date of 1843 has the 3 over a 2 (M.26B). The coin was examined under an Electron Scanning Microscope (ESM) with the benefit of its amazing stereonic photographs. This was the first time the ESM had been used for numismatic purposes and it proved conclusively that at long last an overdate from the London Mint sovereign series had been established. The 1843/2 overdate is certainly a key date within the series and extremely rare, produced as a result of the recoinage of 1842–45.

In 1996 an important auction of mainly gold sovereigns presented a wonderful opportunity for collectors and students—the sale of the *Douro* Cargo.[5] This cargo of some 28,000 gold coins, mainly consisting of sovereigns, was recovered from the RMS *Douro* that sank in the Bay of Biscay in 1882. The cargo included sovereigns of Victoria from 1838 to 1881, 10,000 of which were catalogued as collectable coins, with around 40 key dates and major rarities. However, even a cargo of such a huge quantity as this could not yield all of the extremely rare sovereigns as catalogued within the reign of Victoria—two were thought to be missing. One was the major rarity of the Type IIA series, the 1879 sovereign (M.90), and the other missing sovereign was the 1843/2 overdate from the Type IA series (M.26B). However, some years later an example of this rarity was identified among a small group of bullion sovereigns purchased as one lot from the cargo by a lucky collector. Also amongst the cargo were two varieties of 1863 "827" sovereigns (M.46A), one being from the die number series. A significant point is that they were the only two "827" sovereigns from the catalogued portion of the cargo, and so further endorse the rarity rating they fully deserve.

Another very rare sovereign from the *Douro* cargo was the 1843 (narrow shield) variety (M.26A) which was described as VF except for an obverse edge knock. Few of these sovereigns are known to exist and the *Douro* coin, condition-wise, had been in circulation. There were 13 of the rare key date "Ansell" sovereigns (M.42A) aboard the *Douro*, but only two of these were good grade coins. These two were both EF/GEF and the other examples were all around VF, which endorses the view that this rare key date does occasionally turn up but hardly ever above VF.

The "Ansell" sovereign (M.42A) is so named because of the remarkable efforts of George Frederick Ansell[7] who was employed by the Royal Mint. Thomas Graham, FRS, became Master of the Mint in 1856 and on October 29 of that year he wrote to the Treasury recommending the appointment of Ansell. In accordance with this recommendation to a supernumerary clerkship, he took office in the Rolling Room of the Royal Mint. Graham had described him as *"a person of superior education and ability, and great activity and vigour of character"*. He also had a very significant scientific background.[8] In 1859 a quantity of gold valued at £167,539 was ordered to be melted and returned to the Bank as unfit for coin due to its brittle nature. This gold in fact contained some quantities of antimony, arsenic and lead. Ansell asked to experiment with this gold, and although confronted by several obstacles, including the aversion to change, he was eventually given permission. His experiments brought a successful conclusion and as a result the gold was re-worked at very little additional cost, and without annealing. The new sovereigns were in fact so tough that an ordinary man could not break them even with the aid of a pair of pliers. For his efforts Ansell received a letter of thanks from the Master of the Mint plus £100. The "Ansell" sovereign can be recognised by a small additional line that Ansell had placed in the centre lower edge of the ribbon at the back of Victoria's head.

The other very rare coin from the Type IB die number series is the one dated 1874 (M.58), and seven of these surfaced from the *Douro* in 1996. All except one piece bore the die number 32, which is the number usually seen when this very rare sovereign appears. The highest graded coin of these six was described as AEF. The remaining sovereign bore the so far unrecorded die number of 33, graded GVF. Finally, we had from the *Douro* three sovereigns bearing the date 1841 (M.24), and these extremely rare key date coins were all of variable VF grades.

A variety which remained undetected until quite recently, although none were found among the *Douro* cargo, is the Type IA sovereign dated 1844 (M.27A).[9] This coin displays the figure 4 in its date over an inverted 4 and this is quite remarkable because we now know that this unusual error date was also made in the following years, 1845 and 1846 (M.28A and 29B).

For several years there has been considerable conjecture surrounding the many varieties of the early sovereigns of Queen Victoria, especially those within the Type IA series, and to illustrate the reason for this we can do no better than quote the words of William Wyon himself when addressing the Royal Commission on the Mint in 1848[6]: "*With respect to the dies every die is perfected by the Graver, re-lettered etc., and in fact made an original before it is hardened; so that, in case of a failure of the original matrix, a die could be converted into and used as a matrix, so as to obtain punchoens from it.*"

There are also a number of varieties to be found in the Type IB die number series of sovereigns. One of these varieties also appears in the Type IA group (M.46A) but without die number—it is known as the "827" sovereign. This extremely rare sovereign was first noted in the hoard of coins discovered at Hatton, Derbyshire, on October 6, 1954 by Mr E. H. Pugh. The coin bears the date 1863 and carries the die number 22 on the reverse. To date no other reverse die number for this variety has appeared and on all known examples of this sovereign the second 2 of the die number is weakly struck. It is the obverse of the coin which makes it something very special, for at the bottom of the truncation, where one would expect to see the letters W.W. incuse, there are instead the figures "827" in relief.

To what does 827 relate? It would not be unreasonable to suggest that 827 related to an ingot number, and past Mint records indicate that experiments were carried out in 1863 involving ingots numbered from 816 to 830. However, to establish at least good foundation for the ingot theory, a great deal of searching through existing Royal Mint files and records was necessary. This research was carried out by Mr G. P. Dyer, then Librarian and Curator of the Royal Mint, and full details of this most important research were published in 1977.[10] There cannot be any doubt that the two different varieties of 1863 "827" sovereign are very important key dates within the series, and the Type IA coin without die number (M.46A) is slightly the rarer of the two. Both remain very rare today, and to date, just nine are recorded for the Type IB die number example (M.48A).

Numerous theories have been advanced on the meaning of the die numbers which appear on the reverse of the shield sovereigns struck from 1863 to 1874, but probably the best known is the suggestion that the number was added to produce a record of how many sovereigns a particular die could produce. Another is that they were introduced to enable the Mint to pinpoint the coin press operator in respect of that particular die. However, as scant records exist as to their use, it must remain a little mysterious.

Notes/References
1. Sir John Craig, KCVO, CB, LLD, *The Mint*, Cambridge 1953, pp. 301–14.
2. Sir Geoffrey Duveen and H. G. Stride, *The History of the Gold Sovereign*, London 1962, p. 95.
3. Col J. T. Smith, FRS, *Remarks on a Gold Currency for India and Proposal of Measures for the Introduction of the British Sovereign*, London 1868.
4. M. A. Marsh, *Seaby Coin & Medal Bulletin*. December 1981, pp. 348–49.
5. Spink & Son Ltd., Auction No. 118, The Douro Cargo, London, November 20–21, 1996.
6. Sir Geoffrey Duveen and H. G. Stride, *The History of the Gold Sovereign*, London 1962, p. 86.
7. G. F. Ansell, *The Royal Mint*, third edition, London 1871, pp. 49–52.
8. M. A. Marsh, "The Ansell Sovereign", *Spink Numismatic Circular*, July 1982, pp. 194–95.
9. With grateful thanks to Mr Kenneth Goode of Birmingham, Alabama, USA.
10. G. P. Dyer, "1863 Sovereign Number 827", *Spink Numismatic Circular*, October 1977, p. 421.

SHIELD REVERSE SOVEREIGNS OF QUEEN VICTORIA

Description and details of the Queen Victoria Type IA Shield sovereign

Obverse: Young head of Victoria to left. Hair bound with double fillet and collected up into a knot behind. Legend: VICTORIA DEI GRATIA. Date on field below truncation. The letters W.W. in relief on the bottom of the truncation (these letters appear incuse on some coins).

Reverse: The Ensigns Armorial of the United Kingdom within a plain shield, surmounted by a crown. A branch of laurel is shown on each side of the shield, tied at the bottom by a ribbon. At the bottom the Thistle, Rose and Shamrock are placed with a small flower stop each side. Legend. BRITANNIARUM REGINA FID:DEF:

Edge: Milled.

The coin is struck with a reverse die axis ↑↓. Can sometimes be up to 45 degrees off-centre.

Note. "Small bust" patterns exist dated 1837 and 1838 before the accepted currency design was adopted—see Wilson and Rasmussen no. 255–299 and the Bentley Collection, lot 33.

Description and details of the Queen Victoria Type IB Shield sovereign

Obverse: The same as the first issue Type IA, above.

Reverse: The same as the first issue Type IA, above, except for a die number that is placed on the reverse at the bottom of the coin just above the rose and between the tails of the ribbon.

Edge: The same as the first issue Type IA, above,

The coin is struck with a reverse die axis ↑↓.

Groups within the Type IA and IB Young head/shield series

1. *Sovereigns dated 1838–47 inclusive.*

When the obverse of these coins is studied closely it is noticeable that the Queen's head is small and is well placed in respect of the legend. It does not appear at all cramped and the letters W.W. on the truncation are in relief and with stops. The reverse, although containing far more detail, once again displays the legend quite free of the design.

2. *Sovereigns dated 1848–55 inclusive.*

The borders of these coins are slightly broader than the earlier issue; because of this the legend of the obverse is moved slightly inwards. On the reverse the legend is again forced inwards and is also slightly raised. This gives a very cramped impression of both the laurel branch and legend, and if one looks at the letters T and A in BRITANNIARUM the laurel leaf does in fact encroach between the two letters. Sovereigns dated 1853, 1854 and 1855 within this group can also be found with WW incuse and without stops.

3. *Sovereigns dated 1853–71 inclusive.*

The obverse is similar to that of group 2 coins and the letters WW are incuse and without stops. Sovereigns dated 1870–74 can be found with W.W. in relief and stops. The remaining sovereigns of the Type IB are with W.W. in relief and with stops.

SOVEREIGNS OF VICTORIA, 1837–1901

Pattern Type IA sovereign dated 1837. No currency coins were struck this year

Type IA, group 1

Type IA, group 2

Type IA, group 3

TYPE IA SHIELD SOVEREIGNS OF QUEEN VICTORIA

No.	Date	Type/Variety	Mintage	Rating
21C	1837	Small head pattern. Close spaced legend, plain truncation and edge (WR295)	Very few	R5
21D	1837	As 21C but wider spaced legend	Very few	R5
21E	1837	As 21D but milled edge (WR297)	Very few	R6
21F	1837	As 21D but WW incuse on truncation (WR298)	Very few	R6
21G	1838	Small head pattern as 21F (WR299)	Very few	R5
22	1838	Normal	2,718,694	R
22A	1838	Rev. Narrow Shield. Different arrangement of laurel with top leaves nearer to crown. Rose, shamrock and thistle as 26A but with flower stops	Incl. in above	R3
22B	1838	Plain edge proof (WR300)	Very few	R6
22C	1838	Milled edge proof	Very few	R3
23	1839	Normal	503,695	R2
23A*	1839	Plain edge proof struck en medaille (WR302)	c. 400	R
23B	1839	Plain edge proof, inverted die axis (WR303)	Incl. in above	S
23C	1839	Milled edge proof (WR304)	Very few	R5
23D	1839	Plain edge proof with narrow shield reverse, struck en medaille	Very few	R6
24	1841	Normal	124,054	R3
24A	1841	Unbarred As in GRATIA	Incl. in above	R3
25	1842	Closed 2 in date	4,865,375	N
25A	1842	Open 2 in date	Incl. in above	R2
25B	1842	Unbarred As in GRATIA	Incl. in above	R3
26	1843	Normal	5,981,968	N
26A	1843	Rev. Narrow Shield. Different arrangement of laurel with top leaves nearer to crown. Rose, shamrock and thistle below are larger and finer but without flower stops	Incl. in above	R3
26B	1843/2	3 over 2 in date	Incl. in above	R5
26C	1843	Roman I for 1 in date	Incl. in above	R2
26D	1843	3 over 8 in date	Incl. in above	R5

* 23A is also known struck on a thin flan (WR301).

Type IA SHIELD SOVEREIGNS OF QUEEN VICTORIA *continued*

No.	Date	Type/Variety	Mintage	Rating
27	1844	Spread 4 4 in date	3,000,445	S
27A	1844	First 4 over inverted 4 in date	Incl. in above	R2
27B	1844	Closer 4 4 in date	Incl. in above	R
28	1845	Spread 4 5 in date	3,800,845	S
28A	1845	4 over inverted 4 in date	Incl. in above	R2
28B	1845	Closer 4 5 in date	Incl. in above	R
28C	1845	Roman I for 1 in date	Incl. in above	R2
28D	1845	E of DEI over rotated E	Incl. in above	R3
28E	1845	1 over inverted 1 in date	Incl. in above	R3
29	1846	Normal	3,802,947	S
29A	1846	1 over inverted 1 in date	Incl. in above	R
29B	1846	4 over inverted 4 in date	Incl. in above	R2
29C	1846	Roman I for 1 in date	Incl. in above	R2
30	1847	Normal	4,667,126	N
30A	1847	1 over inverted 1 in date	Incl. in above	R
31	1848	Second larger head	2,246,701	S
31A	1848	Obv. Small head. Group 1	Incl. in above	R2
31B	1848	Last 8 over 7 in date	Incl. in above	R
32	1849	Second larger head. WW raised	1,755,399	R
32A	1849	Roman I for 1 in date	Incl. in above	R3
33	1850	Normal	1,402,039	R
33A	1850	Inverted A for V in VICTORIA	Incl. in above	R4
33B	1850	5 struck over 8 in date	Incl. in above	R5
33C	1850	Roman I for 1 in date	Incl. in above	R3
33D	1850	Wide gap between 1 and 8 in date	Incl. in above	R
33E	1850	With R over E in GRATIA	Incl. in above	R4
34	1851	Normal—date can be quite spread	4,013,624	N
34A	1851	Inverted A for V in VICTORIA	Incl. in above	R3
35	1852	Normal	8,053,435	C
35A	1852	Roman I for 1 in date	Incl. in above	R
35B	1852	Inverted A for V in VICTORIA	Incl. in above	R3
35C	1852	5 over 3 in date	Incl. in above	R4
36	1853	Date can be quite spread. WW raised	10,597,993	C
36A	1853	Milled edge proof (WR305)	Very few	R4
36B	1853	3 over 5 in date	Incl. in above	R4
36C	1853	F struck over E in DEF	Incl. in above	R3
36D	1853	1 over inverted 1 in date	Incl. in above	R2
36E	1853	Inverted A for V in VICTORIA	Incl. in above	R4
36F	1853	WW incuse on truncation	Incl. in above	R2
37	1854	WW incuse on truncation	3,589,611	N
37A	1854	WW raised on truncation	Incl. in above	R2
37B	1854	WW incuse. C of VICTORIA over rotated C	Incl. in above	R3
38	1855	Normal. WW on truncation incuse	8,448,482	C
38A	1855	WW raised on truncation	Incl. in above	R5
38B	1855	WW incuse. 1 over inverted 1 in date	Incl. in above	R2
39	1856	Normal	4,806,160	N
39A	1856	6 over 5 in date	Incl. in above	R2
40	1857	Date can be close or spread	4,495,748	N
40A	1857	Both As in GRATIA only partly barred	Incl. in above	R
41	1858	Normal	803,234	R
41A	1858	8 struck over 7 in date	Incl. in above	R3
41B	1858	Unbarred As in GRATIA	Incl. in above	R2
42	1859	59 sometimes higher than 18 in date	1,380,064	R
42A	1859	"Ansell" (brittle gold)	167,539	R2
43	1860	Normal	2,555,958	S

Type IA SHIELD SOVEREIGNS OF QUEEN VICTORIA *continued*

No.	Date	Type/Variety	Mintage	Rating
43A	1860	E of DEI over rotated higher E	2,555,958	R3
43B	1860	Letter O for zero in date	Incl. in above	R
43C	1860	O of VICTORIA struck over C	Incl. in above	R
43D	1860	Inverted A for V in VICTORIA	Incl. in above	R4
43E	1860	As 43D plus 1 over inverted 1 in date	Incl. in above	R4
43F	1860	E over lower partially rotated E of REGINA	Incl. in above	R3
43G	1860	First A of GRATIA unbarred	Incl. in above	R2
44	1861	Date sometimes more spread	7,624,736	C
44A	1861	First digit in date is a letter I	Incl. in above	R2
44B	1861	C over rotated C in VICTORIA	Incl. in above	R2
44C	1861	O over zero in VICTORIA	Incl. in above	R2
44D	1861	E of DEI over higher rotated E	Incl. in above	R2
44E	1861	E of DEF over higher E	Incl. in above	R2
44F	1861	1 over inverted 1 in date	Incl. in above	R3
44G	1861	First T of legend over tilted T or V	Incl. in above	R3
45	1862	Date can be close or spread	7,836,413	C
45A	1862	F over inverted A over F in DEF	Incl. in above	R2
45B	1862	1 over inverted 1 in date	Incl. in above	R2
45C	1862	R over inverted R in VICTORIA	Incl. in above	R4
45D	1862	R over E in BRIT	Incl. in above	R3
45E	1862	E over F in DEF	Incl. in above	R
46	1863	Normal	Incl. with No. 48	C
46A	1863	"827" (figures on truncation)	Very few	R6
46B	1863	1 over inverted 1 in date	Incl. with No. 48	R2
46C	1863	Proof (WR306)	Very few	R6
47	1872	WW raised on truncation	Incl. with no. 56	C

SOVEREIGNS OF VICTORIA, 1837–1901

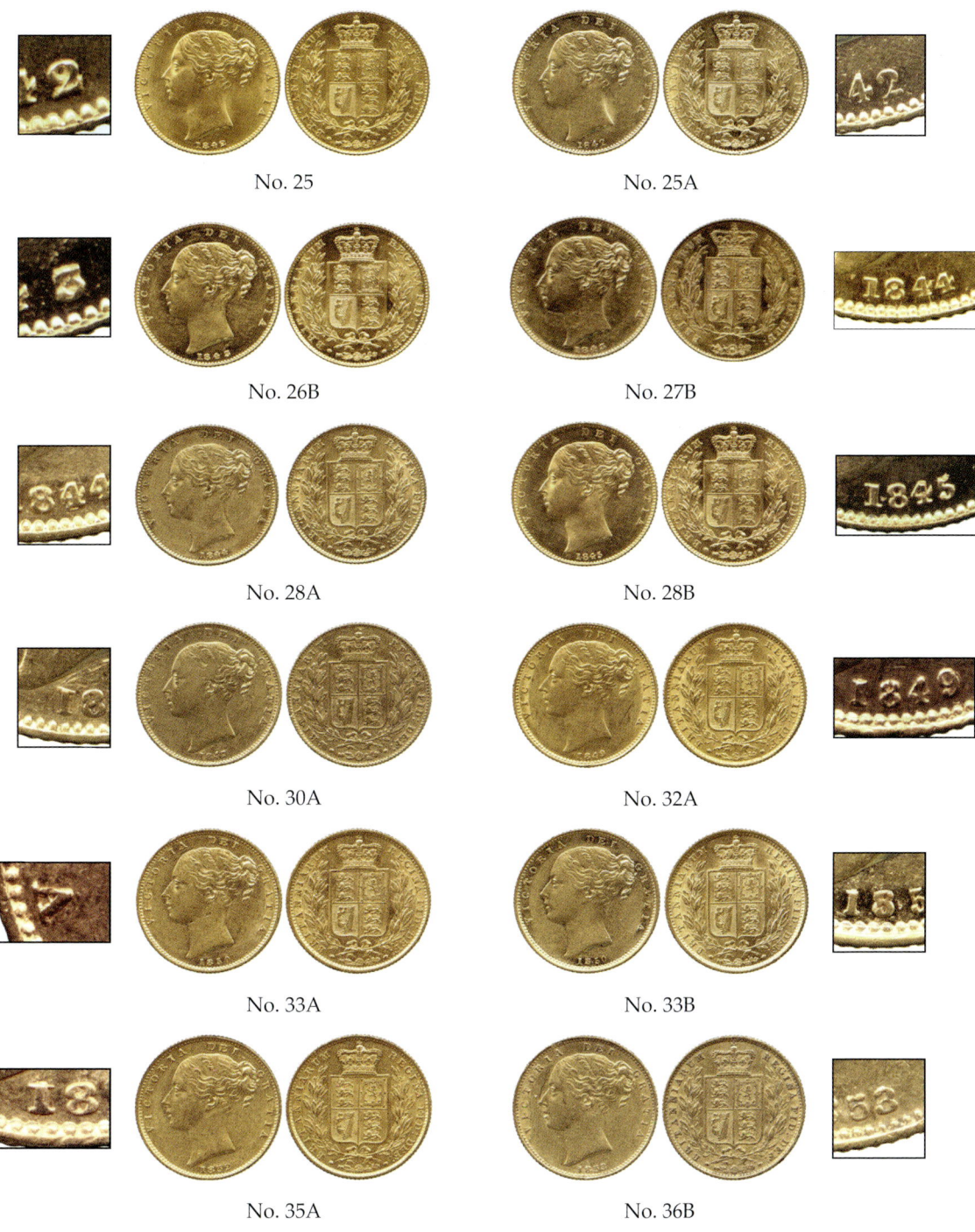

No. 25   No. 25A

No. 26B   No. 27B

No. 28A   No. 28B

No. 30A   No. 32A

No. 33A   No. 33B

No. 35A   No. 36B

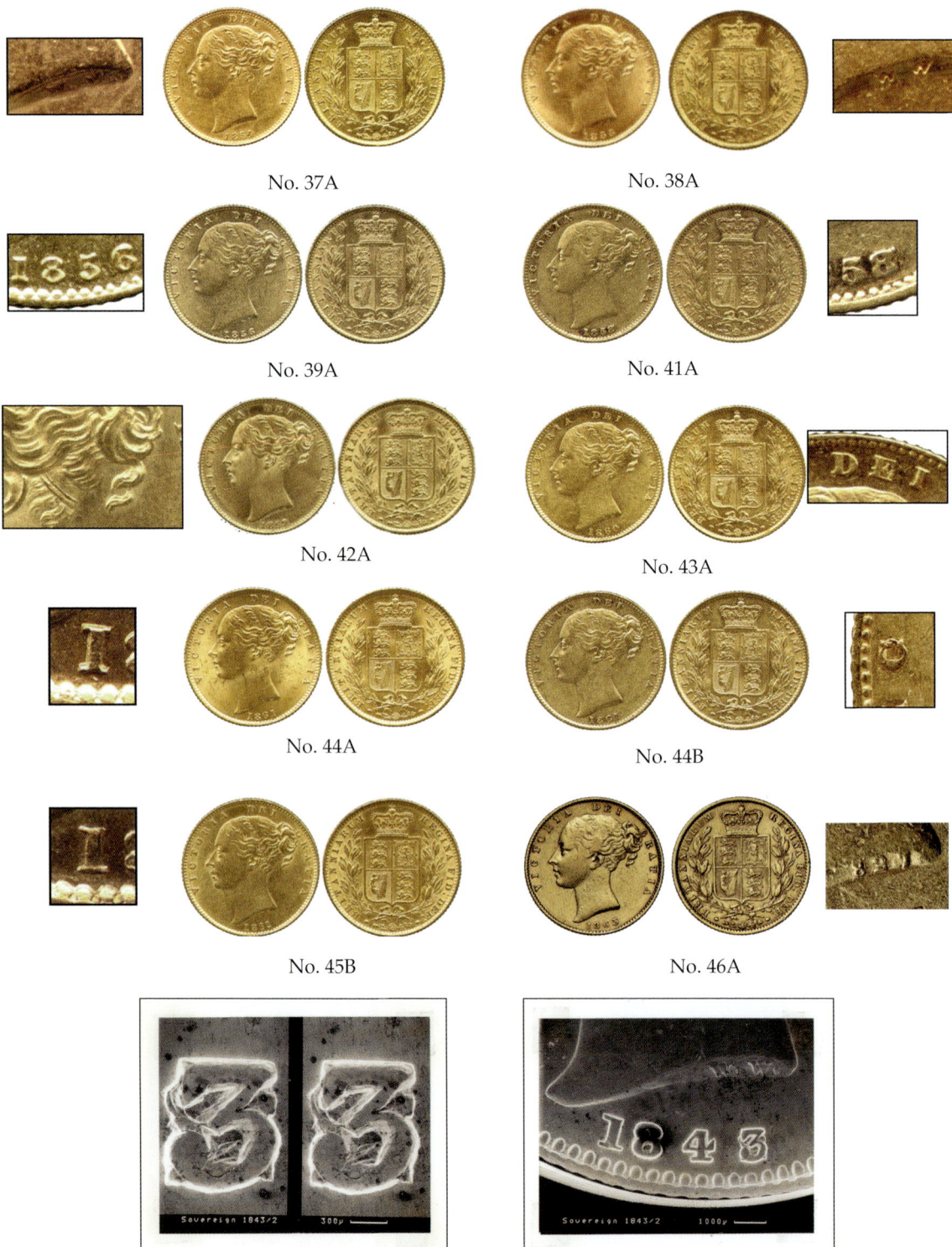

No. 37A No. 38A

No. 39A No. 41A

No. 42A No. 43A

No. 44A No. 44B

No. 45B No. 46A

Scanning Electron Microscope images of detail of M.26B.

TYPE IB (DIE NUMBER) SHIELD SOVEREIGNS OF QUEEN VICTORIA

No.	Date	Type/Variety	Mintage	Rating
48	1863	Normal	5,921,669*	N
48A	1863	"827" (figures on truncation) Rev. die no. 22	Very few	R5
49**	1864	Normal	8,656,352	C
49A	1864	Die number 1. Proof (WR307)	Very few	R7
49B	1864	Die number 79. Proof (WR308)	Very few	R7
50	1865	Normal	1,450,238	S
51	1866†	Normal	4,047,288	C
51A	1866	Die number 9, 11, 17 & 77 with 6 struck over 5 in date	Incl. in above	R2
52	1868	Normal	1,653,384	N
53	1869	Normal	6,441,322	C
53A	1869	Die number 34 struck from "yellow gold"	Incl. in above	R3
53B	1869	Die number 64. Proof (WR312)	Very few	R6
54	1870†	Normal WW incuse on truncation	2,189,960	N
54A	1870	Die number 1. Proof	Very few	R6
54AA	1870	Normal with WW raised on truncation	Incl. in above	N
54B	1870	Pattern with George III reverse (WR313)	Very few	R7
55	1871	Normal	8,767,250*	C
55A	1871	Die number 1. Specimen quality strike	Incl. in above	R5
55B	1871	Milled edge proof. No die number (WR314)	Very few	R7
56	1872	Normal	13,486,708*	C
56A	1872	Die number 65 struck over 64	Incl. in above	R4
57	1873	Normal with bulbous top and bottom to 3	2,368,215*	N
57A	1873	Normal with retracted hooked top to 3	Incl. in above	S
58	1874	Normal	520,713*	R3
58A	1879	Milled edge proof. No die number (WR322)	Very few	R6
58B	1880	Plain edge proof. No die number (WR323)	Very few	R6
58C	1886	Milled edge proof. No die number (WR329)	Very few	R7
58D	1887	Milled edge proof. No die number (WR331)	Very few	R6

*This mintage figure includes those of the Type IA sovereign of the same date.
**1864 sovereign die 49 seen struck en medaille.
†There are different design gold patterns for 1866 and 1870, WR310/313, both very rare.

DIE NUMBERS SO FAR KNOWN

The numbers in brackets and in italics have not been confirmed at the time of publication.

1863 1, 2, 3, 4, 5, 6, 7, 8, 9, 10, 11, 12, 13, 14, 15, 16, 17, 18, 19, 20, 21, 22, 23, 24, (*25*), 26, (*38*)

1864 1, 2, 3, 4, 5, 6, 7, 8, 9, 10, (*11*), 12, 13, (*14*), 15, (*16, 17, 18*), 19, (*20*), 21, 22, 23, 24, 25, 26, 27, 28, 29, 30, 31, 32, 33, 34, 35, 36, 37, 38, 39, 40, 41, 42, 43, 44, 45, 46, (*47*), 48, 49, 50, 51, 52, 53, 54, 55, 56, 57, 58, (*59*), 60, 61, 62, 63, 64, 65, 66, (*68*), 69, 70, 71, 72, 73, 74, 75, 76, 77, 78, 79, 80, 81, 82, 83, 84, 85, 86, 87, 88, 89, 90, 91, 91, 92, 93, 94, 95, 96, 97, 98, 99, 100, 101, 102, 103, 104, 105, 106

1865 1, 2, 3, 4, 5, 6, (*7*), 8, 9, 10, 11, 12, 13, 14, 15, 16, 17, 18, 19, 20, 21, 22, 23, 24, (*25*), 26, 27, 28, 29, (*30*), 31, 32, 33, (*34*), 35, 36, 37, (*38, 39*), 40, (*41, 42*), 44, 45, 51, 54

1866 1, 2, 3, 4, 5, 6, 7, 8, 9, 10, 11, (*12*), 13, 14, 15, 16, 17, 18, 19, 20, 21, 22, 23, 24, 25, 26, 27, 28, 29, 30, 31, 32, 33, 34, 35, 36, 37, 38, 39, 40, 41, 42, 43, 44, 45, 46, 47, 48, 49, 50, 51, 51, 52, 53, 54, 55, 56, 57, 58, 59, 60, 61, 62, 63, 64, 65, 66, 67, 68, 69, 70, 71, 72, 73, 74, 75, 76, 77, 78, (*79*)

1868 1, 2, 3, 4, 5, 6, 7, 8, 9, 10, 11, 12, 13, 14, 15, 16, 17, 18, 19, 20, 21, 22, 23, 24, 25, 26, 27, 28, 29, 30, 31, 32, 33, 34, 35, 36, 37, 38, 39, (*40*), 41, (*47, 48*)

1869 1, 2, 3, 4, 5, 6, 7, 8, 9, 10, 11, 12, 13, 14, 15, 16, 17, 18, 19, 20, 21, 22, 23, 24, 25, 26, 27, 28, 29, 30, 31, 32, 33, 34, 35, 36, 37, 38, 39, 40, 41, 42, 43, 44, 45, 46, 47, 48, 49, 50, 51, 52, 53, 54, (*55*), 56, 57, 58, 59, 60, 61, 62, 63, 64, (*65, 66, 67, 68*), 69, (*70, 71, 72, 73, 74, 75, 76*)

1870 1, (*2, 3, 4, 5, 6, 7, 8, 9, 10, 11, 12, 13, 14, 15, 16, 17, 18, 19, 20, 21, 22, 23, 24, 25, 26, 27, 28, 29, 30, 31, 32, 33, 34, 35, 36, 37, 38, 39, 40, 41, 42, 43, 44, 45, 46, 47, 48, 49, 50, 51, 52, 53, 54, 55, 56, 57, 58, 59, 60, 61, 62, 63, 64, 65, 66, 67, 68, 69, 70, 71, 72, 73, 74, 75, 76, 77, 78, 79*), 80, 81, 82, 83, 84, 85, 86, 87, 88, 89, 90, 91, 92, 93, 94, 95, 96, (*99, 100*), 112, 113, 114, 115, 116, 117, 118, 119, 120, 121, 122, 123

1871 1, 2, 3, 4, 5, 6, 7, 8, 9, 10, 11, 12, 13, 14, 15, 16, 17, 18, 19, 20, 21, 22, 23, 24, 25, 26, 27, 28, 29, 30, 31, 32, 33, 34, 35, 36, 37, 38, 39, 40, 41, 42, 43, 44, 45, (*46*), 47, 48, (*49, 50, 51, 52, 53*), 54, (*55, 56, 57, 58, 59, 60, 61, 62, 63, 64, 65*), 66, 67, 68, (*69*), 70, 71, 72, 73, 74, 75, 76, 77, 78, 79, (*83, 88, 94, 96*), 97, 98, 99, 100, 101, 102, 103, 104, 105, 106, (*107*), 108, 109, 110, 111

1872 1, 2, 3, 4, 5, 6, 7, 8, 9, 10, 11, 12, 13, 14, 15, 16, 17, 18, 19, 20, 21, 22, 23, 24, 25, 26, 27, 28, 29, 30, 31, 32, 33, 34, 35, 36, 37, 38, 39, 40, 41, 42, 43, 44, 45, 46, 47, 48, 49, 50, 51, 52, 53, 54, 55, 56, 57, 58, 59, 60, 61, 62, 63, 64, 65, 66, 67, 68, 69, 70, 71, 72, 73, 74, 75, 76, 77, 78, 79, 80, 81, 82, 83, 84, 85, 86, 87, 88, 89, 90, 91, 92, 93, 94, 95, 96, 97, 98, 99, 100, 101, 102, (*103*), 104, 105, 106, 108, 109, 110, 111, 112

1873 1, 2, 3, 4, 5, 6, 7, 8, 9, 10, 11, 12, 13, 14, 15, 16, 17, 18, 19, 20, 21, 22, (*23*), 24, (*25, 26, 27, 28, 29, 30*), 31, (*32, 33, 34*), 36, (*37, 38, 39, 40, 41, 42, 43, 44, 45, 46, 47, 48, 49, 50, 51, 52, 53, 54, 55, 56, 57, 58, 59, 60, 61, 62, 63, 64, 65, 66, 67, 68, 69, 70, 71, 72, 73, 74, 75, 76, 77, 78, 79, 80, 81, 82, 83, 84, 85, 86, 87, 88, 89, 90, 91, 92, 93, 94, 95, 96, 97, 98, 99, 100*), 103, (*104*), 107

1874 (*12, 15*), 28, 32, 33, (*34*), 35

Note. Original research for the first edition of *The Gold Sovereign* indicated that all the numbers included above had been struck at the Royal Mint. However, it has become clear over the years that many were either struck in small numbers and perhaps subsequently melted down or were never struck. Therefore those not physically seen by the Editor have been included in italics within brackets and their existence may be in some doubt. See the Bentley Collection catalogue Part 1 for a detailed synopsis of die number sovereigns.

SOVEREIGNS OF VICTORIA, 1837–1901

No. 48A

No. 51A

No. 53A

No. 54A

No. 55A

No. 56A

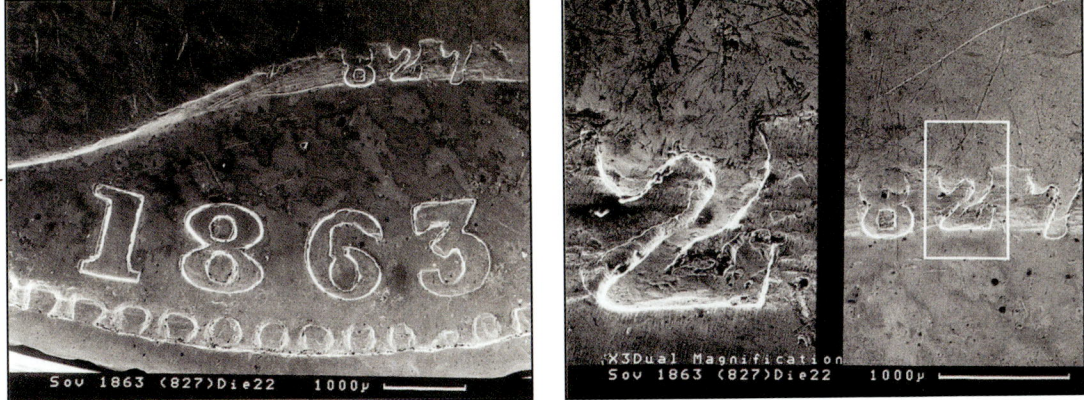

Scanning Electron Microscope images of the obverse detail of No. 48A.

145

THE MELBOURNE AND SYDNEY BRANCH MINT SHIELD SOVEREIGNS OF QUEEN VICTORIA

The Melbourne Type IC and the Sydney Type ID shield sovereigns from the branch mints are the same design as the Type IA sovereign, but they can be identified by the mint mark—an M or S that is placed on the reverse at the bottom of the coin just above the rose.

These two branch mints add a great deal of interest for the collector with the more challenging sovereigns to be found within the Melbourne series. They will present the collector with more than a few problems: those dated 1880, 1883, 1886, 1887 and the 1872/1 overdate are all extremely rare sovereigns which are likely to prove quite expensive.

Perhaps the most intriguing sovereign from the Melbourne series has to be the 1872/1 overdate (M.59A)[11] and it certainly deserves to be described as a remarkable coin simply because the branch mints of neither Sydney nor Melbourne were equipped with engraving staff, indeed they had no need of such staff because all die work for their coins was carried out at the London Mint.

Col E. W. Ward, RE, who later became Major-General Sir Edward Wohlstenholm Ward, KCMG, RE, was the Deputy Master of the Melbourne branch mint. Col Ward had previously been Deputy Master at the Sydney branch mint, and he anticipated that the new Melbourne branch would be ready to open in 1870. This failed to happen and London only supplied dates dated 1871.

The first consignment of these, 100 dies, were sent by the SS *Poonah* from Southampton on September 30, 1871.[12] The *Poonah* was scheduled to make other calls before eventually transferring her package of dies to the Peninsular and Oriental steamer *Rangoon* in Galle Harbour, Ceylon, on November 1, 1871. The existing Melbourne 1872/1 overdate sovereign (M.59A) is evidence that at least some of the 1871 dies arrived in Melbourne, though the *Rangoon* tragically came to grief on the dangerous Cadda rocks shortly after leaving Galle Harbour that evening.

The account reporting the loss of the *Rangoon* appears in Lloyds List of November

23, 1871, column 23, and states: *"Galle 1st Nov. The Peninsular and Oriental Company's steamer* Rangoon, *with mails and passengers for Australia, has struck upon a rock, and is sinking: the passengers have been saved, and the* Baroda *and two Trinity steamers are saving the mails.*

2nd Nov., 3 a.m. The Rangoon *struck on Cadda rock at 6 last evening, in leaving harbour, and sunk at midnight in 15 fathoms; pilot in charge; passengers, crew, a few bags of mails, and a portion of baggage saved"*.

The report also states that *"The* Rangoon *would have had on board the cargo which was shipped at Southampton, per* Poonah, *30th Sept."*, suggesting that some of the dies were delivered.

Despite this set-back new dies for 1872 were sent from London and arrived on April 10 and May 9, 1872, in time for the planned opening of the Melbourne branch mint on June 12, 1872. However, once more events did not go according to plan because the dies sent from London failed to produce the number of sovereigns anticipated. The obverse dies only averaged 8,000 pieces, and the reverse dies 14,000.[13] Experts in London believed that this was because the dies were not placed correctly in the presses. By September the die situation was critical and a local engraver, Julius Hogarth, was employed. This resulted in some of the 1871 dies being altered by Hogarth and are the source of the rare 1872/1 overdate (M.59A) which must be regarded as the most unusual overdate of those we know, and so it is without doubt an extremely rare sovereign, and also a key date of the series. It seems certain that Hogarth's work began towards the end of September, and that he only continued for a few weeks until the new dies arrived at the end of October, so one can reasonably suggest that few examples of his unsuccessful work can exist.

The Type ID Sydney shield sovereigns do not have any coins within the series that can be considered rare, but once again the collector can expect to find most of the sovereigns within this series very expensive in top grade.

Before leaving the Melbourne and Sydney branch mints, it is interesting to note that reference is sometimes made to sovereigns of the Type IC Melbourne shield series dated 1873 and 1879 and of the Type IIC St George series dated 1877. Extensive research regarding these three coins in both Australia and England has revealed no trace of them and the Royal Mint has confirmed that no dies were supplied for any of the three sovereigns in question, so it is difficult to believe that any can exist. Nevertheless mintage figures for such "impossible" calendar years would undoubtedly be consistent with sovereigns dated as the preceding years.

Notes/References
11. M. A. Marsh, "Rare Victorian Sovereigns", *Coin Monthly*, February 1982, pp. 6–11. M.A. Marsh, "A Sovereign Overdate from the Melbourne Mint", *Coin Monthly*, December 1982, pp. 5–7.
12. *Lloyd's List*, November 23, 1871, London 1999.
13. J. Sharples, "The Story of the 1872/1 Sovereign", *Australian Coin Review*, December 1985.

The Sydney Branch Mint opened May 14, 1855.

The Melbourne Branch Mint opened June 12, 1872.

Description and details of the Queen Victoria Melbourne Type IC "shield" sovereign, Melbourne Branch Mint

Obverse: As Type IA.
Reverse: As Type IA except that the mint mark M is placed just above the rose at the bottom of the coin.
Edge. Milled as Type IA.
The coins are struck with a reverse die axis ↑↓.

TYPE IC SHIELD REVERSE SOVEREIGNS OF QUEEN VICTORIA
(MELBOURNE MINT: MINT MARK M)

No.	Date	Type/Variety	Mintage	Rating
59	1872	Normal	748,180*	R
59A	1872/1	Obv. Overdate 2 over 1	Incl. in above	R4
59B	1872	Struck en medaille ↑↑	Incl. in above	R3
60	1874	Normal	1,373,298*	N
61	1880	Normal	3,053,454*	R2
62	1881	Low hairline in line with gap between I and A of VICTORIA, rounded tip to truncation	2,325,303*	R2
62A	1881	High hairline in line with A of VICTORIA, pointed tip to truncation	Inc. in above	R
63	1882	Normal	371,481	S
64	1883	Normal	427,092	R2
64A	1883	Proof	Very few	R7
65	1884	Normal	2,942,630*	N
66	1885	Normal	2,967,143*	N
66A	1885	Proof	Very few	R7
67	1886	Normal	2,902,131*	R3
68	1887	Normal	1,917,048*	R3

*The mintage figures include those of Type IIB sovereigns of the same date.

THE GOLD SOVEREIGN SERIES

Obverse and reverse of the Type IC Melbourne Branch Mint sovereign with overdate 1872/1, No. 59A.

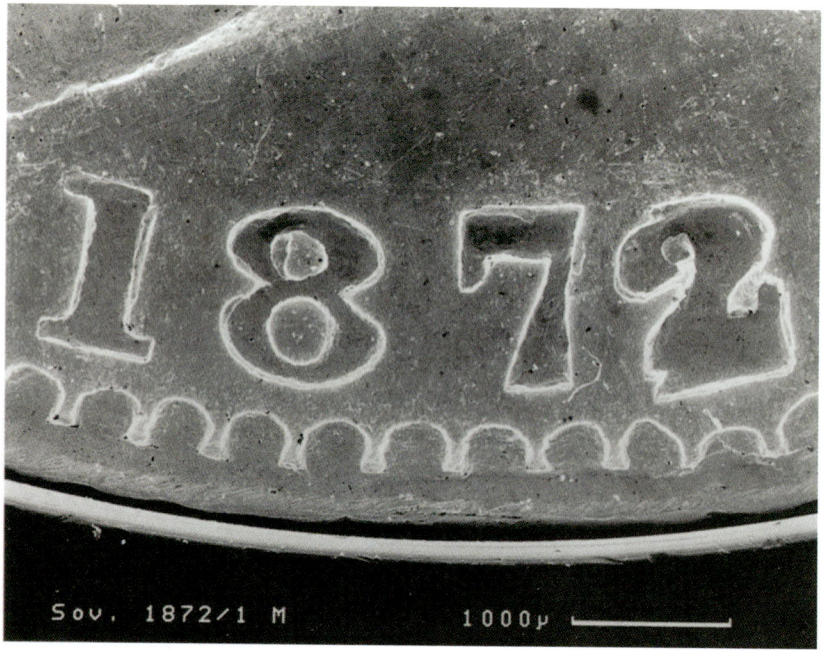

Scanning Electron Microscope photograph of the obverse detail of No. 59A.

SOVEREIGNS OF VICTORIA, 1837–1901

Description and details of the Queen Victoria Sydney Type ID "shield" sovereign, Sydney Branch Mint

Obverse: As Type IA.
Reverse: As Type IA except that the mint mark S is placed just above the rose at the bottom of the coin.
Edge. Milled as Type IA.
The coins are struck with a reverse die axis ↑↓.

TYPE ID SHIELD REVERSE SOVEREIGNS OF QUEEN VICTORIA (SYDNEY MINT: MINT MARK S)

No.	Date	Type/Variety	Mintage	Rating
69	1871	WW incuse on truncation	2,814,000*	S
69A	1871	WW in relief on truncation	Incl. in above	C
70	1872	WW in relief on truncation	1,815,000*	N
71	1873	Normal	1,478,000*	S
72	1875	Normal	2,122,000*	C
73	1877	Normal	1,590,000	N
73A	1877	1 over inverted 1 in date	Incl. in above	R2
74	1878	Normal	1,259,000	S
75	1879	Normal	1,366,000*	N
76	1880	Normal	1,459,000	N
76A	1880	Inverted A for V in VICTORIA	Incl. in above	R2
77	1881	Low hairline in line with gap between I and A of VICTORIA, rounded tip to truncation	1,360,000*	R2
77A	1881	High hairline in line with A of VICTORIA, pointed tip to truncation	Inc. in above	R
78	1882	Normal	1,298,000*	N
79	1883	Normal	1,108,000*	S
79A	1883	Proof	Very few	R7
80	1884	Normal	1,595,000*	N
81	1885	Normal	1,486,000*	S
82	1886	Normal	1,667,000*	S
83	1887	Normal	1,000,000*	S

* Mintage figure includes the total of St George & Dragon reverses.
Note: No. 75, sometimes has letter C of legend flawed shut to look like a letter O (McDonald 126a).

ST GEORGE REVERSE SOVEREIGNS OF QUEEN VICTORIA

Charles Freemantle became the Deputy Master of the Royal Mint in 1868 and during his period of office until 1894 he was very much involved in the re-organisation of the Mint. He later became the Hon Sir Charles Fremantle, KCB. In 1871 following Fremantle's efforts, a new design for the sovereign was suggested and accepted by the Queen, and was authorised by Order in Council on January 14, 1871. Although William Wyon had died in 1851 his Young head bust of the Queen was kept for the new sovereign. The new reverse was to be the return of Pistrucci's St George slaying the dragon, the same design as that used for the first sovereign of George IV. Interestingly there are variations in the length and the apparent thickness of the horse's tail on the reverses which can be clearly identified. These are usually referred to as either long or short tails, but not surprisingly an intermediate tail has also been discovered. The simplest way to spot the differences is to look at the distance between the end of the tail and the end of the lance on the ground line. In addition there are numerous minor varieties identified but these are considered outside the scope of this publication.

The new Type II St George sovereigns of Queen Victoria were first issued in 1871 and struck at the Royal Mint; during the years 1871–74 they ran concurrently with the "shield" sovereign. They were also struck at the Melbourne and Sydney branch mints until 1887, and the series is known as the Type II St George type.

The key date and major rarity from within the whole series of Type II sovereigns, including the branch mints, is unquestionably the 1879 sovereign from the London Mint (M.90). This sovereign, of which only 20,013 were struck, is very worthy of an R4 rating; it rarely appears, and even when it does it is usually in low grade.

Most of the other sovereigns from the Type II series in average grade will not present too many problems for the collector, but high grade examples, especially from the branch mints, are likely to prove more expensive. Surprisingly even the second overdate from the London Mint 1880/70 (M.91A), can only be rated as scarce.

The mint mark for the Type II St George series of Melbourne Type IIB and Sydney Type IIC sovereigns, is a letter M or S, placed on the obverse just below the truncation.

Short tail   Long tail

Description and details of the Queen Victoria Type II St George sovereign

Obverse: The Queen's head to left. Hair bound with a double fillet and collected up into a knot behind. The letters W.W. at the bottom of the truncation standing for William Wyon.* Legend: VICTORIA D:G:BRITANNIAR:REG:F:D:. For the Branch Mint strikings the initial M or S appears in the field below the head.

Reverse: St George armed with a sword, slaying the dragon. The date appears below the exergue or ground line at the bottom with the small letters B.P. (Benedetto Pistrucci) to the right. These letters vary in size for different issues.

Edge: Milled.

The coin is struck with a reverse die axis ↑↓.

* Note that on many of these sovereigns the bottom of the truncation is very narrow, consequently the initials W.W. are often seen encroaching onto the field area with invariably part of them and the stops missing, these initials are then referred to as "buried".

Date area of London Mint Sovereign
No. 84A. (Large B.P.).

Date area of London Mint Sovereign
No. 90. (Normal B.P.).

Date area of Melbourne Mint Sovereign
No. 100. (B.P. similar to London Mint).

Date area of Sydney Mint Sovereign
No. 119. (B.P. can be distinct).

The B.P. normally seen are the small letters with the larger letters being used occasionally. There appear to be no Mint records as to the reason for large or small letters but it makes an interesting study. Occasionally examples are seen where the stops in the B.P. have filled in or are partially filled in on the dies, therefore no stops or only partial stops appear on the coin.

TYPE IIA ST GEORGE REVERSE SOVEREIGNS OF QUEEN VICTORIA (LONDON MINT: NO MINT MARK)

No.	Date	Type/Variety	Mintage	Rating
84	1871	W.W. raised and "buried" in truncation, small B.P., long tail	8,767,250*	C
84A	1871	Large B.P., short tail	Incl. in above	S
84B	1871	Milled edge proof. Large B.P. (WR317)	Very few	R6
84C	1871	Plain edge proof. Large B.P. (WR319)	Very few	R2
84D	1871	Plain edge proof. Small B.P. (WR315)	Very few	R5
84E	1871	Milled edge proof. Small B.P. (WR318)	Very few	R6
85	1872	Small B.P., long tail	13,486,708*	C
86	1873	Small B.P., long tail, date with bulbous top and bottom to 3	2,368,215*	S
86A	1873	Small B.P., short tail, date with hooked top to 3	Inc. in above	R
87	1874	Small B.P., long tail	520,713*	R
88	1876	Small B.P., long tail	3,318,866	C
89	1878	Small B.P., long tail	1,091,275	N
89A	1878	Proof (WR321)	Not known	R6
90	1879	Small B.P., long tail	20,013	R3
91	1880	W.W. "buried", small B.P., short tail	3,650,080	C
91A	1880/70	Rev. overdate, second 8 over 7. W.W. "buried", small B.P., long tail	Incl. in above	S
91B	1880	W.W. buried, no B.P., short tail	Incl. in above	R
91BB	1880/70	Overdate as 91A but no B.P., W.W. "buried", long tail	Incl. in above	R
91C	1880	W.W. clear, no B.P., short tail	Incl. in above	R
91D	1880	W.W. clear, small B.P., long tail	Incl. in above	S
91DD	1880/70	Overdate as 91A, W.W. clear, small B.P., long tail	Incl. in above	R
91E	1880	W.W. clear, small B.P., short tail	Incl. in above	S
91F	1880	W.W. "buried", no B.P.	Incl. in above	S
91G	1880	Milled edge proof. W.W. "buried", long tail (WR325)	Very few	R6
91H	1880	Plain edge proof. W.W. "buried", long tail (WR324)	Very few	R6
92	1884	W.W. "buried", small B.P., short tail	1,769,635	N
92A	1884	W.W. clear, short tail	Inc. in above	S
93	1885	Small B.P., short tail	717,723	S
93A	1887	Milled edge proof. W.W. "buried", short tail (WR332)	Very few	R6

* These mintage figures also include the sovereigns of Type IB.

SOVEREIGNS OF VICTORIA, 1837–1901

TYPE IIB ST GEORGE REVERSE SOVEREIGNS OF QUEEN VICTORIA
(MELBOURNE MINT: MINT MARK M)

No.	Date	Type/Variety	Mintage	Rating
94	1872	W.W. "buried" in thin truncation, long tail	748,180*	S
95	1873	Normal, long tail, date with bulbous top and bottom to 3	752,199	S
95A	1873	Proof WW buried, long tail	Very few	R7
95AA	1873	Normal, long tail, date with retracted hooked top to 3	Incl. above	S
96	1874	Normal, long tail	1,373,298*	S
97	1875	Normal, long tail	1,888,405	N
98	1876	Normal, long tail	2,124,445	S
99	1877	Normal, long tail	1,487,316	N
100	1878	Normal, long tail	2,171,457	C
100A	1878	Melbourne St George with rotated G for D in D:G:	Incl. in above	R4
101	1879	Normal, long tail	2,740,594	C
101A**	1879	Normal, intermediate tail, large last stop in B.P.	Incl. in above	S
102	1880	Normal, long tail	3,053,454*	S
102A**	1880	Normal, intermediate tail	Incl. in above	S
103**	1881	Normal, small B.P., intermediate tail	2,325,303*	N
103A	1881	Normal, small B.P., long tail	Incl. in above	S
103B	1881	Without B.P., short tail	Incl. in above	R
104**	1882	Small B.P., intermediate tail	2,094,300	N
104A**	1882	No B.P., intermediate tail	Incl. in above	S
104B	1882	W.W. clear, small B.P., short tail	Incl. in above	S
104C	1882	W.W. "buried", small B.P., short tail	Incl. in above	S
105	1883	W.W. "buried", small B.P., short tail	1,623,358	N
105A	1883	W.W. clear, short tail	Incl. in above	S
105B	1883	Proof, WW complete, short tail	Very few	R7
106	1884	W.W. "buried", short tail	2,942,630*	C
106A	1884	W.W. clear, short tail	Incl. in above	S
107	1885	W.W. "buried", short tail	2,967,143*	C
107A	1885	W.W. clear, short tail	Incl. in above	C
108	1886	W.W. clear, short tail	2,902,131*	C
109	1887	W.W. clear, short tail	1,917,048*	C

* These mintage figures also include the Type IC Shield type sovereigns.
** The three tail lengths can also be defined to some extent by the presence or absence of one or two spurs of hair in the curved indent midway down the left side of the tail.

TYPE IIC ST GEORGE REVERSE SOVEREIGNS OF QUEEN VICTORIA (SYDNEY MINT: MINT MARK S)

No.	Date	Type/Variety	Mintage	Rating
110	1871	W.W. "buried", small B.P., long tail	2,814,000*	S
110A	1871	Large B.P., short tail	Incl. in above	S
110B	1871	Proof	Very few	R7
111	1872	Small B.P (last stop often missing), long tail	1,815,000*	N
112	1873	Small B.P., long tail	1,478,000*	N
113	1874	Small B.P., long tail	1,899,000	N
114	1875	Small B.P., long tail	2,122,000*	N
115	1876	Small B.P., long tail	1,613,000	S
116	1879	Small B.P., long tail, S mint mark now further from neck	1,366,000*	S
117	1880	W.W. buried, small B.P., long tail	1,459,000*	S
117A	1880	W.W. buried, no B.P., short tail	Incl. in above	S
117B	1880	W.W. complete, small B.P., long tail	Incl. in above	S
117C	1880	W.W. complete, no B.P., long tail	Incl. in above	S
118	1881	W.W. buried, no B.P., short tail	1,360,000*	S
118A	1881	W.W. complete, no B.P., short tail	Incl. in above	S
119	1882	W.W. complete, small B.P., short tail	1,298,000*	N
119A	1882	W.W. complete, no B.P., short tail	Incl. in above	S
120	1883	Short tail	1,108,000*	N
121	1884	Short tail	1,595,000*	N
122	1885	Short tail	1,486,000*	N
123	1886	Short tail	1,667,000*	N
124	1887	Short tail	1,000,000*	N

* These figures also include the Type ID Shield type sovereigns. Refer also to "Note" after Sydney mint "AUSTRALIA" sovereigns.

THE SYDNEY BRANCH MINT *AUSTRALIA* REVERSE SOVEREIGNS OF QUEEN VICTORIA

With large tracts of gold being discovered in the Australian interior, west of the young Sydney colony, the colonial government of New South Wales sought approval from Britain to open a branch of the Royal Mint. Approval was granted in August 1853, and several pattern sovereigns were struck in London for consideration. These patterns, dated 1853, bore a uniquely Australian design: the obverse carried a new rendition of the Queen by James Wyon, while the words SYDNEY MINT ONE SOVEREIGN with a crowned AUSTRALIA within a wreath of banksia graced the reverse. This was the first time anywhere in the Empire that the coin stated its denomination.

Meanwhile, in Sydney, work had begun on establishing the premises of the new mint. The facility occupied the south wing of the old "Rum" hospital, and was opened on May 14, 1855. The transformation of raw gold from the gold fields into coinage begun in earnest, and by the end of 1856 over a million of the new colonial sovereigns had been struck.

In 1856, Leonard Charles Wyon, who had designed the reverse a few years earlier, was ordered to begin redesigning the obverse, perhaps in response to criticism that the obverse bust of the Queen was somewhat too mature. The new design, which featured a younger Queen wreathed in native Australian banksia, appeared on an 1856 pattern and later on currency issue coins dated 1857. This well-received design graced the Australian sovereign until 1870.

THE GOLD SOVEREIGN SERIES

Description and details of the Sydney Branch Mint Queen Victoria AUSTRALIA type sovereign with First type bust

Obverse: Young head of Victoria to left. Hair bound with double fillet and collected into a knot behind by James Wyon. Legend. VICTORIA D:G:BRITANNIAR:REGINA F:D: Date below truncation.

Reverse: AUSTRALIA across the centre with a small crown above. A branch of laurel leaves on either side joined at the bottom by a knotted bow. ONE SOVEREIGN at the bottom, and SYDNEY MINT displayed at the top.

Edge. Milled.

The coin is struck with a reverse die axis ↑↓.

SYDNEY BRANCH MINT SOVEREIGNS OF QUEEN VICTORIA
AUSTRALIA REVERSE, FIRST TYPE BUST

No.	Date	Type/Variety	Mintage	Rating
A358	1853	Pattern	Very few	R6
A359	1855	Pattern	Very few	R6
A360	1855	Normal	502,000	R
A361	1856	Normal	981,000	R

SOVEREIGNS OF VICTORIA, 1837–1901

Description and details of the Sydney Branch Mint Queen Victoria AUSTRALIA type sovereign with Second type bust

Obverse: Smaller Young head of Victoria to left by L. C. Wyon. The hair is bound and collected into a knot behind and plaited at the side, the plait falls below the ear and is gathered into the knot at the back of the head which is crowned with a wreath of native Banksia. Legend: VICTORIA D:G:BRITANNIAR:REG:F:D:. Date below truncation.

Reverse: As First type.

Edge: Milled. The coin is struck with a reverse die axis ↑↓.

SYDNEY BRANCH MINT SOVEREIGNS OF QUEEN VICTORIA
AUSTRALIA REVERSE, SECOND TYPE BUST

No.	Date	Type/Variety	Mintage	Rating
A360A	1855	Pattern	Very few	R6
A361A	1856	Pattern, plain edge	Very few	R5
A362	1857	Normal	499,000	R
A362A	1857	Proof, milled edge	Very few	R7
A362B	1857	Proof, plain edge	Very few	R6
A363	1858	Normal	1,101,500	R
A364	1859	Normal	1,050,500	N
A365	1860	Normal	1,573,500	R
A365A	1860	60 struck over 59 in date	Incl. in above	R3
A366	1861	Normal	1,626,000	N
A366A	1861	1 struck over 0 in date	Incl. in above	R3
A367	1862	Normal	2,477,500	N
A368	1863	Normal	1,255,500	N
A369	1864	Normal	2,698,500	N
A370	1865	Normal	2,130,500	N
A370A	1865	5 struck over 4 in date	Incl. in above	R6
A371	1866	Normal	2,911,000	N
A371A	1866	Proof	Very few	R6
A372	1867	Normal	2,370,000	N
A373	1868	"Yellow" gold, alloyed with 8.33% silver	1,117,000	N
A373A	1868	With 8 struck over 6	Incl. in above	R3
A374	1869*	Dated 1868. "Red" gold, alloyed with 8.33% copper	1,202,000	N
A375	1870	Normal	1,220,000	N
A375A	1870	Proof	Very few	R7

Note: We know that the Sydney branch mint often struck sovereigns for a particular year and then continued the same date well into the next year and also their records failed to indicate which type they were, therefore mintage figures in general must be accepted as the calendar year not the date on the coin.

*No dies were supplied for this year so the coins struck continued to be dated 1868.

THE GOLD SOVEREIGN SERIES

No. 365A

No. 366A

Below: A group of early Sydney AUSTRALIA sovereigns from a hoard discovered in the UK.

No. 370A

TYPE IIIA—JUBILEE SOVEREIGNS OF QUEEN VICTORIA

Boehm's new effigy of the Queen was adopted for the "Jubilee" coinage including that struck at the branch mints, with Pistrucci's St George and dragon retained for the reverse. The sovereigns and half sovereigns were struck at the London Mint and the branch mints of Melbourne and Sydney.

A survey of examples from all three mints has confirmed that there is a second legend type within the Victorian "Jubilee" series of currency sovereigns and that it began in the very first year of issue (1887). The first legend type displays the last colon of D:G: in the legend with a distinct gap between it and the edge of Victoria's crown, the crown is seen slightly encroaching into the toothing above. The letters J.E.B. are shown clearly within the lower line of the shoulder truncation. On the second legend type the same colon of D:G: this time appears very close to Victoria's crown, and the top of the crown does not interfere with the toothing above. The letters J.E.B. are again on the lower shoulder truncation but can be clearly seen intruding onto the field area and here again several differing types have been found. In addition to these a number of other varieties have been identified and most are listed here with their DISH numbers[1].

Notes/References
1. David Iverson and Steve Hill, *The Jubilee Head Gold Sovereign, 1887–93*, revised and updated by Sovereign Rarities, London 2018.

THE GOLD SOVEREIGN SERIES

Description and details of the Queen Victoria Jubilee head sovereign

Obverse: Bust of the Queen facing left wearing small crown, veiled and with ribbon and star of the Garter and the Victoria and Albert Order. The small letters J.E.B. for Joseph Egar Boehm in relief at the bottom of the bust. Legend: VICTORIA D:G:BRITT:REG:F:D:

Reverse: St George slaying the dragon. The date is shown below the exergue ground line, with the small letters B.P. to right.

Edge. Milled.

The coin is struck with an upright die axis ↑↑.

TYPE IIIA JUBILEE SOVEREIGNS OF QUEEN VICTORIA (LONDON MINT: NO MINT MARK)

No.	Date	Type/Variety	Mintage	Rating
125	1887	First legend, hooked J with J. higher than E.B. (DISH.L1)	est. 6,305‡	R5
125A	1887	First legend, hooked J with B. higher than J.E. (DISH.L2)	est. 6,305‡	R5
125B	1887	First legend, hooked J, spread initials in straight line (DISH L3)	est. 6,305‡	R5
125C	1887	First legend, hooked J, closer initials in straight line (DISH L4)*	est. 6,305‡	R5
125D	1887	First legend, with imperfect J (DISH L7)	1,079,756	C
125E	1887	Proof. Second legend, G: closer to crown (WR333)	797	S
125F	1887	Pattern. 14 pearls in necklace	Very few	R6
125G	1887	Pattern. 14 pearls in necklace. P of B.P. an inverted triangle	Not known	R6
125H***	1887	Pattern. 13 pearls, first legend with higher bust, fuller garter star	Not known	R7
125I	1887	First legend, hooked J, high J with low stop, lower E.B. (DISH L5)	c.6,304	R6
126	1888	First legend, G: distant from crown (DISH.L8)	16,850	R5
126A	1888	Second legend, G: close to crown (DISH.L9)	2,260,574	C
126B	1888	Proof (WR335)	Very few	R7
127	1889**	Second legend (DISH.L11)	7,257,455	C
127A	1889	Proof (WR336)	Very few	R7
128	1890**	First legend, G: distant from crown (DISH.L12). Not yet seen	32,649	R4
128A	1890	Second legend G: close to crown (DISH.L13)	6,497,238	N
128B	1890	Second legend O instead of 0	Incl in above	C
129 †	1891	Reverse horse with short tail (DISH.L14)	est. 6,329	R4
129A †	1891	Reverse horse with long tail (DISH.L15)	6,323,147	C
129B	1891	Proof. Horse with long tail (WR337)	Very few	R6
130	1892	Normal (DISH.L16)	7,104,720	C
130A	1892	Proof. Horse with short tail (WR338)	Very few	R7

Notes: A number of patterns and trial pieces by Boehm from 1881 to 1885 exist, gold versions of which are listed by Wilson & Rasmussen, WR326–328.

*In addition to the four hooked J varieties listed here DISH lists two more, L5 and L6, but these have not been seen despite a record of six dies being produced.

**The "first legend" type dated 1889 and 1890 (DISH.L.10) is thought unlikely to exist as none have come to light.

***Refer to "Discoveries" article, *Coin News*, by S. Hill, January 2023 and *The Numismatist*, May 2024.

SOVEREIGNS OF VICTORIA, 1837–1901

† There are in fact three tail varieties which can be defined to some extent by the presence or total absence of one or two spurs of hair in the curved indent midway down the left side of the tail, but as they are not always obvious as dies wear it would be foolhardy to delineate them further.

‡ The Royal Mint reports of 1887 reveal that 1,657,067 sovereigns were struck for this date using 141 obverse dies, equating to an average life of 11,752 coins. However, the report goes on to state that 545,787 of the coins were rejected as not suitable to be released for circulation bringing the average output per obverse die down to 7,881 pieces, though in practise the amounts would vary from this mean average one way or the other.

First legend
with G: distant from crown

Second legend
with G: closer from crown

No. 125
(DISH L1)

No. 125B
(DISH L3)

No. 125C
(DISH L4)

No. 125D
(DISH L7)

No. 126
(DISH L8)

No. 125

No. 125D

No. 126

No. 126A

No. 127

No. 128A

163

THE GOLD SOVEREIGN SERIES

Description and details of the Queen Victoria Jubilee head sovereign, Melbourne Branch Mint

Obverse: As type IIIA.
Reverse: As type IIIA except that the M mint mark appears in the centre of the ground line above the date.
Edge. Milled.
The coin is struck with an upright die axis ↑↑.

TYPE IIIB JUBILEE SOVEREIGNS OF QUEEN VICTORIA (MELBOURNE MINT: MINT MARK M)

No.	Date	Type/Variety	Mintage	Rating
131	1887	First legend, hooked J, letters in straight line with raised stops (DISH.M1)	c. 42,727	R5
131A	1887	First legend, hooked J, space between J.E. and B. (DISH.M2)	c. 42,727	R5
131B	1887	First legend, hooked J, E. higher than J. and B. (DISH.M3)	c. 42,727	R5
131C	1887	First legend, hooked J, stops lower than letters (DISH.M4)*	c. 42,727	R5
131D	1887	First legend, imperfect J (DISH.M7)	c. 598,184	S
131E	1887	Second legend, imperfect J, G: closer to crown (DISH.M8)	c. 170,908	R
131F	1887	Pattern in silver with 14-pearl necklace	Unique?	R7
131G	1887	Proof	Very few	R7
132	1888	First legend, G: distant from crown (DISH.M9)	c. 28,306	R4
132A	1888	Proof	Very few	R6
132B	1888	Second legend, G: closer to crown (DISH.M10)	c. 2,802,306	C
133	1889	First legend, G: distant from crown (DISH.M11)	c. 55,152	R3
133A	1889	Second legend, G: closer to crown (DISH.M12)	c. 2,677,438	C
133B	1889	Proof, second legend, plain edge	Very few	R7
134	1890**	Second legend, G: closer to crown (DISH.M14)	2,473,537	N
134A	1890	Proof, second legend	Very few	R7
134AA***	1890	Second legend, with letter O for figure 0 in date	Incl. in above	C
135	1891	Reverse horse with short tail (DISH.M15)	2,749,592	R3
135A	1891	Reverse horse with long tail (DISH.M16)	Incl. in above	C
136***	1892	Normal (DISH.M17)	3,488,750	C
137	1893	Normal (DISH.M18)	1,649,352	S
137A	1893	Proof	Very few	R7

*In addition to the four hooked J varieties listed here DISH lists two more, M5 and M6, but these have not been seen despite a record of six dies being produced.
** The "first legend" type dated 1890 (DISH M.13) is thought unlikely to exist as none have come to light.
*** There are in fact three tail varieties which can be defined to some extent by the presence or total absence of one or two spurs of hair in the curved indent midway down the left side of the tail, but as they are not always obvious as dies wear it would be foolhardy to delineate them further.

Short and long tail variation

Short tail   Long tail

No. 131 (DISH M1)   No. 131A (DISH M2)   No. 131B (DISH M3)   No. 131C (DISH M4)

No. 131   No. 133

No. 134   No. 135

No. 135A   No. 136

No. 137

THE GOLD SOVEREIGN SERIES

Description and details of the Queen Victoria Jubilee head sovereign, Sydney Branch Mint

Obverse: As type IIIA.
Reverse: As type IIIA except that the S mint mark appears in the centre of the ground line above the date.
Edge. Milled.
The coin is struck with an upright die axis ↑↑.

TYPE IIIC JUBILEE SOVEREIGNS OF QUEEN VICTORIA (SYDNEY MINT: MINT MARK S)

No.	Date	Type/Variety	Mintage	Rating
138	1887	First legend, hooked J, with low E. and high B. (DISH.S1)	c. 62,000	R3
138A	1887	First legend, hooked J, with stops lower than letters (DISH.S2)	c. 62,000	R3
138B	1887	First legend, hooked J, J.E.B. low on truncation with E. lowest (DISH.S3)	c. 62,000	R4
138C	1887	First legend, hooked J, J.E.B. at bottom of junction of truncation with field (DISH.S4)	c. 62,000	R4
138D	1887	First legend, hooked J, J.E.B. higher up on truncation (DISH.S5)*	c. 62,000	R4
138E	1887	Specimen finish (a polished die version of 138)	Very few	R5
138F	1887	Proof from the true proof dies	Very few	R6
138G	1887	Proof, plain edge	Very few	R7
138H	1888	First legend, hooked J, with closer initials (DISH.S8***)	Not known	R7
139	1888	First legend, hooked J in wide spread J.E.B. (DISH.S7)	c. 65,000	R3
139A	1888	First legend, angled J in J.E.B. (DISH.S9)	87,480	R2
139B	1888	Second legend, G: closer to crown (DISH.S10)	2,034,520	C
140	1889	First legend, G: distant from crown (DISH.S11)	97,860	R3
140A	1889	Second legend, G: closer to crown (DISH.S12)	3,164,140	C
141	1890	First legend, G: distant from crown (DISH.S13)**	52,160	R4
141A	1890	Second legend, G: closer to crown (DISH.S14)**	2,751,840	C
142	1891	Second legend, reverse with long tail horse (DISH.S15)	2,596,000	C
142A	1891	First legend, reverse with long tail horse	Incl. in above	R7
143	1892	Second legend, reverse with long tail horse (DISH.S16)	2,837,000	C
144	1893	Second legend, reverse with long tail horse (DISH.S17)	1,498,000	C
144A	1893	Proof, plain edge	Very few	R7

*In addition to the four hooked J varieties listed here DISH also lists another, S6, but this has not been seen despite a record of six dies being produced. It is thought that this could be S7 (dated 1888) therefore its assumed mintage has been added to S7.

**The mintmark "S" on 141 and 141A appears to be double-struck over a 9 or 5.

*** Note this coin may be a re-use of the obverse of 138B of 1887 (DISH S3).

SOVEREIGNS OF VICTORIA, 1837–1901

No. 138 (DISH S1) No. 138A (DISH S2) No. 138B (DISH S3) No. 138C (DISH S4)

No. 138D (DISH S5) No. 139 (DISH S7) No. 139A (DISH S9)

No. 138 No. 139 No. 139A

No. 139B No. 140 No. 140A

No. 141 No. 141A No. 142

No. 143 No. 144

167

TYPE IVA—OLD HEAD SOVEREIGNS OF QUEEN VICTORIA

The final type of Queen Victoria's sovereigns are known as the "Old Head" or occasionally the "Veiled Head" series, from the style of the veiled image of the Queen on the obverse by Thomas Brock, RA, which would be used on the obverse of all gold and silver coins of the realm. As is customary his initials, T.B., appear on the truncation. Like the Jubilee series before it, Pistrucci's St George slaying the dragon was retained for the reverse of the sovereign and the initials B.P. can be found to the right in the exergue.

An important event during the last period of Victoria's reign was the opening of the last of Australia's branch mints, the Perth branch in Western Australia. The Deputy Master J. F. Campbell's report to the Royal Mint of March 1, 1900 stated that the Perth buildings were finished by November 1898 and that the installation of machinery, etc. was completed in May 1899.[1] The same report listed the local deposits of gold received and went on to describe the opening of the new branch mint at Perth on June 20, 1899. The first gold sovereigns struck at the Perth branch mint bear the date of that year.

As with the earlier Jubilee sovereigns, the branch mint mark for the "Old Head" series of Melbourne, Sydney and Perth, a letter M, S or P, is placed in the centre of the exergue/ground line on the reverse.

The only coins in the "Old Head" series that can be difficult to obtain are the 1899 Perth sovereign (M.171), and the 1896 Sydney coin (M.165). However, we must again stress that branch mint sovereigns, particularly in the better grades, can be very difficult for the collector to find, and so may well be costly.

Notes/References
1. J. E. Campbell, "Perth branch mint report", *Royal Mint Report,* 1899, pp. 132–36.

SOVEREIGNS OF VICTORIA, 1837–1901

Description and details of the Queen Victoria Old head sovereign

Obverse: Bust of the Queen facing left, crowned, veiled and draped, wearing ribbon and star of the Garter. The small letters T.B. appear below the bust. Legend: VICTORIA.DEI.GRA.BRITT.REGINA. FID.DEF.IND.IMP.*

Reverse: Pistrucci's St George slaying the dragon as previous type.

Edge. Milled.

The coin is struck with an upright die axis ↑↑.

*The words IND.IMP. for Empress of India appear in the legend for the first time.

TYPE IVA—OLD HEAD SOVEREIGNS OF QUEEN VICTORIA (LONDON MINT: NO MINT MARK)

No.	Date	Type/Variety	Mintage	Rating
145	1893*	Normal	6,898,260	C
145A	1893	Milled edge proof (WR341)	773	R
146	1894	Normal	3,782,611	C
147	1895	Normal	2,285,317	C
148	1896	Normal	3,334,065	C
149	1898	Normal	4,361,347	C
150	1899	Normal	7,515,978	C
151	1900	Normal	10,846,741	C
152	1901	Normal	1,578,948	N

*Note. There are patterns by Allan Wyon dated 1893 of extreme rarity (WR339 and 340).

Description and details of the Queen Victoria Old head sovereign, Melbourne Branch Mint

Obverse: As Type IVA.
Reverse: As Type IVA except that the M mint mark appears in the centre of the ground line above the date.
Edge. Milled.
The coin is struck with an upright die axis ↑↑.

TYPE IVB—OLD HEAD SOVEREIGNS OF QUEEN VICTORIA
(MELBOURNE MINT: MINT MARK M)

No.	Date	Type/Variety	Mintage	Rating
153	1893	Normal	1,914,000	N
153A	1893	Proof	Very few	R6
154	1894	Normal	4,166,874	C
154A	1894	Proof	Very few	R6
155	1895	Normal	4,165,869	S
155A	1895	Proof	Very few	R7
156	1896	Normal	4,456,932	C
156A	1896	Proof	Very few	R7
157	1897	Normal	5,130,565	C
157A	1897	Proof	Very few	R7
158	1898	Normal	5,509,138	C
158A	1898	Proof	Very few	R7
159	1899	Normal	5,579,157	C
159A	1899	Proof	Very few	R6
160	1900	Normal	4,305,904	C
160A	1900	Proof	Very few	R7
161	1901	Normal	3,987,701	C
161A	1901	Proof	Very few	R7

SOVEREIGNS OF VICTORIA, 1837–1901

Description and details of the Queen Victoria Old head sovereign, Sydney Branch Mint

Obverse: As Type IVA.
Reverse: As Type IVA except that the S mint mark appears in the centre of the ground line above the date.
Edge. Milled.
The coin is struck with an upright die axis ↑↑.

TYPE IVC—OLD HEAD SOVEREIGNS OF QUEEN VICTORIA (SYDNEY MINT: MINT MARK S)

No.	Date	Type/Variety	Mintage	Rating
162	1893	Normal	1,346,000	N
162A	1893	Proof	Very few	R6
163	1894	Normal	3,067,000	C
164	1895	Normal	2,758,000	C
165	1896	Normal	2,544,000	S
166	1897	Normal	2,532,000	C
167	1898	Normal	2,548,000	C
168	1899	Normal	3,259,000	C
169	1900	Normal	3,586,000	C
170	1901	Normal	3,012,000	C

THE GOLD SOVEREIGN SERIES

Description and details of the Queen Victoria Old head sovereign, Perth Branch Mint

Obverse: As Type IVA.
Reverse: As Type IVA except that the P mint mark appears in the centre of the ground line above the date.
Edge. Milled.
The coin is struck with an upright die axis ↑↑.

TYPE IVD—OLD HEAD SOVEREIGNS OF QUEEN VICTORIA (PERTH MINT: MINT MARK P)

No.	Date	Type/Variety	Mintage	Rating
171	1899	Normal	690,992	R
171A	1899	Proof	Very few	R7
172	1900	Normal	1,866,089	N
173	1901	Normal	2,889,333	N
173A	1901	Proof	Very few	R6

EDWARD VII 1901–10

Mint Engraver, George William de Saulles, modelled and engraved the obverse for the sovereign of Edward VII and his initials DeS. are placed under the truncation. Pistrucci's St George slaying the dragon was retained for the reverse and his initials appear in the exergue.

In 1900, following the discovery of gold in the Yukon,[1] the Canadian Government asked for the right to coin sovereigns. To enable them to do so the new mint that they had already planned would need to be a branch of the Royal Mint.

In 1901 the Canadian House of Commons agreed to fund a branch mint in Ottawa and this received Royal assent. However, building of the new mint premises did not begin until 1905 and the first sovereigns were not struck until 1908, and then for only two more years to the end of Edward's reign although it continued to operate into the reign of George V and, of course, today is one of the leading mints of the world.

The first Deputy Master for the Ottawa branch mint was James Bonar, and its coins are identified by a letter C placed on the reverse in the centre of the exergue line.

Sovereigns for the reign of Edward VII were struck at the London Mint and the branch mints of Melbourne, Sydney, Perth and Ottawa; the mint marks were a letter M, S, P or C respectively placed in the centre of the exergue line or ground on the reverse immediately under the horse's rear hoof.

For the collector the currency sovereigns of neither the London Mint nor the branch mints of Australia for Edward VII will present many problems, although some difficulty may be encountered in obtaining really choice examples. However, coins from the newly-opened branch mint of Ottawa may well cause problems as sovereigns were struck for only three years of the reign at the Canadian branch mint and all three dates are hard to find with the first of these, dated 1908 (M.183), being quite rare. The Deputy Master of the Ottawa branch mint, James Bonar, submitted his report for 1908[2] to the Royal Mint on March 25, 1909, and in this report he stated that the Melting and Coining Departments had struck 678 gold sovereigns for the year 1908. In Appendix B of this report

173

the statement of the weight and value of gold bullion received for coinage and resultant coins struck, shows that only 633 sovereigns were in fact issued. It is reasonable to suggest, therefore, that the remaining 45 sovereigns were rejected as being unsuitable for issue. It would appear that all 633 sovereigns were struck with a satin finish, unlike those for the following year when over 16,000 were struck as currency with a very small unrecorded number of specimens produced with a satin finish. However, over the years the Bank of Canada has disposed of much of its holding of gold, and this of course included Edward VII and George V sovereigns. Consequently coins which were once rated as being extremely rare can today be classified as simply rare or scarce. This, perhaps surprisingly, includes examples of the coveted 1908 sovereign which is still a difficult coin to track down but is no longer as prized as it was, although Canadian coin-series collectors also demand it, keeping the still limited supply of high value in top grades.

The Ottawa Branch Mint opened in January 1908.

Notes/References
1. J. Sharples, "Sovereigns of the overseas branches", *Royal Sovereign 1489–1989*, Royal Mint, p. 72.
2. J. Bonar, "Ottawa branch mint report", *Royal Mint Report,* 1908, pp. 138–142.

Description and details of the Edward VII sovereign

Obverse: The bare head of the King facing right. The small letters DeS (for De Saulles) below the truncation. Legend: EDWARDVS VII D:G:BRITT:OMN:REX:F:D:IND:IMP:
Reverse: St George mounted slaying the dragon, the date below the exergue line, with B.P. in small letters to right.
Edge: Milled.
The coin is struck with an upright die axis ↑↑.

EDWARD VII SOVEREIGNS
(LONDON MINT: NO MINT MARK)

No.	Date	Type/Variety	Mintage	Rating
174	1902	Normal	4,737,796	C
174A	1902	Matt proof (WR408)	15,123	S
174B	1902	Non matt finish proof (WR407)	Not known	R7
175	1903	Normal	8,888,627	C
176	1904	Normal	10,041,369	C
177	1905	Normal	5,910,403	C
178	1906	Normal	10,466,981	C
178A	1906	Matt proof (WR409)	Not known	R6
179	1907	Normal	18,458,663	C
180	1908	Normal	11,729,006	C
181	1909	Normal	12,157,099	C
182	1910	Normal	22,379,624	C

THE GOLD SOVEREIGN SERIES

Description and details of the Edward VII Ottawa Branch Mint sovereign

Obverse: As London Mint.
Reverse: As London Mint except that the C mint mark appears in the centre of the ground line above the date.
Edge: Milled.
The coin is struck with an upright die axis ↑↑.

SOVEREIGNS OF EDWARD VII
(OTTAWA MINT: MINT MARK C)

No.	Date	Type/Variety	Mintage	Rating
183	1908*	Satin finish	633	R
184	1909	Normal	16,300	C
184A	1909	Satin finish	Not known	R6
185	1910	Normal	28,020	C

* The milled edge reeding and spacing matches that as used on the London 1902 matt proof issue.

Description and details of the Edward VII Melbourne Branch Mint sovereign

Obverse: As London Mint.
Reverse: As London Mint except that the M mint mark appears in the centre of the ground line above the date.
Edge: Milled.
The coin is struck with an upright die axis ↑↑.

SOVEREIGNS OF EDWARD VII
(MELBOURNE MINT: MINT MARK M)

No.	Date	Type/Variety	Mintage	Rating
186	1902	Normal	4,267,157	C
186A	1902	Proof	Very few	R7
187	1903	Normal	3,521,780	C
188	1904*	Normal	3,743,897	C
189	1905	Normal	3,633,838	C
190	1906	Normal	3,657,853	C
191	1907	Normal	3,332,691	C
192	1908	Normal	3,080,148	C
193	1909	Normal	3,029,538	C
194	1910	Normal	3,054,547	C
194A	1910	Proof	Very few	R7

* Though records indicate there was provision for a 1904 M proof Sovereign to be struck, it is not known if any were and there are no known survivors.

THE GOLD SOVEREIGN SERIES

Description and details of the Edward VII Perth Branch Mint sovereign
Obverse: As London Mint.
Reverse: As London Mint except that the P mint mark appears in the centre of the ground line above the date.
Edge: Milled.
The coin is struck with an upright die axis ↑↑.

SOVEREIGNS OF EDWARD VII
(PERTH MINT: MINT MARK P)

No.	Date	Type/Variety	Mintage	Rating
195	1902*	Normal	4,289,122	C
196	1903	Normal	4,674,783	C
197	1904	Normal	4,506,756	C
198	1905	Normal	4,876,193	C
199	1906	Normal	4,829,817	C
200	1907	Normal	4,972,289	C
201	1908	Normal	4,875,617	C
202	1909	Normal	4,524,241	C
203	1910	Normal	4,690,625	C

* NGC have graded an example of the 1902 Perth as having no "DES" below the bust.

SOVEREIGNS OF EDWARD VII, 1901–10

Description and details of the Edward VII Sydney Branch Mint sovereign
Obverse: As London Mint.
Reverse: As London Mint except that the S mint mark appears in the centre of the ground line above the date.
Edge: Milled.
The coin is struck with an upright die axis ↑↑.

SOVEREIGNS OF EDWARD VII
(SYDNEY MINT: MINT MARK S)

No.	Date	Type/Variety	Mintage	Rating
204	1902	Normal	2,813,000	C
204A*	1902	Matt proof	Very few	R6
204B*	1902	Brilliant proof	Very few	R7
205	1903	Normal	2,806,000	C
206	1904	Normal	2,986,000	C
207	1905	Normal	2,778,000	C
208	1906	Normal	2,792,000	C
209	1907	Normal	2,539,000	C
210	1908	Normal	2,017,000	N
211	1909	Normal	2,057,000	N
212	1910	Normal	2,135,000	N

* These previously were numbered, incorrectly, as 205A and 205B.

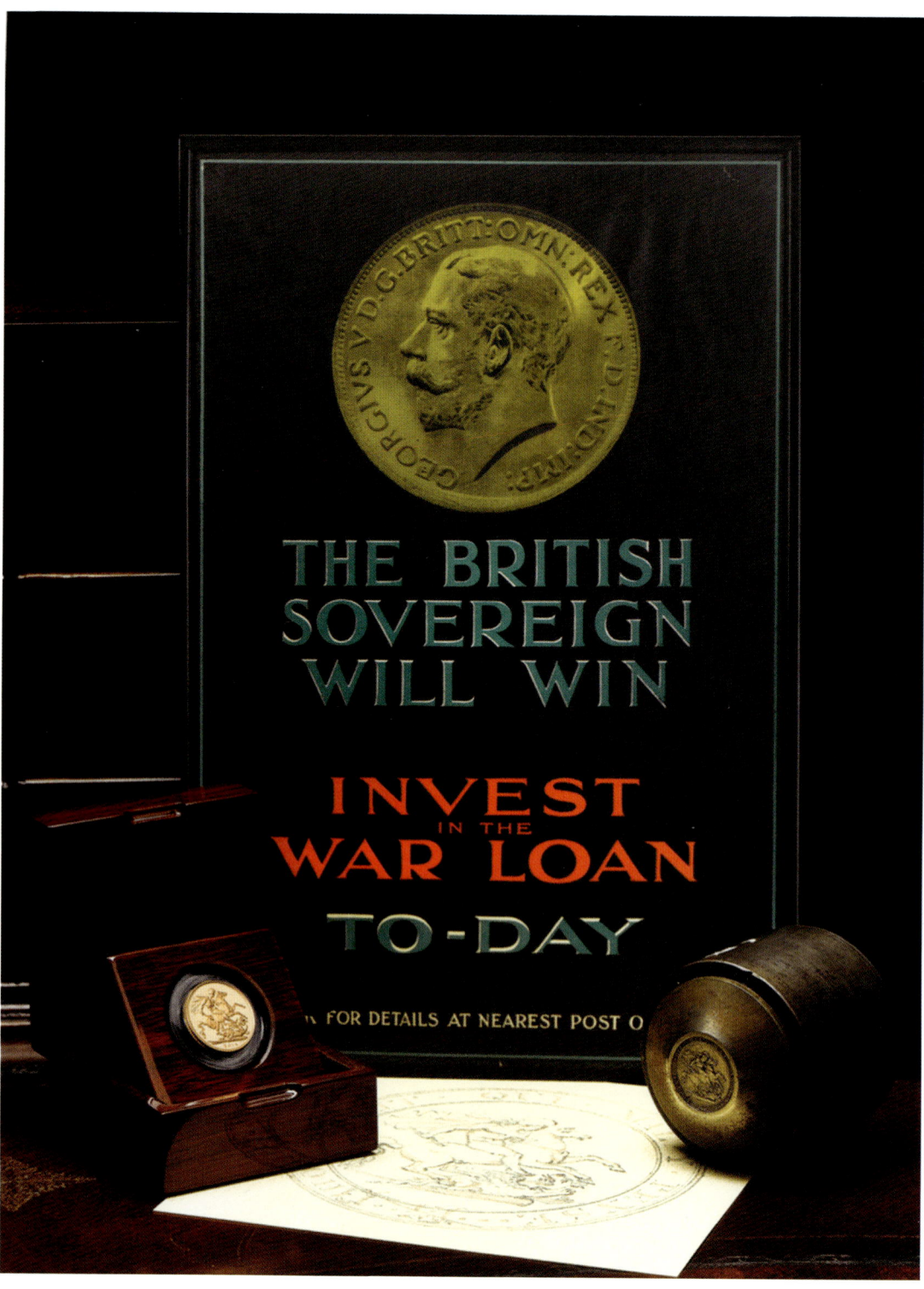

During World War I posters such as this exhorted the public to save.

GEORGE V, 1910–36

The reign of George V is remembered for many important events, the most dramatic being the outbreak of war in 1914. As a result of the need for economy, and to boost the war effort, the Government issued Treasury banknotes to the value of £1 and 10 shillings to replace the sovereign and its half. In a short time the new notes took the place of the circulating gold coinage. However, many sovereigns were struck during the war years and they became part of the gold reserve held by the Bank of England.

During the war the country's debts to the United States of America were considerable and following the war there is little doubt that large quantities of sovereigns were used in payment of these debts. Bearing in mind that the United States were not legally permitted to hold non-US gold coins as such at that time, it is almost certain that any sovereigns they received would have been melted down and made into ingots. Further to this, the Gold Standard Act of 1925 made currency notes no longer exchangeable for gold coins so notes continued as the preferred method of payment. The price of gold continued to rise making the sovereign worth far more than its face value of £1 and as a result it is recorded that sovereigns alone worth £100,441,000 were melted during 1929 and 1930. This is undoubtedly the reason why some dates such as 1916 and 1917 sovereigns from the London Mint are rare today. 1917 was the last year of manufacture of the sovereign at the London Mint, although a small quantity were struck in 1925 but not released. However, during the reign of George VI (1936–52), sovereigns dated 1925 and bearing the head of George V were issued.

As will be seen in the accompanying tables, the branch mints between them produced George V sovereigns for various years with the new Pretoria mint striking coins dated as late as 1932.

The new Bombay branch mint[1] opened in 1918 after building work was completed in May of that year and the dies, plant and machinery arrived from London in June. Automatic weighing machines and two coining presses arrived in early August and the first coinage was issued on August 15, 1918, under the new Deputy Master, R. R. Kahan. A total of 1,294,372 sovereigns were struck for that year and although this branch mint continued to operate in 1919 no more sovereigns were struck there.

By a Royal proclamation of December 14, 1922, the last branch mint to be opened was at Pretoria in South Africa.[3] The new mint was to open officially on January 1, 1923, but because of delays in erecting the machinery and equipping the various departments, coining was not possible until later that year.

The new Deputy Master, Mr R. Pearson, in his report dated February 4, 1924, for the year of 1923 said, "*During the period covered by this report only one deposit of gold was received at the mint. This consisted of old jewellery, which after the Rand Refinery's charge for refining, and the Mint charges, was found to be of the net value of £406 0s 9d. The resulting sovereigns were delivered to the depositor*".

The first currency sovereign of 1923 (M.287) from the new branch mint of Pretoria is without question a very rare piece. In 1979 the Director of the Suid-Afrikaanse Munt of Pretoria confirmed Deputy Master Pearson's report, stating that the sovereigns sent to the depositor must have been currency pieces. He also revealed that the South African Mint collection contained an example of the 1923-dated currency sovereign.

The mint mark for the new Bombay branch mint is the letter I for India, and for the Pretoria branch mint the letters SA for South Africa. The branch mints of Melbourne, Perth and Sydney as well as the Ottawa branch mint also struck sovereigns during this reign and their mint marks, as previously described, can be found on the reverse of the coin in the centre of the exergue ground line.

There are two distinctly different obverse busts: the "large head" type being the first to appear and the "small head" type being used only for the last three years of the Melbourne and Perth issues and the last four years of the South African issues. The "small head" series appears to be slightly less strongly struck than the more common larger bust. There are also slight variations on the reverse, most notable being St George's head appears to be very close to the mane of the horse and there are tighter folds on his cape.

From the London Mint the 1917 coin is by far the rarest currency issue and is seldom seen and the 1916 date will perhaps prove difficult to find.

All the coins from the Ottawa mint were difficult to find but following the disposal of a large part of the gold holdings of the Bank of Canada many of the rarities, including the 1916 (M.224) sovereign, although still scarce, are no longer considered as extremely rare.

Surprisingly there are quite a number of rarities in the Melbourne series: 1920, 1921, 1922, 1927 and 1928 are the rarest, and all three coins of the later issue "small head" type are scarce.

Of the Perth Mint series the most difficult may well prove to be the 1926 sovereign, and several other coins that are rated "S" could also prove hard to find. The three coins of the "small head" group will not be easy to obtain, especially the 1930 date.

Six dates of sovereigns from the Sydney Mint are notably very rare—1920, 1921, 1922, 1923, 1924 and 1926, with the lead taken by the extremely rare 1920-dated issue of which only seven examples remain known in commerce with perhaps a few more yet to discover, having the lowest mintage at this mint. The most up to date and full account of the 1920 Sydney Sovereign was written up by Howard Hodgson in *Coin News*

Notes/References
1. *Royal Mint Report* 1918, "Bombay branch mint", Deputy Master R. R. Kahan, pp. 144–145.
2. *Royal Mint Report* 1923, "Pretoria branch mint", Deputy Master R. Pearson, pp. 132–36.
3. G. P. Dyer, "The Existence of 1923 SA Currency Sovereign", *Spink Numismatic Circular,* March 1985, pp. 42–43.

First (large) head.

Small head.

magazine in two parts (April and May 2021) where it is recorded 360,121 were struck in this calendar year, all of this date. It would seem the overwhelming majority of this issue was subsequently melted down in the culls of 1926, 1930 and 1931. The surviving population we have today seems to be almost exclusively that which were originally ordered by the politician Jacob Garrard for his Golden Wedding anniversary that year and given out to relatives who attended on April 15, 1920, and if it were not for that occasion, it may well have been possible that the whole mintage would not have survived till the present day.

As already mentioned above, the Pretoria Mint sovereign of 1923 (M.287) was without doubt a very rare coin, but in recent years a number of examples have surfaced, reducing its rarity in the collector market.

Britain's abandonment of the Gold Standard in the 1930s was to begin a process whereby today no country bases its currency on gold. Sir Robert Johnson, Deputy Master of the Royal Mint, famously stated that ". . . as far as the Mint is concerned gold coinage as currency is for ever dead . . .". As a result millions of sovereigns were melted down and formed into ingots—nearly 106 million coins were melted, containing 24 million ounces of fine gold with a value of around £42.5 billion at today's prices.

The melting pot was indiscriminate and undoubtedly many rarities joined their worn and well-used fellow currency coins. This sad occurrence in our history, especially from the numismatist's point of view, is fully explained by Howard Hodgson in the Addendum at the end of this book.

Description and details of the George V sovereigns

Obverse: The King's bare head facing left. The letters B.M. in relief at the bottom of the truncation standing for Bertram Mackennal. Legend: GEORGIVS V D.G.BRITT:OMN:REX F.D.IND:IMP:

Reverse: St George mounted and slaying dragon with sword. Date at the bottom with small letters B.P. (Benedetto Pistrucci) to right. Those of the various Branch Mints carry the relevant initial mint mark in the centre of the exergue ground line.

Edge: Milled.

The coin is struck with an upright die axis ↑↑.

SOVEREIGNS OF GEORGE V
(LONDON MINT: NO MINT MARK)

No.	Date	Type/Variety	Mintage	Rating
213	1911	Normal	30,044,105	C
213A	1911	Proof (WR416)	3,764	R
213B	1911	Matt proof (WR417)	Not known	R7
214	1912	Normal	30,317,921	C
215	1913	Normal	24,539,672	C
216	1914	Normal	11,501,117	C
217	1915	Normal	20,295,280	C
218	1916	Normal	1,554,120	R
219	1917	Normal	1,014,714	R3
220	1925*	Normal	3,520,431*	C

*An additional 886,000 sovereigns dated 1925 (No. 220) were struck during the reign of George VI (*qv*).

Description and details of the George V sovereign, Ottawa Branch Mint

Obverse: As London Mint.:
Reverse: As the London Mint but with C mint mark in the centre of the exergue ground line.
Edge: Milled.
The coin is struck with an upright die axis ↑↑.

SOVEREIGNS OF GEORGE V
(OTTAWA MINT: MINT MARK C)

No.	Date	Type/Variety	Mintage	Rating
221	1911	Normal	257,048	C3
221A	1911	Specimen finish	Not known	R4
222	1913	Normal	3,717	C
223	1914	Normal	14,900	C2
224	1916	Normal	6,119	R2
225	1917	Normal	58,845	C2
226	1918	Normal	106,570	C2
227	1919	Normal	135,957	C2

Note: After 1919 the Ottawa Branch Mint began to produce gold bars rather than coins, though four Sovereign reverse dies dated 1920 were despatched from the Royal Mint on February 6, 1920 to Canada but subsequently were never used. An intention to strike Sovereigns occurred again with dies ordered and despatched for 1925 and 1926, but again neither date with the C mint mark were ever used, with gold bar production continuing through the decade. The Ottawa Branch Mint became the Royal Canadian Mint on December 1, 1931. For further reading see "The Canadian Sovereigns of 1925 and 1926—almost" by Howard Hodgson, *Coin News*, May 2024.

THE GOLD SOVEREIGN SERIES

Description and details of the George V sovereign, Bombay Branch Mint

Obverse: As London Mint.:
Reverse: As the London Mint but with I mint mark in the centre of the exergue ground line.
Edge: Milled.
The coin is struck with an upright die axis ↑↑.

SOVEREIGNS OF GEORGE V
(BOMBAY MINT: MINT MARK I)

No.	Date	Type/Variety	Mintage	Rating
228	1918	Normal	1,295,372	N
228A	1918	Specimen finish	12	R7

SOVEREIGNS OF GEORGE V, 1910–36

Description and details of the George V sovereign, Melbourne Branch Mint

Obverse: As London Mint.:
Reverse: As the London Mint but with M mint mark in the centre of the exergue ground line.
Edge: Milled.
The coin is struck with an upright die axis ↑↑.

SOVEREIGNS OF GEORGE V
(MELBOURNE MINT (FIRST HEAD): MINT MARK M)

No.	Date	Type/Variety	Mintage	Rating
229	1911	Normal	2,851,451	C
229A	1911	Proof	Very few	R7
230	1912	Normal	2,469,257	C
231	1913	Normal	2,323,180	C
232	1914	Normal	2,012,029	C
233	1915	Normal	1,637,839	N
234	1916	Normal	1,272,634	N
235	1917	Normal	934,469	S
236	1918	Normal	4,909,493	C
237	1919	Normal	514,257	S
238	1920	Normal	530,266	R2
239	1921	Normal	240,121	R3
240	1922	Normal	608,306	R2
241	1923	Normal	511,129	R
242	1924	Normal	278,140	R
243	1925	Normal	3,311,662	C
244	1926	Normal	211,107	C
Mintage for the year 1927 was all dated 1926			310,156	—
246	1928	Normal	413,208	R2
246A	1928	Specimen proof	Very few	R7

(MELBOURNE MINT ("SMALL HEAD") MINT MARK M)

No.	Date	Type/Variety	Mintage	Rating
247	1929	Normal	436,938	R3
247A	1929	Specimen proof	Not known	R6
248	1930	Normal	77,588	R
248A	1930	Specimen proof	Very few	R6
249	1931	Normal	57,809	R2
249A	1931	Specimen proof	Very few	R6

Note: In 1934 four reverse Sovereign dies were ordered from London in anticipation of striking some more Sovereigns and were received in Melbourne by April 1934, but it seems they were never used and subsequently destroyed in December 1934.

THE GOLD SOVEREIGN SERIES

Description and details of the George V sovereign, Perth Branch Mint

Obverse: As London Mint.:
Reverse: As the London Mint but with P mint mark in the centre of the exergue ground line.
Edge: Milled.
The coin is struck with an upright die axis ↑↑.

SOVEREIGNS OF GEORGE V
(PERTH MINT (FIRST HEAD): MINT MARK P)

No.	Date	Type/Variety	Mintage	Rating
250	1911	Normal	4,373,165	C
251	1912	Normal	4,278,144	C
252	1913	Normal	4,635,287	C
253	1914	Normal	4,815,996	C
254	1915	Normal	4,373,596	C
255	1916	Normal	4,096,771	S
256	1917	Normal	4,110,286	S
257	1918	Normal	3,812,884	C
258	1919	Normal	2,995,216	C
259	1920	Normal	2,421,196	C
260	1921	Normal	2,314,360	C
261	1922	Normal	2,298,884	C
262	1923	Normal	2,124,154	C
263	1924	Normal	1,464,416	N
264	1925	Normal	1,837,901	S
265	1926	Normal	1,313,578	R
266	1927	Normal	1,383,544	S
267	1928	Normal	1,333,417	S

(PERTH MINT ("SMALL HEAD") MINT MARK P)

No.	Date	Type/Variety	Mintage	Rating
268	1929	Normal	1,606,625	S
269	1930	Normal	1,915,352	R
270	1931	Normal	1,173,568	S
270A	1931	Specimen proof	Not known	R6

Description and details of the George V sovereign, Sydney Branch Mint
Obverse: As London Mint.:
Reverse: As the London Mint but with S mint mark in the centre of the exergue ground line.
Edge: Milled.
The coin is struck with an upright die axis ↑↑.

SOVEREIGNS OF GEORGE V
(SYDNEY MINT: MINT MARK S)

No.	Date	Type/Variety	Mintage	Rating
271	1911	Normal	2,519,000	C
272	1912	Normal	2,227,000	C
273	1913	Normal	2,249,000	C
274	1914	Normal	1,774,000	C
275	1915	Normal	1,346,000	S
276	1916	Normal	1,242,000	N
277	1917	Normal	1,666,000	C
278	1918	Normal	3,716,000	C
279	1919	Normal	1,835,000	N
280	1920*	Normal	360,121*	R6
280A	1920	Specimen proof	Very few	R7
281	1921	Normal	839,000	R3
282	1922	Normal	578,000	R3
282A	1922	Specimen proof	Very few	R6
283	1923	Normal	416,000	R4
283A	1923	Specimen proof	Very few	R6
284	1924	Normal	394,000	R3
285	1925	Normal	5,632,000	S
286	1926	Normal	1,031,050	R3
286A	1926	Specimen proof	Very few	R6

* This figure shows the number of coins struck in 1920, however, it seems all the surviving Sydney coins dated 1920 are from those that were specifically minted for New South Wales politician Jacob Garrard on the occasion of his Golden Wedding anniversary and remain extremely rare. For the full factual story see articles by Howard Hodgson *Coin News* April and May 2021.

THE GOLD SOVEREIGN SERIES

Description and details of the George V sovereign, Pretoria Branch Mint

Obverse: As London Mint.:
Reverse: As the London Mint but with SA mint mark in the centre of the exergue ground line.
Edge: Milled.
The coin is struck with an upright die axis ↑↑.

SOVEREIGNS OF GEORGE V
(PRETORIA MINT (FIRST HEAD): MINT MARK SA)

No.	Date	Type/Variety	Mintage	Rating
287	1923	Normal	406	R3
287A	1923	Proof	655	R2
288	1924	Normal	2,660	R2
289	1925	Normal	6,086,264	C
290	1926	Normal	11,107,611	C
291	1927	Normal	16,379,704	C
292	1928	Normal	18,235,057	C
292A	1928	Matt proof	Not known	R6

(PRETORIA MINT ("SMALL HEAD"): MINT MARK SA)

No.	Date	Type/Variety	Mintage	Rating
293	1929	Normal	12,024,107	C
293A	1929	Proof	Not known	R6
294	1930	Normal	10,027,756	C
295	1931	Normal	8,511,792	C
296	1932	Normal	1,066,680	N

SOVEREIGNS OF GEORGE V, 1910–36

The Perth Branch Mint opened June 20, 1899.

The Pretoria Branch Mint opened February 1923.

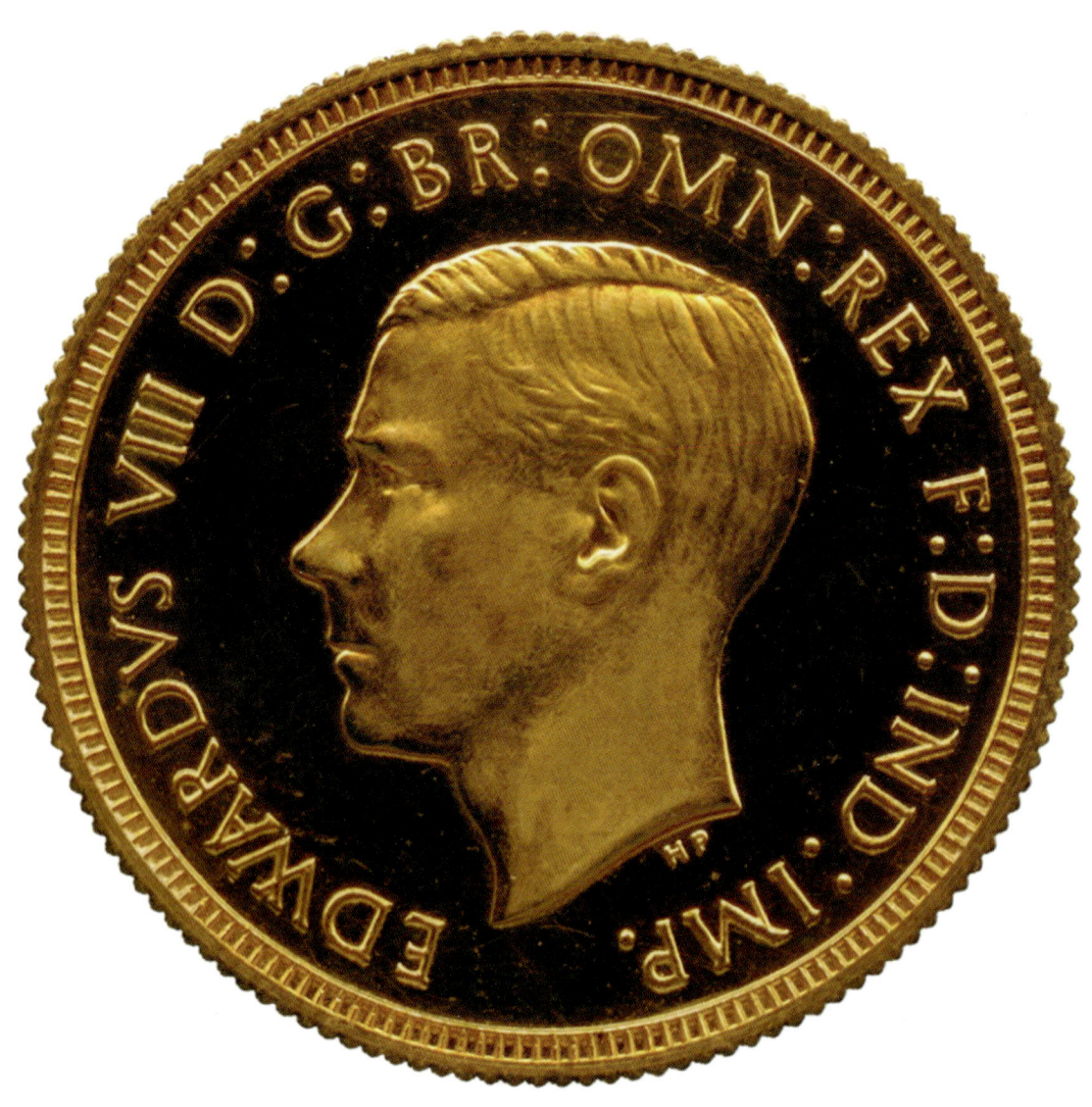

The legendary sovereign of Edward VIII
which was sold at the sale of the "Hemisphere" Collection
on May 8, 2014 at Baldwin's where it realised a total of £516,000.
Since then it has been graded by NGC as PF63 and was sold in a public offering
by the Royal Mint to one of its clients for £1 million in January 2020.

EDWARD VIII (JANUARY–DECEMBER 1936)

Though Edward VIII abdicated in late 1936, coinage proposals were well advanced and only a small quantity of complete proof sets were ever struck from designs by Humphrey Paget, thus making the sovereign one of the greatest rarities in the series. As the other coins of Edward VIII, the King is shown facing to the left, breaking the tradition of successive monarchs facing opposite directions as George V had also faced to the left. The engraver's initials, HP, appear on the truncation of the King's bust. The reverse carries the familiar figure of St George armed with a sword slaying the dragon by Benedetto Pistrucci, whose initials appear to the right in the exergue.

Description and details of the Edward VIII sovereign

Obverse: Bareheaded bust of the king facing left. Initials HP on truncation. Legend: EDWARDVS VIII D: G: BR: OMN: REX: F: D: IND: IMP.
Reverse: Pistrucci's St George slaying the dragon. Date below exergue ground line and initials B.P. on right.
Edge: Milled.
The coin is struck with an upright die axis ↑↑.

SOVEREIGNS OF EDWARD VIII

No.	Date	Type/Variety	Mintage	Rating
296A	1937	Edward VIII pattern (WR434)	6	R6

GEORGE VI, 1936–52

The only sovereign bearing the bust of George VI is dated 1937 and it is a specimen coin with plain edge struck to commemorate the Coronation, with a mintage of 5,501. The effigy on the obverse was modelled by Humphrey Paget from a personal sitting. As the sovereigns of George V, the reverse displays Pistrucci's St George slaying the dragon.

Little can be written concerning the currency sovereigns of George VI as the only examples struck during the reign were from George V dies that were all dated 1925. Prior to this the 1925 sovereign had been somewhat scarce, and so it is easy to imagine the dismay this must have caused numismatists at that time.

Description and details of the George VI sovereign

Obverse: The bare head of the King facing left. The small letters HP standing for Humphrey Paget on truncation. Legend: GEORGIVS VI D: G: BR: OMN: REX F: D: IND: IMP.
Reverse: St George slaying the dragon. Date below exergue ground line and initials B.P. on right.
Edge: Plain.
The coin is struck to proof standard "with mirror-like" fields and an upright die axis ↑↑.

SOVEREIGNS OF GEORGE VI

No.	Date	Type/Variety	Mintage	Rating
296B	1937	Plain edge proof (WR439)	5,501	S
296C	1937	Matt proof (WR440)	Very few	R6

Note: The Royal Mint Museum has some trial pieces in varying alloys of the 1937 George VI Sovereign in their collection, each unique.

Many George V currency sovereigns dated 1925 were struck during the reign of George VI and are the same design and date as those listed as No. 220 in the reign of George V. They were struck in the following years:

No.	Date struck	Type/Variety	Mintage
220	1949	Normal	138,000*
220	1951	Normal	318,000*
220	1952	Normal	430,000*

*These figures have not been included in the mintage given for sovereign No. 220 of George V (*qv*).

ELIZABETH II, 1952–2022

The first sovereign struck in Queen Elizabeth II's reign was a proof coin dated 1953 with a laureate image of Her Majesty on the obverse by Mary Gillick. It was decided to continue using Pistrucci's iconic image of St George and the dragon for the reverse. As the rest of the coinage, the obverse legend included BRITT: OMN: (All Britains) in reference to the Commonwealth at the time. Only a few examples of this sovereign in proof quality with a finely milled edge were struck for the National collections.

In 1957 the first currency type sovereign for the reign was struck and the bust used for this new second issue was again the work of Mary Gillick, however, the title BRITT: OMN: was omitted from the Queen's titles owing to the changing status of many Commonwealth territories. This currency issue continued to be struck until 1968 when the country began transit towards the decimal system.

For the first few years of the decimal period no sovereigns were struck but in 1974 a new bust of the Queen was introduced, in keeping with the rest of the then new decimal currency. The image, in which the Queen is shown wearing a tiara, was the work of the sculptor Arnold Machin, a member of the Royal Academy and their Master sculptor from 1959 until 1966. Machin was selected to sculpt the new effigy of the Queen and he was granted personal sittings by the Queen for his work. His much admired bust continued to adorn our gold sovereign until it was replaced in 1985. The Machin effigy was also used on other denominations of our coinage and on many of those of the Commonwealth, and for a long period millions of our postage stamps also carried the Machin bust of our Queen. Interestingly, the very last coin to be struck at the Royal Mint, Tower Hill, London, was a "Machin" gold sovereign bearing the date 1974 and was struck on November 10, 1975.

The fourth issue, in 1985, saw the introduction of the third new portrait of the Queen designed by Raphael David Maklouf. The first sovereigns bearing the new bust, on which the Queen is wearing a crown and a pearl necklace, were dated 1985 and they were struck for every year up to and including 1997 except for the year 1989. All are proof coins and were issued in relatively small quantities.

In 1989 a special proof sovereign was struck to mark the "500th anniversary of the Sovereign 1489–1989". This sovereign, the work of sculptor Bernard Sindall, is a splendid example of both design and engraving. The obverse features the enthroned effigy of the monarch wearing a crown and robed in superb regal splendour. On the reverse the Royal arms are placed in the centre of a large Tudor rose with the crown above. The legend on both sides is in Tudor-style lettering.

In 1998 the fourth bust was introduced for all of the country's coinage including the sovereign. This new effigy was the work of sculptor and medallist Ian Rank-Broadley. The bust portrays a mature couped image of Her Majesty once more wearing a tiara. The new sovereign was issued as a proof coin only for 1998 and 1999 but in 2000 partly because of the popularity and the increasing price of gold it was decided to strike currency coins once more—a move which has proved popular with collectors and investors alike and which continues, although in 2002, 2005 and 2012 the reverse designs were different.

Strictly speaking these coins are no longer used as currency, and so in this modern age they are now more properly and certainly better known as bullion sovereigns. However, the same coins are also available as proofs, usually issued in a padded box with an accompanying certificate of authenticity.

Another interesting fact relating to the new bullion issue and reflecting its modern status as a collector's coin is that it is available directly from the Royal Mint. Distribution was previously handled by the Bank of England, and indeed one has to go back to the hey-day of the sovereign considerably before World War I to find instances of sovereigns being issued by the Royal Mint to bodies other than the Bank of England.

In keeping with the rest of the coinage of 2002, the obverse of the sovereign issued that year in celebration of Her Majesty's Golden Jubilee carries the fifth bust, the work of the talented sculptor and medallist Ian Rank-Broadley. He was the winner of the Royal Mint competition in 1997 to design the new effigy of Her Majesty the Queen to be used on United Kingdom coinage from 1998. He was also successful in another Royal Mint competition the following year for the Queen Mother's hundredth birthday crown.

The reverse of the Jubilee sovereign features a beautifully adapted design of the Victorian shield reverse sovereign with the date 2002 below the new design. It is the creation of the heraldic artist Timothy Martin Noad who has worked largely for the College of Arms, London since 1986. In 1996 his entry for the Royal Mint competition for the design of the new circulating £2 coin reached the final short list. In the year 2002 his design for the Jubilee sovereign reverse was accepted by the Royal Mint.

For the sovereign of 2005 Timothy Noad was once again chosen to design the reverse and his modern interpretation of St George slaying the dragon created a great deal of publicity at the time. However, the stylised image of St George and the dragon which appears on the reverse of the 2012 sovereigns issued in commemoration of Her Majesty's Diamond Jubilee was a complete shift from Pistrucci's iconic design. Not everyone was in favour of Paul Day's St George—even though his lance was reinstated for the first time since 1820 and the date offset to the left side of the design, many collectors can be forgiven for being a little bemused.

In 2007 the Royal Mint decided that it was time to take a look at the reverse that had remained the same for so many years and the dies were re-engraved. However, the sovereigns dated 2007 were struck in lower relief than their predecessors—a feature that was changed for the following year.

In 2009 it was decided to completely overhaul the reverse design so the image of St George was re-engraved omitting the streamer that had flown from his helmet since the sovereigns of Queen Victoria's Jubilee coinage.

An interesting precedent was set in 2013 when the Royal Mint decided to strike 2,013 sovereigns on the day of the birth of our future King, Prince George. These were issued in special packaging with a certificate of authenticity and they were snapped up by an eager collecting audience. A Royal Mint statement declares that *"The sovereign is closely associated with the monarch and the Royal Mint strike limited numbers of the coin on the day of the most special Royal occasions, tying them to that special moment in history*". Interestingly, in 2017 the Mint struck just 750 sovereigns on the actual day of the Sapphire (65th) anniversary of Her Majesty the Queen's accession, which were also accompanied by a special certificate. Surprisingly, other than the certificates of authenticity accompanying the coins, there is no way to identify these special sovereigns, although the later ones have special privy marks. However, the popularity of these strike on the day coins has prompted the Royal Mint to continue the practice on a regular basis. A full list of the dates and identifying features of these issues is included later.

By 2015 Her Majesty the Queen was approaching her 90th year so it was decided to "age" her image on the coinage with the introduction of the fifth bust, by Royal Mint engraver Jody Clark, and it was his work that appeared on Prince George's special issues. However, in 2016 a new image by James Butler graced a special issue to commemorate Her Majesty's 90th birthday.

In 2017 on the 200th anniversary of the introduction of the "modern" sovereign, the Royal Mint produced a red-gold sovereign based on the design of 1817 but bearing the new obverse bust by Jody Clark. However, the reverse is faithful to the original, showing St George carrying a broken lance and with his streamers flowing from his helmet, surrounded by the garter and motto. To mark the auspicious occasion, on July 1, 2017, a limited edition of just 1,817 sovereigns were struck on the anniversary of the actual day of the proclamation that revived the sovereign in 1817. In addition, for the very first time in history the Royal Mint produced a proof piedfort edition of the same coin. Piedfort comes from the French meaning "heavy measure" and the coin has been produced twice the thickness of the ordinary issue. Also to mark the occasion a special issue of the bullion sovereign (M.345) with "200" in a shield privy mark was struck.

Undoubtedly the re-introduction of the "Bullion" sovereign in 2000 created a renewed interest in the series and this has fuelled demand which the Royal Mint continues to meet with its usual professionalism. As a result the quantities struck continue to rise, but despite this, most years the demand outstrips the supply and the secondary market for the sovereign remains buoyant. Since 2015 there have been two different grades of uncirculated sovereigns available, the first are classed as bullion whilst the others are referred to as Brilliant Uncirculated and are sold in limited numbers to collectors suitably packaged in a similar way to the Proof edtions. As they are both uncirculated grades there has been no attempt to differentiate between them in the listings and both are referred to as "Normal".

In 2019 the Royal Mint started to produce some special edition Brilliant Uncirculated sovereigns with a matt surface thereby adding a third type of format.

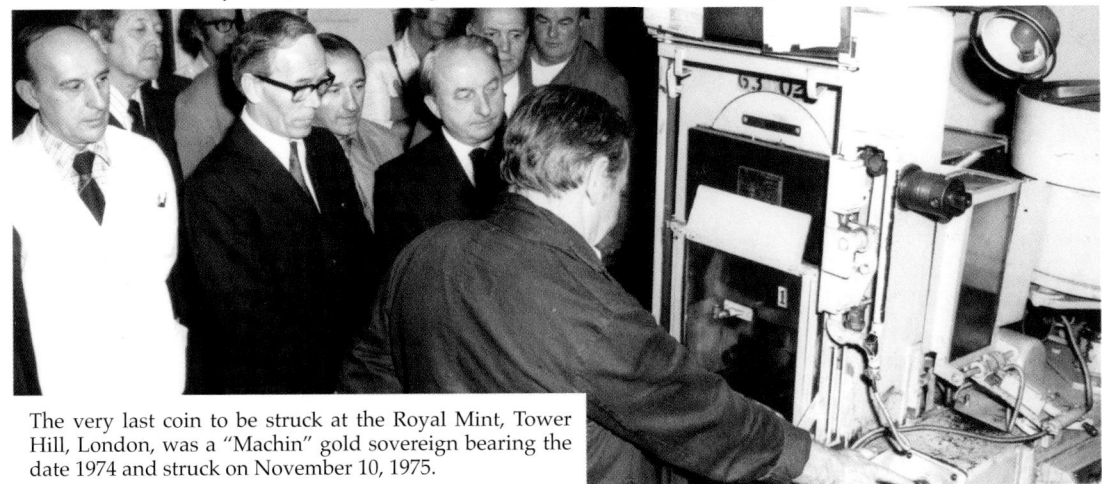

The very last coin to be struck at the Royal Mint, Tower Hill, London, was a "Machin" gold sovereign bearing the date 1974 and struck on November 10, 1975.

Description and details of the Elizabeth II First bust, First type sovereign

Obverse: Laureate head of the Queen facing right, with tie at the back of the hair, by Mary Gillick.
  Legend: ELIZABETH II DEI GRA:BRITT:OMN:REGINA F:D:+
Reverse: St George slaying the dragon. Date below exergue ground line with the small letters B.P. to the right.
Edge: Finely milled.
The coin is struck with an upright die axis ↑↑.

The first type sovereign of Elizabeth II which was only struck for presentation to select institutions. However, an example (ex the National Museum of Wales) sold in the Hemisphere Collection (lot 2081) for £320,000 hammer in 2014.

FIRST BUST SOVEREIGNS OF ELIZABETH II (FIRST TYPE)

No.	Date	Type/Variety	Mintage	Rating
296D	1953	Proof. BRITT:OMN: legend (WR448)	Small number	R6

Description and details of the Elizabeth II First bust, Second type sovereign

Obverse: Laureate head of the Queen facing right with tie at the back of hair, by Mary Gillick. Legend: ELIZABETH·II·DEI·GRATIA·REGINA·F:D:+

Reverse: St George slaying the dragon. Date below exergue ground line with the small letters B.P. to right.

Edge: Milled. The edge milling on the 1957 sovereign is slightly less coarse than the other issues of the series.

The coin is struck with an upright die axis ↑↑.

FIRST BUST SOVEREIGNS OF ELIZABETH II (SECOND TYPE)

No.	Date	Type/Variety	Mintage	Rating
297	1957	Finer edge graining	2,072,000	N
297A	1957	Proof (WR449)	Very few	R7
298	1958	Normal	8,700,140	C
298A	1958	Specimen striking	Not known	R5
298B	1958	Proof (WR450)	Very few	R4
299	1959	Normal	1,385,228	N
299A	1959	Proof (WR451)	Very few	R6
299B	1959	Specimen striking	Not known	R5
300	1962	Normal	3,000,000	C
300A*	1962	Proof	Not known	R6
301	1963	Normal	7,400,000	C
301A	1963	Proof (WR452)	Very few	R4
301B	1963	Matt proof (WR453)	Not known	R7
302	1964	Normal	3,000,000	C
303	1965	Normal	3,800,000	C
303A	1965	Matt proof	Not known	R5
304	1966	Normal	7,050,000	C
305	1967	Normal	5,000,000	C
306	1968	Normal	4,203,000	C

* The only known examples of this Proof coin are housed in the Hunterian Museum, Glasgow, National Museum of Scotland and two in the Royal Mint Museum, as featured in an article in a BNS blog article of May 2024, by Cameron Maclean.

Description and details of the Elizabeth II Second bust type sovereign

Obverse: Shoulder-length bust of the Queen facing right, wearing a tiara and off the shoulder dress, by Arnold Machin. Legend: ELIZABETH·II·DEI·GRATIA·REGINA·F:D:
Reverse: St George slaying the dragon. Date below exergue ground line with small letters B.P. to right.
Edge: Milled.
The coin is struck with an upright die axis ↑↑.

SECOND BUST SOVEREIGNS OF ELIZABETH II
(FIRST DECIMAL PERIOD)

No.	Date	Type/Variety	Mintage (+extra included in sets)	Rating
307	1974	Normal	5,002,566	C
308	1976	Normal	4,045,056	C
308A	1976	Brilliant proof (no frosting)	Very few	R7
309	1978	Normal	6,550,000	C
310	1979	Normal	9,100,000	C
310A	1979	Proof	50,000	N
311	1980	Normal	5,100,000	C
311A	1980	Proof	81,200 (+10,000)	N
312	1981	Normal	5,000,000	C
312A	1981	Proof	32,960 (+4,187)	N
313	1982	Normal	2,950,000	C
313A	1982	Proof	20,000 (+2,500)	N
313B	1983	Proof	21,250 incl. those in sets	N
313C	1984	Proof	12,880 (+7,095)	N

Note: The mintage figures given show coins additionally issued in the Year Proof Sets where relevant.

Description and details of the Elizabeth II Third bust type sovereign

Obverse: Bust of the Queen facing right and wearing a coronet, by Raphel Maklouf, the letters RDM on the truncation. Legend: ELIZABETH II DEI·GRA·REG·F·D.
Reverse: St George slaying the dragon. Date below the exergue ground line with the small letters B.P. to right.
Edge: Milled.
The coin is struck with an upright die axis ↑↑.

THIRD BUST SOVEREIGNS OF ELIZABETH II

No.	Date	Type/Variety	Mintage (+extra included in sets)	Rating
313D	1985	Proof	11,393 (+5,849)	N
313E	1986	Proof	5,079 (+12,500)	N
313F	1987	Proof	9,979 (+12,500)	N
313G	1988	Proof	7,670 (+11,192)	N
313H	1989	See special issues for details*		
313I	1990	Proof	4,767 (+3,658)	N
313J	1991	Proof	4,713 (+2,488)	N
313K	1992	Proof	4,772 (+2,132)	N
313L	1993	Proof	4,349 (+1,741)	N
313M	1994	Proof	4,998 (+2,167)	N
313N	1995	Proof	7,500 (+1,830)	N
313O	1996	Proof	7,500 (+1,610)	N
313P	1997	Proof	7,500 (+1,677)	N

*As this design carries the obverse and reverse by Bernard Sindall, strictly speaking it should not be included with the third bust types.

Description and details of the Elizabeth II Fourth bust, First reverse type sovereign

Obverse: Bust of the Queen facing right and wearing a tiara, by Ian Rank-Broadley, the letters IRB below the truncation. Legend: ELIZABETH·II·DEI·GRA REGINA·FID·DEF
Reverse: St George slaying the dragon. Date below exergue ground line with small letters B.P. to right.
Edge: Milled.
The coin is struck with an upright die axis ↑↑.

FOURTH BUST SOVEREIGNS OF ELIZABETH II (FIRST REVERSE)

No.	Date	Type/Variety	Mintage (+extra included in sets)	Rating
313Q	1998	Proof	10,000 (+1,349)	N
313R	1999	Proof	10,000 (+1,903)	N
314	2000	Normal	129,069	N
314A	2000	Proof	9,909 (+2,250)	N
315	2001	Normal	49,462	N
315A	2001	Proof	8,915 (+1,891)	N
316	2002	See special issues for details		
316A	2002	See special issues for details		
317	2003	Normal	43,230	N
318	2003	Proof	12,433 (+3,787)	N
319	2004	Normal	30,688	N
320	2004	Proof	10,175 (+2,510)	N
321	2005	See special issues for details		
322	2005	See special issues for details		
323	2006	Normal	33,012	N
324	2006	Proof	9,195 (+2,290)	N
Reverse re-engraved in lower relief, small date and tiny B.P				
325	2007	Normal	27,628	N
326	2007	Proof	8,199 (+3,219)	N
Reverse further revised for 2008, larger date				
327	2008	Normal	58,894	N
328	2008	Proof	7,735 (+3,137)	N

Description and details of the Elizabeth II Fourth bust, Second reverse type sovereign

Obverse: Bust of the Queen facing right and wearing a tiara, by Ian Rank-Broadley, the letters IRB below the truncation. Legend: ELIZABETH·II·DEI·GRA REGINA·FID·DEF

Reverse: Similar to the 1821 issue. St George slaying the dragon. No streamer flying from helmet. Date below exergue ground line with small letters B.P. to right.

Edge: Milled.

The coin is struck with an upright die axis ↑↑.

FOURTH BUST SOVEREIGNS OF ELIZABETH II (SECOND REVERSE)

No.	Date	Type/Variety	Mintage (+extra included in sets)	Rating
329	2009	Normal	60,292	N
330	2009	Proof	7,354 (+2,416)	N
331	2010	Normal	243,158	N
332	2010	Proof	6,809 (+2,019)	N
333	2011	Normal	253,773	N
334	2011	Proof	7,181 (+1,028)	N
335**	2012	See special issues for details		
336	2012	See special issues for details		
337**	2013	Normal	261,581 (+5,732)	N
337A	2013	Normal. Indian minting*	94,790	C
338	2013	Proof	8,243 (+1,915)	N
339**	2014	Normal	261,216	N
339A	2014	Normal. Indian minting	60,471	N
340	2014	Proof	3,263 (+1,350)	N
341**	2015	Normal	131,177	N
341A	2015	Normal. Indian minting	64,500	N
342	2015	Proof	4,546 (+1,499)	N

* For the first time in many years, the Indian Mint produced sovereigns. These can be identified by the appearance of I for India as a mintmark on the reverse. The number minted given for 2013 does not include those struck in India. These were sold in India and are seldom seen in the UK.

** 335, 337, 339 and 341 also include "Struck on the Day" coins—see listing on page 217.

Description and details of the Elizabeth II Fifth bust type sovereign

Obverse: Bust of the Queen facing right and wearing a tiara, by Jody Clark, the letters JC below the truncation. Legend. ELIZABETH·II·DEI·GRA REGINA·FID·DEF
Reverse: St George slaying the dragon. Date below exergue ground line with small letters B.P. to right.
Edge: Milled.
The coin is struck with an upright die axis ↑↑.

FIFTH BUST SOVEREIGNS OF ELIZABETH II

No.	Date	Type/Variety	Mintage (+extra included in sets)	Rating
344	2015	Proof	7,494 (+1,046)	N
345	2016	Normal	1,251 (+bullion issue)	N
345A	2016	Normal. Indian minting	45,000	S
346	2016	See special issues for details (James Butler portrait)		
346A	2017	Normal. Indian minting	Not known	S
347	2017	See special issues for details (200th Anniversary)		
348	2017	See special issues for details (200th Anniversary)		
349	2017	See special issues for details (200th Anniversary)		
350	2017	Normal, with 200 privy mark (200th Anniversary)	Not known	S
351	2018	Normal (including bullion issue)	Not known	S
352	2018	Proof, with 65 mintmark	10,633 (+2,566)	N
352A	2018	*Normal, plain edge, with 65 mintmark (SOTD)	323	R
353	2018	Proof piedfort, with 65 mintmark	1,930	R
354	2018	*Normal, plain edge, no privy mark (SOTD)	457	R
354A	2018	Normal, Indian minting	Not known	S
355	2019	Normal, matt finish, milled edge	1,124 (+390)*	N
355A**	2019	Normal, Brilliant finish, bullion issue	Not known	N
355B**	2019	Proof	9,538 (+2,103)*	N
355C**	2019	Proof, piedfort	656	S
356	2019	Matt finish, VR privy mark (SOTD)	Limit 650	S
357	2019	Matt finish, plain edge, VA privy mark (SOTD)	Limit 650	S
357A**	2019	Normal, Indian minting	Not known	S
358	2020	Normal,	1,139 (+360)	N
359	2020	Proof, with GR cypher privy mark	Issued 7,992 (+1,878)	N
359A	2020	Matt finish, with GR cypher, milled edge	Edition 12,000	C

360	2020	BU, matt finish, plain edge, crowned portcullis privy mark (SOTD)	Edition 1,500	N
360A	2020	BU, Matt finish, plain edge, VE75 privy mark (SOTD)	Edition 750	N
360B	2020	BU, Matt finish, plain edge, VJ75 privy mark (SOTD)	Edition 750	N
360C	2020	Normal. Indian minting	Not known	S
361	2021	Normal	Not known	C
361A	2021	Normal, matt finish, milled edge	9,850	C
362	2021	Proof, with 95 in crown privy mark, 95 edge mills	7,988 (+1,739)	C
363	2021	BU, matt finish, plain edge, with 95 privy mark (SOTD)	Edition 1,295	N

364, 365, 366, 367—See Special Issues (Platinum Jubilee).

* These quantities also include "Struck on the Day" coins—see listing on page 217.
** For 2019 Normal, Proof, Piedfort and Indian production add six to mintage of each to account for Trial of the Pyx varieties sold to the public.

ELIZABETH II SOVEREIGNS —SPECIAL ISSUES

500th ANNIVERSARY OF THE SOVEREIGN 1489–1989. Obverse and reverse by Bernard Sindall

No.	Date	Type/Variety	Mintage (+extra included in sets)	Rating
313H	1989	Proof	10,535 (+12,936)	S

GOLDEN JUBILEE OF HER MAJESTY QUEEN ELIZABETH II. Shield reverse by Timothy Noad

No.	Date	Type/Variety	Mintage (+extra included in sets)	Rating
316	2002	Normal	75,264	N
316A	2002	Proof	12,500 (+6,947)	N

Paul Day's original model for the reverse of the special sovereign issued in commemoration of the Diamond Jubilee of Her Majesty Queen Elizabeth II in 2012.

THE GOLD SOVEREIGN SERIES

MODERN INTERPRETATION OF ST GEORGE. New reverse for 2005 by Timothy Noad

No.	Date	Type/Variety	Mintage (+extra included in sets)	Rating
321	2005	Normal	45,542	N
322	2005	Proof	12,500 (+2,958)	N

DIAMOND JUBILEE OF HER MAJESTY QUEEN ELIZABETH II. Stylised reverse by Paul Day

No.	Date	Type/Variety	Mintage (+extra included in sets)	Rating
335	2012	Normal	432,925 (+6,668)	C
336	2012	Proof	5,501 (+2,597)	N

90th BIRTHDAY OF HER MAJESTY THE QUEEN. Obverse portrait by James Butler

No.	Date	Type/Variety	Mintage (+extra included in sets)	Rating
346	2016	Proof	7,995 (+1,666)	N

200th ANNIVERSARY OF THE SOVEREIGN. Jody Clark obverse. Reverse as 1817 sovereign

No.	Date	Type/Variety	Mintage (+extra included in sets)	Rating
347	2017	Proof	10,493 (+2,198)	N
348	2017	As M.347 but Proof-like with Plain edge	1,793 issued	R
349	2017	Piedfort	3,484	R

THE GOLD SOVEREIGN SERIES

PLATINUM JUBILEE OF HER MAJESTY QUEEN ELIZABETH II.
Royal Arms reverse by Timothy Noad

No.	Date	Type/Variety	Mintage (+extra included in sets)	Rating
364	2022	Normal	Not known	C
365	2022	Proof	Edition 10,500 (+2,200)	C
366	2022	Proof, piedfort	Edition 3,360	N
367	2022	BU, matt finish, plain edge (SOTD)	Edition 1,200	N

Note: SOTD = Struck on the day—see list of all these editions on page 217.

CHARLES III, 2022–

Upon the death of Her Majesty Queen Elizabeth II on September 8, 2022, Charles, Prince of Wales, immediately became King Charles III. The 73-year-old King had been the longest ever Monarch-in-waiting in British history. Preparations for his new coinage, as well as banknotes and stamps, had been ongoing for some time though and it wasn't long before the new obverse design for coinage, including the Sovereign series, was announced. Martin Jennings, a sculptor famous for figurative works in bronze and stone that can be seen across Britain, produced two computer generated initial portraits, a bare headed effigy, very reminiscent of the 20th century kings, which will appear on the definitive coinage (it also appears on stamps), and a crowned head design for special Coronation issues. Special edition reverse designs for Sovereign series gold has so far been produced for a Memorial design to the Late Queen as well as the Coronation Sovereign. The familiar St George and dragon design by Benedetto Pistrucci has since returned to the series for the 2024-dated issues.

Description and details of the Charles III bare head sovereign, Memorial reverse

Obverse: Bare head effigy of King Charles III left by Martin Jennings, raised initials below neck MJ. Legend CHARLES III. DEI. GRA. REX. FID. DEF.

Reverse: Royal heraldic coat of arms with crowned lion and unicorn supporters, crowned helm above, banner motto below DIEU ET MON DROIT with date.

Edge: Milled.
The coin is struck with a straight upright die axis ↑↑.

MEMORIAL FOR THE LATE QUEEN
Martin Jennings obverse, Jody Clark Royal Arms reverse.

No.	Date	Type/Variety	Mintage	Rating
368	2022	Normal	Not known	C
369	2022	Proof	17,271 (+3,127)	C
370	2022	Proof, piedfort	Edition 1,915	N

Description and details of the Charles III crowned head sovereign

Obverse: Bare head effigy of King Charles III left by Martin Jennings, raised initials below neck MJ. Legend CHARLES III. DEI. GRA. REX. FID. DEF.

Reverse: Pistrucci's St George armed with sword slaying the dragon. The date in the exergue below the ground line with B.P. in small raised letters to upper right.

Edge: Milled.
The coin is struck with a straight upright die axis ↑↑.

CORONATION OF KING CHARLES III
Crowned bust left by Martin Jennings.

No.	Date	Type/Variety	Mintage	Rating
371	2023	Normal	Not known	C
372	2023	Proof	Edition 15,000 (+2,875)	C
373	2023	Proof, piedfort	Edition 1,260	N
374	2023	Matt Proof	Edition as a set 23	R3
375	2023	BU, Matt finish, plain edge	Edition 1,250	N

THE GOLD SOVEREIGN SERIES

Description and details of the Charles III bare head sovereign

Obverse: Bare head effigy of King Charles III left by Martin Jennings, raised initials below neck MJ. Legend CHARLES III. DEI. GRA. REX. FID. DEF.

Reverse: Pistrucci's St George armed with sword slaying the dragon. The date in the exergue below the ground line with B.P. in small raised letters to upper right.

Edge: Milled.

The coin is struck with a straight upright die axis ↑↑.

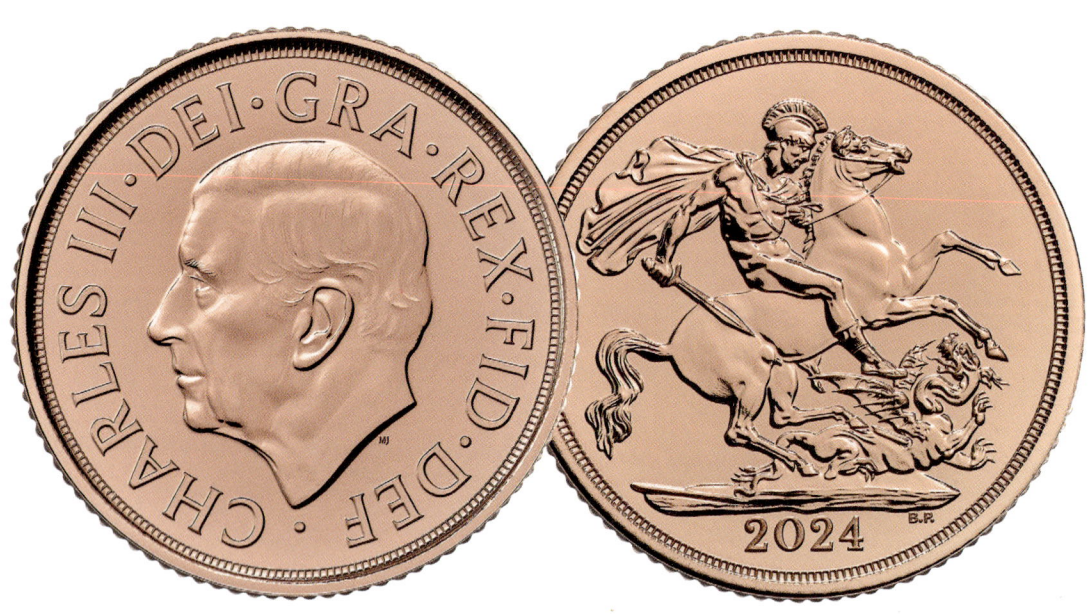

REGULAR SOVEREIGN DESIGN KING CHARLES III
Bare head left by Martin Jennings. Reverse Pistrucci's St George and dragon with date in exergue

No.	Date	Type/Variety	Mintage	Rating
376	2023	BU, normal, struck for 75th Anniversary of the King	Edition 860	N
377	2024	Normal	Not known	C
378	2024	Proof	Edition 7,500 (+1,450)	C

STRUCK ON THE DAY

To commemorate certain special occasions the Royal Mint strike a limited number of sovereigns on the day of the event. Listed below are the events so marked and the quantities issued. Some are only identified by a special certificate issued with the coin, but most of the later issues are marked with a special privy mark appropriate to the occasion. The first strike on the day was to mark the Diamond Jubilee of Her Majesty the Queen on June 2, 2012, followed by the 60th anniversary of the Coronation the following year. Since then various occasions have been celebrated and this has generated a great deal of interest among collectors, with the generally low quantities struck reflected in their values if kept in their original box accompanied by the certificate.

The practice has continued with the change of monarch to King Charles III.

Date	Occasion	Quantity issued	Type	Privy mark
June 2, 2012	Diamond Jubilee of Her Majesty the Queen	1,990	BU	—
June 2, 2013	60th anniversary of the Coronation	900	BU	—
July 22, 2013	Birth of Prince George	2,013	BU	—
July 22, 2014	First Birthday of Prince George	398	BU	—
May 2, 2015	Birth of Princess Charlotte	743	BU	—
July 22, 2015	Second Birthday of Prince George	301	BU (Jody Clark obv.)	—
June 11, 2016	90th Birthday of Her Majesty the Queen	499	BU	—
February 6, 2017*	Sapphire Jubilee—65th anniversary of the accession of Her Majesty the Queen	739	BU	—
July 1, 2017	200th anniversary of the issue of the 1817 sovereign	1,793	BU, plain edge	—
November 20, 2017*	Platinum Wedding of Her Majesty the Queen and Prince Philip	745	BU	—
June 2, 2018	65th anniversary of the Coronation	323	BU, plain edge	65
July 22, 2018	5th Birthday of Prince George	457	BU, plain edge	—
May 24, 2019	200th anniversary of birth of Queen Victoria	Limit 649	Matt, plain edge	VR
August 26, 2019	200th anniversary of birth of Prince Albert	Limit 647	Matt, plain edge	VA
January 31, 2020	"Brexit" Day	Limit 1,500	Matt, plain edge	Crowned portcullis
May 8, 2020	75th anniversary of VE Day	Limit 750	Matt, plain edge	VE75
August 15, 2020	75th anniversary of the End of WWII	Limit 750	Matt, plain edge	VJ75
April 21, 2021 (June 12, 2021**)	The 95th Birthday of Her Majesty the Queen	Limit 1,295	Matt, plain edge	95 in Crown
February 6, 2022	Queen's Platinum Jubilee	Limit 1,200	Matt, plain edge	
May 6, 2023	King's Coronation Day	Limit 1,250	Matt, plain edge	
November, 14 2023	King's 75th Birthday	Limit 860	Matt, plain edge	
June 6, 2024	80th Anniversary of D-Day	Limit 1,000,	Matt plain edge	Helmet above "80" in upper left of exergue

* We note, the milled edge cross section profiles differ between these two issues.
** Issue postponed to June 12, 2021 owing to the passing of HRH The Duke of Edinburgh on April 9, 2021.

Saint George and the Dragon by Gustave Moreau (courtesy of the National Gallery).

THE HALF-SOVEREIGN

Half-sovereign of Elizabeth II
(enlarged x2 and actual size).

The great recoinage of 1816 reintroduced the Sovereign at 20 shillings, and it was logical, considering the popularity of the Guinea fractionals (halves and thirds) that had been in use up until this time, to reintroduce the ten shilling Half-Sovereign too. There were no plans, as far as we know, to introduce a third Sovereign coin even though there was precedence for a coin of that denomination with the Noble and the Angel having both previously been valued at 6s 8d.

A ten-shilling denomination remained in circulation, either as a gold coin or a note, up until 1968 when the introduction of the seven-sided 50p replaced it, (although for the next few years the coin was used as a ten-shilling piece in everyday transactions). In 1971 decimalisation meant that the shilling denomination was scrapped altogether, but the Half Sovereign carried on being legal tender, keeping its "half a pound" value making it nominally worth just 50p. It remains legal tender at that value today.

The Half Sovereign, as its name suggests, was exactly half the weight of the full Sovereign at 3.994 grams (61.637 grains) although it was not half its diameter, coming in at 19.30mm as opposed to the 22.047 of its bigger brother. It was after all, a coin that had to be used as currency and making it too small would not have been popular. The reduction in weight was instead achieved by making the coin 1/2mm thinner than the Sovereign at 1.02mm rather than 1.52mm.

In keeping with the rest of the gold coins struck today, the Half Sovereign has maintained the same dimensions, i.e., size, weight and fineness since it was first introduced.

Unlike the post-1816 Sovereign, which, of course, showcased Benedetto Pistrucci's St George and the Dragon design before being replaced by a crowned Shield of Arms in 1825, the Half featured a shield from the start. It wasn't until the introduction of the "Old Head" obverse bust in 1893 that Pistrucci's St George and the Dragon was used on the reverse at all (although the Branch Mint at Melbourne produced 1893 Half Sovereigns with the Jubilee Head and

Shield Reverse). This ensured that all of the coins in the Sovereign series finally had a common design.

In recent years, the design of the Half Sovereign has changed when the full Sovereign reverse changed, so there were new designs in 1989, 2002, 2005, 2012, 2017, and two in 2022 (one for the Platinum Jubilee, one as a memorial to Her Majesty Queen Elizabeth II) with a one-off obverse change with a new portrait by James Butler in 2016. There were also a number of Privy Marks used.

As with the full Sovereign, the Half fell out of general use when Treasury notes replaced gold at the beginning of World War I, and none were produced as currency coins at the Royal Mint past 1915. There were issues past that date from the Branch Mints in Australia and South Africa, with Sydney minting them until 1916, Perth until 1920 (all dated 1918) and Pretoria for two years in 1925 and 1926, (a small number of proofs having been minted there in 1923). Just over 5,500 proofs were minted to celebrate the Coronation of George VI in 1937, but there were to be no Elizabeth II pre-decimal Half Sovereigns at all.

The coin made a welcome return in 1980 when it was issued as a proof for the collector market. In 1982 some 2,500,000 non-proof coins were minted in addition to nearly 22,000 proofs, but after that, and for the next 18 years, only proof coins were minted, often in small quantities of less than 10,000. In 2000 that changed, and a bullion Half Sovereign was released in greater numbers. Today both a proof and bullion Half Sovereigns are available.

Specifications of the Half Sovereign:
Weight: 3.994 grams.
Fineness, 22 carat: 11/12 fine gold, 1/12 alloy (this means that each Half Sovereign contains 3.6612 grams of pure gold).
Millesimal fineness: 916.66.
Thickness: 1.02mm.
Diameter: 19.30mm.

GEORGE III, 1760–1820

Before Thomas Wyon's death on September 22, 1817, Benedetto Pistrucci had already carried out a great deal of work on the new proposed coinage, and his effigies of the King had already been cut for the sovereign, shilling, sixpence and the halfcrown. He then produced a model in wax of St George slaying the dragon to serve as a model for the reverse of the sovereign, and he further suggested that this should also be used for the rest of the new gold coinage. However, it was William Wyon who designed and modelled the reverse for the first half-sovereign of 1817.

The first gold coins of the new modern coinage were the sovereign and the half-sovereign both bearing the date of 1817. The new sovereign was made current by a Royal Proclamation on July 1, 1817. However, the new half-sovereign was not made current until October 10 of the same year. The obverse again carried the Pistrucci bust of George III surrounded by the inscription GEORGIUS III DEI GRATIA with the date of the year below, but the reverse by Wyon features the Ensigns Armorial of the United Kingdom contained in an angular shield surmounted by the royal crown. The Hanoverian arms within an escutcheon surmounted by a smaller royal crown appear in the centre of the Ensigns Armorial. The surrounding legend begins at the bottom and reads BRITANNIARUM REX FID:DEF. Ruding[1] describes the edge as: *"with a new invented graining on the edge of the piece"*, this we know of today as the milled edge.

The fineness of the new gold coinage remained at 22 carat (11/12 fine gold 1/12 alloy) the same as the guineas, and the weight of the new half-sovereign was to be not less than 61.637 grains. The coin's value was ten shillings, and it was the smallest gold coin in circulation and replaced the seven shilling piece or quarter guinea.

Currency half-sovereigns were only issued for the years 1817, 1818 and 1820, none being issued for 1819. A good example of the first two dates should not prove too difficult for the serious collector to obtain, however, the half-sovereign for 1820 will not be so easy to acquire, especially in high grade, and this is without doubt because a low mintage of only 35,043 of this date were struck.

THE GOLD SOVEREIGN SERIES

Finally, in this short period of only three currency issues we come to the only variant that we have on record for George III half-sovereigns: the overdate 1818/7 (M.401A). This coin shows the second figure 8 having been entered over the figure 7, and it is probably the earliest overdate known within the modern series of gold coins. It is difficult to understand how this particular overdate managed to slip through, especially given the care with which the coins were made in the gold coin department. Indeed, it was an honourable job few would achieve at the Royal Mint in those days. However, as very few half-sovereigns of this overdate are known (we know of only nine), we feel the rarity rating of R5 for this coin is fully justified. This solitary variant amongst the half-sovereigns of George III is without doubt the key coin within this small series, and any collector who is able to fill this gap in their tray will certainly be most fortunate and he or she may well have to spend a four-figure sum to achieve it.

Description and details of the George III half-sovereign

Obverse: The King's head facing right, laureate, hair short; the tie of the laurel wreath has a loop and two hanging ends; the neck is bare. Legend commencing at the bottom of the coin, GEORGIUS III DEI GRATIA. The date is at the bottom of the coin below the truncation.

Reverse: An angular shield surmounted by the royal crown, bearing the Ensigns Armorial of the United Kingdom. The Hanoverian arms within an escutcheon surmounted by the royal crown in the centre of the shield. Legend beginning at the bottom reads BRITANNIARUM REX FID:DEF: and is interrupted by the crown at the top.

Edge: Milled.

The coin is struck with a reverse die axis ↑↓.

HALF-SOVEREIGNS OF GEORGE III

No.	Date	Type/Variety	Mintage	Rating
400	1817	Normal	2,080,197	C
400A	1817	Proof (WR204)	Very few	R3
401	1818	Normal	1,030,286	R
401A	1818	Proof (WR205)	Very few	R5
401B	1818/17	Obv. Overdate final 8 over 7 (top right of 7 visible)	Not known	R5
402	1820	Normal (note: the zero sometimes varies in shape)	35,043	R2
402A	1820	Patterns (WR206–7)	Very few	R5

Note: There are gold patterns dating to 1816 that led to the 1817 currency issue (WR201–3).

Reference
1. The Rev. Rogers Ruding, *Annals of the Coinage of Great Britain and its Dependencies*, Third Edition, Vol. II, London 1840, pp. 121–123.

GEORGE IV, 1820–30

The first change to affect the new sovereign coinage during the reign of George IV was brought about on February 6, 1821 by a Proclamation that stated that the allowance made in previous proclamations for reasonable wear of the sovereign and half-sovereign had been found by experience to be too small for general practice. So the new Proclamation stated that the least current weight for the sovereign should be 122.5 grains, and 61.125 grains for the half-sovereign. Finally an Order in Council dated March 5, 1821 decreed that sovereigns and half-sovereigns should be struck for that year, and another Proclamation made these coins current on May 5, 1821.

So the first half-sovereign for the reign of George IV was issued in 1821. It carried a truly magnificent laureate head bust of the King, and its reverse featured an equally impressive design that displayed the Ensigns Armorial of the United Kingdom beautifully garnished and surmounted by a large crown. The Hanoverian arms within an escutcheon are again placed in the centre of the shield, and the word ANNO is placed to the left of the garnishing and the year 1821 on the right side. This coin is without doubt a splendid example of both engraving and design by Pistrucci, but sadly it will grace few collections because it was quickly withdrawn. The reason for this was because of its likeness to the current sixpence which was being gilded and passed as a half-sovereign. However, this bust of George IV survived and was not only used for the next issue of half-sovereigns, but on several other coins including the magnificent silver crown of 1821. Pistrucci had been much criticised for his engraving of the coinage for George III, but freely admitted he had never before engraved on steel and further stated it would take ten years to achieve the ability to do so. Time has indeed told us this truly great engraver mastered this art of his trade much earlier, and even Vivant Denon, director of the French Mint described the earlier silver crown of 1818 as "the handsomest coin in Europe".

The half-sovereign was next issued in 1823 with the same Type I obverse by Pistrucci, but the Ensigns Armorial of the United

Kingdom surmounted by a crown are this time shown within a plain square shield on the reverse. The date of 1823 is placed in a similar position as on the first issue of 1821, and this second type was further struck for the years of 1824 and 1825.

At this point major changes were about to be made and a new coinage was ordered on June 14, 1825, the gold coins requested being a five pound piece, two pound piece, sovereign and half-sovereign. However, by this time it seemed the King was looking for a change of bust, and some two years earlier a bust of the King had been prepared by Sir Francis Chantrey for a medal which had very much impressed his Majesty. The King requested that the Chantrey bust should be used for the new coinage and Pistrucci was asked to copy the bust and proceed with the work. Pistrucci refused to obey the order and said it was well beneath his dignity to copy another man's work, but this time the King would not tolerate such behaviour and Pistrucci took no further part in coinage preparation. However, prior to this on June 23, 1824, the Master of the Mint recommended that Jean Baptiste Merlen be employed to prepare the design and engrave the dies for the new series of gold and silver coins, and William Wyon the Second Engraver was also asked to prepare designs and engrave the obverse dies for the new coinage. So all in fact had been put into place for the new coinage of George IV.

The new Type III half-sovereign features the Chantrey bust of the King bare headed and engraved by William Wyon, the date placed below the truncation. The legend reads GEORGIUS IV DEI GRATIA and begins and ends with a small oval flower stop. The reverse carries a beautifully garnished shield containing the Ensigns Armorial of the United Kingdom surmounted by a crown. The Hanoverian arms within an escutcheon with a crown above are placed in the centre of the shield as the earlier issues. The inscription reads BRITANNIARUM REX FID:DEF:. This reverse was designed and engraved by Merlen. The Type III bare head half-sovereigns were first issued bearing the date of 1826 and were also struck for the next two years.

There are three variants in this small group spanning only three years, and these occur because two slightly different busts were prepared by William Wyon in 1826. These busts only differ in the arrangement of the hair curls of the King. On some variants the small cluster of the curls near the front top part of the ear appear to have had another curl added. At the back of the bust where the hair begins at the top of the nape three separate clusters of curls are clearly defined. It is worth noting that Wyon seems to have made various other hair changes to different bare-head denominations of George IV coinage in this period.

The unique 1829 half-sovereign, which can be seen in the Ashmolean Museum, is the result of a request to the Royal Mint made in 1891 by E. B. Nicholson, Librarian at the Bodleian Library, Oxford. The request for a number of coins to complete the Bodley's coin cabinet resulted in a number of individual coins being struck from original dies, in gold, silver and bronze.[1] Naturally when the Bodley's cabinet was transferred to the Ashmolean's Heberden Coin Room, these coins, including the 1829 specimen were included.

Half-sovereigns are becoming increasingly more difficult to find, and without doubt those of George IV will be very hard for the collector to acquire. In fact the first issue, the 1821 half-sovereign M.403, very rarely appears. Probably the two coins in this series most likely to be found are those dated 1825 (M.406) and 1828 (M.409), although in extremely fine condition they would command a fairly high premium.

Reference
1. Roderick Farey, "The 1829 Half-Sovereign", *British Numismatic Journal*, Vol. XXXIX, 1970.

HALF-SOVEREIGNS OF GEORGE IV, 1820–30

Description and details of the George IV Laureate Head Type I half-sovereign

Obverse: The King's bust facing left, laureate, tie with loop and two ends, hair short and bare neck. B.P. in small letters below truncation standing for Benedetto Pistrucci. Legend: GEORGIUS III D:G: BRITANNIAR: REX F:D:

Reverse: A heavily garnished shield, surmounted by the royal crown, bearing the Ensigns Armorial of the United Kingdom. The Hanoverian arms within an escutcheon surmounted by the royal crown in the centre of the shield. The shield surrounded by roses, thistles and shamrocks. ANNO to the left reading downwards, the date on the right reading upwards. The letters W.W.P. standing for William Wellesley Pole, then Master of the Mint, appear in the centres of three of the shamrock leaves.

Edge: Milled.
The coin is struck with a reverse die axis ↑↓.

Type I.

TYPE I LAUREATE HEAD HALF-SOVEREIGNS OF GEORGE IV

No.	Date	Type/Variety	Mintage	Rating
403	1821	Normal	231,288	R3
403A	1821	Proof (WR244)	Very few	R3

Note: There are patterns in gold dated 1820–21 (WR239–243) that led to the 1821 currency issue.

Description and details of the George IV Laureate Head Type II half-sovereign

Obverse: As Type I.
Reverse: A plain square shield, surmounted by the royal crown, bearing the Ensigns Armorial of the United Kingdom. The Hanoverian arms within an escutcheon surmounted by the royal crown in the centre of the shield. ANNO to the left reading upwards, the date on the right reading downwards. Below the shield are a thistle and shamrock emerging from a rose
Edge: Milled.
The coin is struck with a reverse die axis ↑↓.

Type II.

TYPE II LAUREATE HEAD HALF-SOVEREIGNS OF GEORGE IV

No.	Date	Type/Variety	Mintage	Rating
404	1823	Normal	224,280	R2
404A	1823	Proof (WR245)	Very few	R5
405	1824	Normal	591,538	S
405A	1824	Proof (WR246)	Very few	R5
406	1825	Normal	761,150	N

HALF-SOVEREIGNS OF GEORGE IV, 1820–30

Description and details of the George IV Bare Head Type III half-sovereign

Obverse: The King's bare head facing left. Date below truncation. Legend: GEORGIUS IV DEI GRATIA begins and ends with a small oval flower stop.

Reverse: A garnished shield, surmounted by the royal crown, bearing the Ensigns Armorial of the United Kingdom. The Hanoverian arms within an escutcheon surmounted by the royal crown in the centre of the shield. Legend: BRITANNIARUM REX FID: DEF:

Edge: Milled.

The coin is struck with a reverse die axis ↑↓.

Type III.

TYPE III BARE HEAD HALF-SOVEREIGNS OF GEORGE IV

No.	Date	Type/Variety	Mintage	Rating
406A	1825	Proof (WR248)	Very few	R4
407	1826	Normal	344,830	R
407A	1826	Proof (WR249)	c. 400	S
407B	1826	Hair curls differ*	Incl. in 344,830 above	R
407C	1826	Proof. Hair curls differ	Inc. in 407A	S
408	1827	Normal	492,014	S
408A	1827	Proof (WR250)	Very few	R6
408B	1827	Hair curls differ	Incl. in 492,014 above	S
409	1828	Normal	1,244,754	N
409A	1828	Proof (WR251)	Very few	R6
409B	1828	Hair curls differ	Incl. in 1,224,754 above	S
409C	1829	Proof (WR252)	Unique †	R7
409D	1829/1823	Mule. Pattern (WR253)	Miniscule	R7

Note: There is a record of a further 4,205 Half-Sovereigns being struck in the calendar year for 1829, which are presumably all dated 1828.

* The hair curl is most visible as an extra tuft of hair immediately to the left of ear, as shown in the illustration of the 1826 piece above, the normal variety being without such an extra lower tuft of hair.

† This coin, in the Ashmolean Museum, was struck by the Royal Mint in 1891 at the request of the Bodleian Library curator E. B. Nicholson.

WILLIAM IV, 1830–37

William IV succeeded to the throne upon the death of his elder brother on June 26, 1830, and no currency gold coins were issued for that year. However, an Order in Council, dated November 22, 1830, specified that a double sovereign, sovereign and half-sovereign be struck in gold. These in fact became current by Proclamation on April 13, 1831.

Although plain edge proofs were issued of both the sovereign and half-sovereign, bearing the date of 1831, and also a currency sovereign for the same year, the half-sovereign was not issued as a currency piece for this reign until 1834. There are important facts that should be mentioned regarding this half-sovereign: first the obverse was engraved by William Wyon (1795–1851) from a superb bust of William IV by Sir Francis Chantrey (1781–1841). The reverse features a beautifully garnished shield modelled and engraved by Jean Baptiste Merlen (1769–c.1850) and finally it should be noted that this particular half-sovereign has a diameter of only 17.9mm. This was considerably smaller than any other half-sovereign previously struck during the modern era, which measured 19.4mm. A Treasury order dated April 14, 1835 requested that the half-sovereign should be struck at a reduced size but the only half-sovereigns of this size to be produced are those dated 1834, although they are of the same weight and fineness as previous issues (61.637 grains and 916.66 fineness).

Although only five currency issues of half-sovereigns were made during this short reign, two of these bear the same date of 1836, and one of these (M.412) can most certainly be described as a normal issue. However, the other dated 1836 (M.412A) deserves special mention, for this displays a bust of William IV that was struck from a sixpence die in error.[1] Prior to this, in the reign of George IV sixpences and shillings were being gilded in an attempt for them to be passed as half-sovereigns and sovereigns by dishonest people. However, Mint ledgers record that half-sovereigns with a value of £60,000 or 120,000 coins dated 1834 had been recalled and melted. This was probably as a result of complaints relating to their being very similar to the seven shilling or third guinea pieces. Further to this both reverse designs of the shilling and sixpence of William IV now clearly displayed their denominational values.

It is unlikely the sixpence obverse was used intentionally, but had it been so, this would certainly have saved many hours of work and of course a considerable sum of money. However, history has revealed that Wyon would go on and repeat a similar piece of engraving. On this occasion in the reign of Victoria he used a farthing die for the obverse of a Type IA sovereign, but again this could have been in error.

Another interesting point that should be noted is on the reverse of the William half-sovereigns, and here we refer to the band that holds the lower garnishing around the shield together. This horizontal band on the 1834 coin (M.410) has a plain void centre area and is only defined by its outer edges, but on the other normal size issues (M.413) it can be seen that a central incuse line has been added running from end to end across the bar. The final general observation of the William half-sovereign leads us to the conclusion that this very short series of coins is made up from only one type of obverse bust, and this also includes the bust used for the sixpence die.[2] The bust used on the William half-sovereigns is, we believe, that which has previously been described as the Second Bust in the sovereign series. Easy points of recognition that identify the William half-sovereign bust are: the hair on the nape of the neck has a clear gap between it and the neck; and the hair arrangement at the top of the forehead is a single curl laying almost flat and bending gently backwards towards a small cluster of curls behind; finally the top part of the ear is clearly visible.

Even though this very short reign has only produced five different currency issues it may well take the collector a very long time to complete the series and even if he does, he may well have to accept very low grades. The half-sovereigns of William IV very seldom appear, and even in only fine grade examples of the three easier dates of 1835, 1836 and 1837 can be expensive. However, the key coin of this small group is without doubt the 1836 half-sovereign with its obverse struck from a sixpence die (M.412A). This coin even in fine grade may well cost a heavy four-figure sum.

M.412A with obverse struck from sixpence die.

Notes/References
1. G. P. Dyer, "The Small Half-Sovereigns of William IV", *Spink Numismatic Circular*, October 1978, pp. 470–471.
2. M. A. Marsh, "William IV Sovereign. A Different Bust and a New Variety", *Spink Numismatic Circular*, May 1984, pp. 118–119.

Description and details of the William IV half-sovereign

Obverse: The bare head of the King facing right. Legend: GULIELMUS IIII D:G:BRITANNIAR:REX F:D:

Reverse: A garnished shield surmounted by a royal crown, bearing the Ensigns Armorial of the United Kingdom. The Hanoverian arms within an escutcheon surmounted by the royal crown in the centre of the shield. The date is shown in the field at the bottom of the right side, the word ANNO appears in a similar position on the left side.

Edge: Milled.

The coin is struck with a reverse die axis ↑↓.

HALF-SOVEREIGNS OF WILLIAM IV

No.	Date	Type/Variety	Mintage	Rating
409E	1831	Small size proof plain edge (WR 267)	c. 225	S
409F	1831	Small size Milled edge proof (WR 268)	Very few	R6
410*	1834	Small size (17.9mm)	133,899	R2
411	1835	Normal size 19.4mm	772,554	S
412	1836	Normal size 19.4mm	146,865	R3
412A	1836	Obv. struck from sixpence die (19.4mm)	Incl. in above	R5
413	1837	Normal size 19.4mm	160,207	R
413A	1837	Proof (WR 269)	Very few	R6

* Ongoing research suggests that as many as 120,000 coins of this smaller size issue were subsequently melted down.

Segment of reverse of M.410 showing horizontal band on lower garnishing without central line.

Segment of reverse of M.413 showing horizontal band on lower garnishing with central line.

VICTORIA, 1837–1901

The first gold currency half-sovereign for the new reign of Queen Victoria was issued bearing the date of 1838, and its obverse carried the young head bust of the Queen facing to the left, engraved by William Wyon. The reverse by J. B. Merlen featured an ornate garnished shield containing the Ensigns Armorial of the United Kingdom similar to the previous reign, but it should be noted that the escutcheon containing the Hanoverian arms has now been omitted. The reason for this being because the right to the Kingdom of Hanover was limited to only the male line of succession.

Similar to the sovereign (*qv*) the half-sovereign was produced throughout the Queen's reign, between 1838 and 1901. The first type, the shield reverse half-sovereigns commenced in 1838 and, as will be seen, this series offers the collector a number of interesting varieties. It was during this reign that the various branch mints were introduced and, like the sovereigns, produced an interesting series of coins avidly sought after today.

There are a number of good reasons that contribute to the general rarity of our gold coinage during the Victorian period but the main cause is that as the gold coins became worn they were withdrawn and melted down. An example is one of the major rarities in the Type IA series of half-sovereigns, M.428: we know that the recorded mintage figure for this 1854 coin was quite large (1,125,144), but even so it is hardly ever seen. Perhaps because of its small size it would have been even more susceptible to wear and so more likely to have been withdrawn.

SHIELD REVERSE HALF-SOVEREIGNS OF QUEEN VICTORIA

Type IA Shield reverse half-sovereigns London Mint dated 1838–71

OBVERSE 1. The bust on these coins is the smallest of all Type I half-sovereigns and displays the young head of Victoria to the left. Hair bound with double fillet and collected into knot behind, all held in place by ribbons. Legend VICTORIA DEI GRATIA. Date displayed in field below truncation. The front ribbon on the top of the bust is noticeably wider than the other ribbons, and the lower truncation does not enter into the area of the legend. The date figures are occasionally found intermingled with different size figures, probably caused by the engraver not noticing which punch he had entered. However, it seems that the larger figures were used on a more regular basis from 1883 onwards. Surprisingly, unlike the larger sovereign, the engraver, William Wyon's initials do not appear on the truncation of the half-sovereigns.

Reverse. The Type A reverse is very similar to the sovereign, the Ensigns Armorial of the United Kingdom within a shield surmounted by a crown, except that on the half-sovereign the wreath of laurel is replaced by ornate garnishing and the Thistle, Rose and Shamrock that were centrally placed between two small flower stops at the bottom of the sovereign are omitted. The flower stops are, however, still present on either side of the lower garnishing at the bottom of the coin. The reverse engraving is by J. B. Merlen.

OBVERSE 2. This slightly larger bust was first used in 1858. The bust is slightly larger than obverse 1 and because of this the hair at the back of Victoria's head can be clearly seen closer to the G in GRATIA, and also the small strand of hair showing from behind the bun has been removed.

Reverse. This is the normal A type except for one interesting change, and this is the addition of a small dot that is placed just above the centre of the crossed lines that divide the Ensigns Armorial.

In general, the collector will find that the Type IA half-sovereigns will not be easy to acquire, and even the common dates in around extremely fine condition are becoming expensive. However, there are six coins within this series that are extremely rare and may well cause the collector much difficulty to find, and even then the price may be prohibitive! Indeed the collector may well have to find a large four figure sum to acquire any of these coins: 1845 (M.419), 1850 (M.424), 1854 (M.428), 1862 (M.436), 1871 (M.438) and the overdate of 1848/7 (M.422A). Finally another rarity in the list of Type IA half-sovereigns is an overdate 1856/5 (M.430A). This was first discovered by Steve Hill when at Spink in 2003 and since then a few more examples have come to light.

The half-sovereign of 1871 (M.438) with its obverse 2 variant has a slightly turned bust causing Victoria's nose to point just above the letter T, and its reverse not having the dot on the vertical line of the crossed lines that divide the Ensigns Armorial. This coin is without doubt one of the major rarities within the Type IA series.

The first overdate of the Type IA series (M.422A) is special as it was first discovered in 1981 when Mr Marsh was given the opportunity to work on the Scanning Electron Microscope by Dr R. S. Paden of CAMSCAN Electronics Ltd of Cambridge. This enabled him to establish the very first overdate to be recorded in the sovereign series.

HALF-SOVEREIGNS OF VICTORIA, 1837–1901

M.422A. The overdate on Type IA, obverse 1.

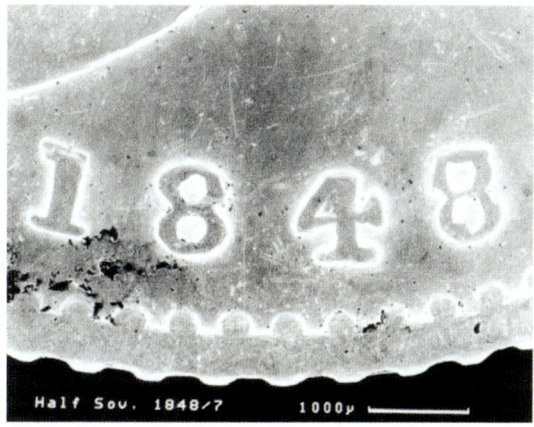 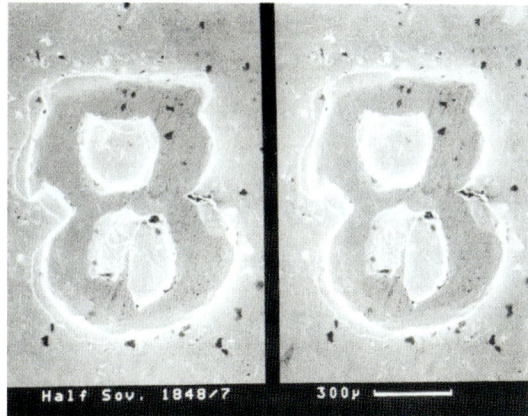

Full date.   Stereo pair of the figure 8.

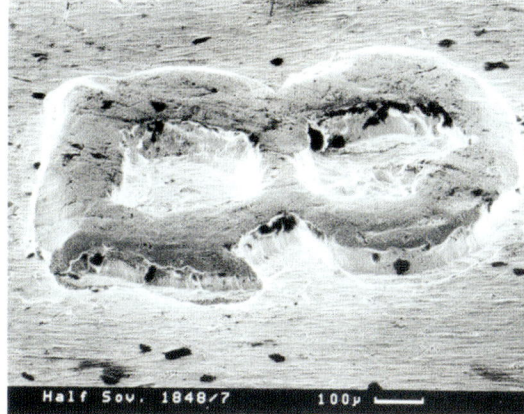 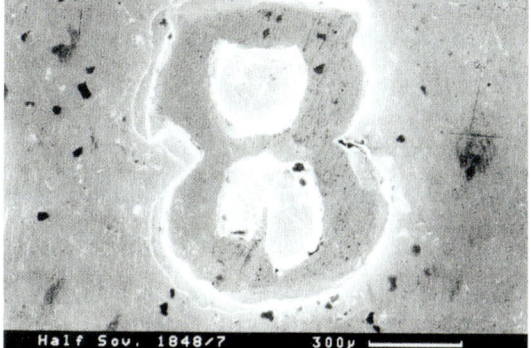

Angled side view of figure 8.   Normal view of figure 8.

Scanning Electron Microscope images of the 1848 8 over 7 overdate M.422A, which was the very first overdate identified in the half-sovereign series.

THE GOLD SOVEREIGN SERIES

M.431. Type IA, obverse 1—first small young head.

M.435. Type IA, obverse 2—second larger young head.

M. 438. Type IA, obverse 2A—transitional obverse, head lower .

M.442. Type IB, obverse 2—second larger young head with die number on reverse.

M.446C & M.446D, Type IB, obverse 2B

M.449. Type IB, obverse 3—third larger young head, bun closer to G.

M.452. Type IB, obverse 4—fourth young head, hair fillets of equal width.

Type IB (Die Number) Shield reverse half-sovereigns London Mint dated 1863–80

OBVERSE 2, 3 and 4. This Type IB series brings us into the interesting area that was introduced by the Royal Mint, which was simply to add a number that appears between the flower stops on the reverse of the half-sovereign. Although there is no documentary evidence available, today it is generally accepted that the addition of this number meant that the Mint could establish at least two very important things. First and foremost, they would be able to identify the coin press operator and secondly, they would be in a position to locate the particular die used to strike a specific coin.

To accommodate the new die number it was necessary to raise the shield on the reverse, and in doing this the upper part of the crown can be now seen slightly encroaching into the beading at the top of the coin. So this change in the position of the garnished shield occurs throughout the die number series of half-sovereigns. The next point of note is that the dot originally introduced by Merlen for the reverse of the earlier obverse 2 Type IA half-sovereigns continues to be used on the next type, and on the Type IB die number half-sovereigns it is again positioned just above the centre of the crossed lines that divides the Ensigns Armorial, and it is used at the beginning of this series from 1863 to 1871.

The next important change in this series occurs on coins from 1872 to 1876 when a third slightly larger bust was introduced; this bust is slightly larger than the type 2 obverse, and this causes the bun of Victoria's hair to be much closer to the G in GRATIA and the lower point of the truncation is well past the top line of the date figures. The fourth and final bust of the series appears on the half-sovereigns dated 1876 to 1880 and this bust is similar in size to the third bust, but a very noticeable change has been made to the ribbon that holds in place Victoria's hair. This is quite narrow compared to that shown on any of the earlier busts.

Final observations on the Type IB (Die Number) series of half-sovereigns bring us to the last coin of the series, that of 1880 (M.455), with the bust similar in size and detail to the fourth bust described, but the bust itself struck in very low relief compared to other young head busts seen from this series. This coin should be classified as a variant rather than a new bust.

Finally, there are two important and extremely rare variants in this die number series, and they are without doubt the key dates. The first is dated 1870 (M.445A) and the other 1871 (M.446A); except for different die numbers both these variants are similar coins. They are both obverse 2 with the busts slightly turned causing Victoria's nose to point between the letters T and O in the legend; they are also placed well out of the central position clearly nearer to the left side of the flan. The border beading is larger and this creates a much coarser effect, but only on M.446B is the dot placed on the reverse crossed lines.

Aside from the first half-sovereign in the series, 1863 (M.439), most of the other coins will not be difficult for the collector to acquire. However, the two variants are both extremely rare coins and they will be exceptionally difficult to find, and if they do appear in extremely fine condition then a large four-figure sum may well be necessary.

Type IC (No Die Number) Shield reverse half-sovereigns London Mint dated 1880–85

OBVERSE 5. This fifth head is the largest of the entire series of Victoria's young head busts, and this variety does not carry a die number.

This half-sovereign features a large bust struck in very low relief and encroaching into the legend area, the rear of Victoria's bun can be seen very much engulfing the lower part of the G in GRATIA. The bottom point of the truncation also intrudes well into the same area, and the beading on both obverse and reverse is larger and so makes the thickening of the rim most evident. Because of this thicker edge the top of the crown on the reverse is almost buried under the beading, and the flower stops together with the legend area are also very close to the beading.

Only the first and last issues of this very small Type IC series will present the collector with problems. The three other half-sovereigns 1883, 1884 and 1885 can be quite easily acquired in around extremely fine condition and are not expensive. The 1880 half-sovereign, although rare, does sometimes appear and in extremely fine grade would probably cost about double the price of the later coins in the group. However, the most difficult coin in the group is the 1885/3 overdate (M.459A) and it will not be at all easy to find, if it does appear it may well cost a four-figure sum.

M.457. Type IC, obverse 5—fifth young head, bun nearly touches G.

Victoria Young Head half-sovereign—summary of obverse varieties
(note some obverses overlap in use for certain dates)

Obverse 1—1838–58 inclusive—Smallest Young head left, pointed tip to front of neck with sharper truncation, nose points between T and O but nearer to O, front fillet in hair thick, rear fillet thinner and points between D and E but nearer to E, rear hair bun most distant from G of legend and with single hair strand curving out to right. Obverse in use for Type 1A only."

Obverse 2—1858–72 inclusive—Slightly larger with re-engraved hair, bun closer to G without single hair strand at right, nose points similar to 1 but a little more towards O, thinner rear fillet in hair more towards E. Obverse in use for Types 1A and 1B and usually with the reverse with a raised dot on the upper vertical of the shield division crosshair.

Obverse 2A—transitional obverse between 2 and 3—1871 (438)—with coarse beading, bust a little lower on coin so nose points between T and O but nearer to T, thinner rear fillet in hair points between D and E but nearer to E, hair bun closer to G. Obverse in use for type 1A.

Obverse 2B—Transitional obverse between 2 and 3—1871 and 1872 (446C and 446D)—similar to 2 but with different orientation to legend, nose points between C and T but more towards T, thinner rear fillet in hair points between D and E but nearer to D. Obverse in use for type 1B.

Obverse 3—1872–76 inclusive—Head a little larger, nose points between T and O but nearer to O, right side of thick front hair fillet points closer to left of D, thinner rear hair fillet points between E and I but nearer to E, bun of hair closer to G. Obverse in use for type 1B.

Obverse 4—1876–80 inclusive—Hair reengraved now with two hair fillets of equal thickness, nose points between T and O but just a little closer to O, rear hair fillet points between E and I but closer to E, hair bun close to G. Obverse in use for types 1B and 1C (1880).

Obverse 5—1880–87 inclusive—Enlarged head so the front of truncation nearly touches 1 of date and bun nearly touches G, nose points midway between T and O, both hair fillets of equal size, rear fillet points between E and I but more towards E. Obverse in use for types 1B (1880 only) and 1C.

The same busts varieties (2, 3, 4 and 5) can be applied to the Sydney and Melbourne Young Head series though they are currently numbered by obverses defined mainly by rim teeth numbers as per Australian convention.

Description and details of Queen Victoria half-sovereigns Type 1A Shield reverse (no Die numbers)

Obverse: Young head of Victoria to left. Hair bound with double fillet and collected into knot behind. Legend: VICTORIA DEI GRATIA. Date is shown in field below truncation.

Reverse: The Ensigns Armorial of the United Kingdom within a garnished shield surmounted by a crown. A small flower stop appears in the field either side of the lower garnishing at the bottom of the coin. Legend: BRITANNIARUM REGINA FID:DEF:

Edge: Milled.
The coin is struck with a reverse die axis ↑↓.

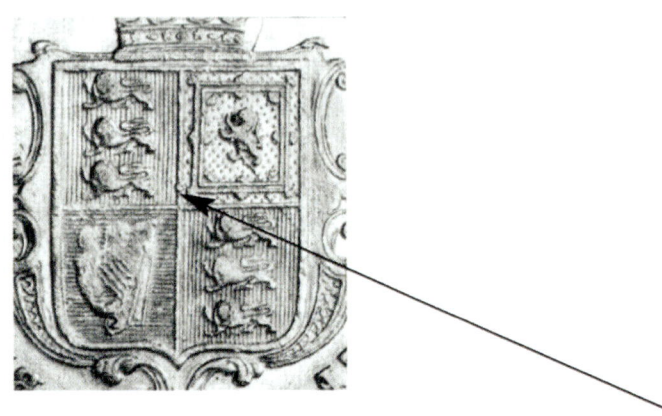

The dot found on the reverse of Type IA Shield half-sovereigns dated from 1858 to 1871.

TYPE IA SHIELD HALF-SOVEREIGNS OF QUEEN VICTORIA, LONDON MINT (NO MINT MARK)

No.	Date	Type/Variety	Mintage	Rating
414	1838	Obv. 1. Small bust	273,341	R
414A	1839	Plain edge proof. Die axis ↑↓ (WR343)	c. 400	S
414B	1839	Plain edge proof. Die axis ↑↑ (WR344)	Incl. in above	S
414C	1839	Milled edge proof (WR345)	Very few	R6
415	1841*	Normal	508,835	R2
416	1842	Normal	2,223,352	N
417	1843	Normal	1,251,762	R2
418	1844	Normal	1,127,007	R
419	1845	Normal. Date figures can vary in spacing and level	887,526	R3
420	1846	Normal	1,063,928	R
421	1847	Normal	928,656	R2
422	1848	Normal (close grouped date figures)	410,595	S
422A	1848/7	Obv. 1. Overdate. 8 over 7	Incl. in above	R3
422B	1848	Wide spaced date figures	Incl. in above	R
422C	1848	Now re-classified as 422 above	Incl. in above	S
423	1849	Normal	845,112	R
424	1850	Normal	179,275	R3
425	1851	Normal	773,575	S
426	1852	Normal	1,377,671	N
427	1853	Normal	2,708,796	N
427A	1853	Proof. Small date (WR346)	Very few	R4
427B	1853	Proof. Large date (WR347)	Very few	R6
428	—	†	1,125,144	R6
429	1855	Normal	1,120,362	N
429A	1855	With second 5 in date over 1 or 3	Incl. in above	R3
430	1856	Normal	2,391,909	N
430A	1856/5	Obv. 1. Overdate. 6 over 5	Incl. in above	R3
431	1857	Normal	728,223	S
432	1858‡	Obv. 2. Slightly larger bust. Rev. Garnished shield with dot	855,578	R
433	1859	Normal	2,203,813	N
434	1860	Normal	1,131,500	N
435	1861	Normal	1,130,867	N
436	1862	Normal	Not known	R5
437	1863	Normal	See Type IB	N
438	1871	Obv. 2A. Head a little lower on obverse. Rev. no dot on shield	Not known	R6
438A	1876	Obv. 2. Rev. no dot on upper vertical of shield crosshair	Not known	R6

* There is a pattern in gold dated 1841 (WR377) which is a mule of the 1841 obverse with the reverse of an 1841 sixpence (R7).

† No coins dated 1854 were minted therefore the recorded mintage were all probably dated 1853 or 1855.

‡ Both Obv. I and Obv. 2 can be found with this date.

Note: There are non-die number proofs and patterns dated 1870 (WR348), 1871 (WR349–350), 1872 (WR351), 1877 (WR352), 1878 (WR353) and 1880 (WR353) as well as an 1880 pattern with a St George reverse (WR354).

Coins dated between 1853 and 1862 often come with date figures doubled.

THE GOLD SOVEREIGN SERIES

Description and details of Queen Victoria half-sovereigns Type 1B Shield reverse with Die numbers

The appearance of this series is exactly as before but with the addition of a small die number which appears immediately below the bottom of the garnishing of the reverse shield.

TYPE IB (DIE NUMBER) SHIELD HALF-SOVEREIGNS OF QUEEN VICTORIA, LONDON MINT (NO MINT MARK)

No.	Date	Type/Variety	Mintage	Rating
439	1863	Obv. 2. Rev. Garnished shield with dot	1,351,574*	R2
440	1864	Normal	1,758,490	N
441	1865	Normal	1,834,750	N
442	1866	Normal	2,058,776	N
443	1867	Normal	992,795	N
444	1869	Normal	1,861,764	N
445	1870	Obv. 2. Normal beading. Rev. with dot	981,408	N
445A	1870	Obv. 2. Coarse beading. Rev. no dot	Incl. in above	R4
445B	1871	Obv. 1 nose points toward T (dies 65/68 noted)	Incl. below	R3
446	1871	Obv. 2. Normal beading	2,217,760	N
446A	1871	Obv. 2. Coarse beading. Rev. no dot Rosettes closer to border	Incl. in above	R4
446B	1871	Obv. 2. Coarse beading. Rev. with dot	Incl. in above	R
446C	1871	Obv. 2B. Transitional between 2 and 3	Incl. in above	R2
446D	1872	Obv. 2B. Similar to above	Incl. in above	R2
447	1872	Obv. 3. Slightly larger bust. Rev. no dot	3,235,112	N
447A	1872	Roman I for 1 in date (noted with die 95)	Incl. in above	R4
447B	1872	New obv. With bunched legend, nose points below T (noted with die 79)	Incl. in above	R5
448	1873	Normal. The 3 of date perhaps varies in size	2,003,464	N
449	1874	Normal	1,884,432	N
450	1875	Normal	516,240	R2
450A	1876	Obv. 3. With wider front fillet in hair	Incl. in above	N
451	1876	Obv. 4. With narrow front fillet in hair	2,804,187	N
452	1877	Normal	1,962,800	N
453	1878	Normal	2,317,506	N
454	1879	Normal	35,201	R4
455	1880	Normal	See Type IC No. 456	N
455A	1880	Obv. 5. Bust in very low relief	Incl. in above	R
455B	1880	With 8 over 7 in date (seen die no. 129)	Incl. in above	R4

*This mintage figure includes those of the Type IA half-sovereigns of the same date.

Note: The normal beading on a half sovereign consists of 117 denticles obv. and 120 rev. The coarse beading only has 98 denticles obv. and 101 rev. with no dot on shield line at centre of rev.

DIE NUMBERS SO FAR KNOWN

Year	Die numbers
1863	1, 2, 3, 4, 6, 7, 9
1864	2, 4, 5, 7, 8, 9, 10, 12, 13, 14, 15, 16, 17, 18, 19, 20, 21, 22, 23, 24, 25, 26, 27, 28, 29, 30, 31, 32, 33, 34, 35, 36, 37, 38, 39, 41
1865	1, 2, 3, 4, 5, 6, 7, 8, 9, 10, 11, 12, 13, 14, 15, 16, 17, 18, 19, 20, 21, 22, 23, 24, 25, 26, 27, 29, 30, 32, 33, 37, 38, 39, 40, 44, 45, 47, 48, 49, 50, 52, 53, 54, 57
1866	1, 2, 3, 4, 5, 6, 7, 8, 9, 11, 12, 13, 14, 15, 16, 17, 18, 19, 21, 22, 23, 24, 25, 26, 27, 28, 30, 31, 32, 33, 34, 35, 36, 38, 40
1867	1, 2, 3, 4, 5, 6, 7, 8, 9, 10, 11, 12, 13, 14, 15, 17, 18, 19, 20, 21
1869	1, 3, 4, 5, 6, 7, 8, 9, 10, 11, 12, 13, 14, 16, 17, 18, 19, 20, 21, 22, 23, 24, 25, 26, 28, 29
1870	1, 2, 3, 4, 5, 6, 7, 23, 33, 34, 35, 36, 37, 38, 39, 40, 41, 42, 43, 44, 45, 46
1871	1, 4, 5, 6, 7, 8, 9, 10, 11, 12, 13, 14, 17, 18, 19, 26, 28, 33, 34, 35, 36, 37, 38, 41, 42, 45, 47, 49, 50, 52, 53, 55, 56, 57, 58, 59, 60, 61, 62, 63, 64, 65, 66, 67, 68, 69, 70, 71, 74, 78, 81, 89, 90, 92, 163
1872	4, 6, 11, 12, 17, 20, 25, 28, 29, 30, 32, 34, 37, 38, 40, 41, 42, 43, 49, 50, 57, 62, 65, 68, 69, 70, 73, 74, 75, 76, 77, 78, 79, 80, 82, 85, 86, 87, 93, 94, 95, 97, 99, 100, 102, 104, 105, 106, 109, 110, 111, 112, 114, 119, 120, 121, 124, 126, 129, 136, 138, 141, 143, 150, 151, 154, 162, 163, 165, 172, 173, 179, 186, 192, 195, 196, 198, 200, 202, 203, 212, 214, 223, 240, 243, 245, 246, 251, 254, 255, 260, 271, 274, 279, 289, 283, 291, 293, 296, 297, 304, 308, 312, 320, 326, 331, 335, 338, 341, 346, 349, 350, 353, 354, 357, 363, 369, 378, 380, 391, 398
1873	3, 4, 8, 14, 15, 20, 29, 31, 32, 36, 49, 56, 65, 89, 94, 99, 103, 112, 113, 147, 157, 158, 171, 172, 184, 185, 197, 201, 205, 208, 220, 226, 233, 235, 238, 241, 245, 246, 247, 249, 257, 258, 259, 260, 263, 265, 268, 269, 275, 278, 279, 280, 281, 283, 286, 289, 290, 295, 296, 299, 300, 301, 302, 303, 306, 308, 312, 314, 315, 319, 320, 328, 334, 335, 394, 406, 407, 414
1874	1, 2, 3, 4, 8, 10, 12, 13, 14, 15, 16, 17, 18, 19, 21, 22, 23, 24, 25, 26, 27, 28, 29, 31, 32, 33, 35, 37, 38, 41, 44, 45, 47, 50, 54, 56, 60, 66, 68, 69, 74, 75, 78, 212, 238, 338, 341, 342, 350
1875	2, 3, 5, 6, 8, 11, 12, 15, 16, 17, 22, 23, 24, 26, 38, 47, 53, 72, 76, 96, 199, 280, 344, 395
1876	1, 2, 3, 5, 6, 9, 10, 11, 12, 13, 14, 15, 17, 20, 21, 22, 25, 27, 29, 30, 33, 34, 37, 41, 42, 43, 44, 45, 47, 49, 51, 52, 55, 56, 57, 58, 62, 63, 64, 65, 69, 71, 72, 73, 74, 75, 76, 77, 78, 79, 80, 81, 82, 83, 84, 85, 86, 87, 88, 89, 98, 101, 414
1877	1, 2, 3, 10, 11, 16, 20, 21, 22, 23, 25, 26, 28, 29, 31, 32, 33, 37, 39, 40, 43, 46, 47, 49, 51, 52, 53, 54, 55, 56, 57, 58, 61, 62, 63, 64, 65, 66, 68, 69, 71, 73, 74, 80, 81, 85, 88, 91, 92, 94, 95, 96, 97, 100, 102, 103, 105, 108, 109, 110, 114, 115, 120, 123, 124, 125, 126, 127, 130, 134, 135, 136, 137, 138, 139, 141, 143, 147, 148, 149, 150, 151, 152, 154, 155, 157, 159, 160, 171, 245
1878	2, 4, 6, 7, 8, 9, 10, 11, 13, 14, 15, 17, 19, 20, 21, 22, 23, 24, 25, 28, 29, 32, 33, 34, 35, 36, 37, 38, 40, 41, 44, 45, 46, 48, 50, 51, 52, 53, 55, 56, 57, 59, 62, 65, 66, 67, 69, 70, 71, 72, 73, 76, 78, 81, 89, 91, 93, 94, 97, 98, 99, 100, 101, 105, 106, 108, 113, 130, 141, 147, 149, 156, 158, 162, 167, 197
1879	57, 58, 80, 87, 88, 89, 95, 112, 119, 161, 180
1880	3, 12, 75, 78, 80, 87, 103, 104, 108, 110, 111, 114, 115, 118, 119, 121, 123, 124, 125, 129, 130, 131, 132

Description and details of Queen Victoria Type 1C Shield reverse half-sovereign

Obverse: Young head of Victoria to left. Hair bound with double fillet and collected into knot behind. Legend: VICTORIA DEI GRATIA. Date is shown in field below truncation.

Reverse: The Ensigns Armorial of the United Kingdom within a garnished shield surmounted by a crown. A small flower stop appears in the field either side of the lower garnishing at the bottom of the coin. Legend: BRITANNIARUM REGINA FID:DEF:

Edge: Milled.

The coin is struck with a reverse die axis ↑↓.

TYPE IC SHIELD HALF-SOVEREIGNS OF QUEEN VICTORIA (NO DIE NUMBER) BUST IN LOW RELIEF

No.	Date	Type/Variety	Mintage	Rating
456	1880	Normal	1,008,362*	R
456A	1880	With Arabic 1 in REGINA	Incl. in above	R3
457	1883	Normal	2,807,411	C
458	1884	Normal	1,121,600	N
459	1885	Normal	4,533,605	C
459A	1885/3	Overdate 5 over 3	Incl. in above	R3
459B	1886	Proof (WR358)	Very few	R6
463C	1887	Proof (WR359, WR360)	Very few	R6

*This mintage figure includes those of the Type IB half-sovereign of the same date.

THE BRANCH MINTS

An Order in Council of August 19, 1853 authorised the establishment of the first Branch Mint in Sydney. However, many problems were still to be resolved, including the building of the new Branch Mint itself. In the meantime patterns for the new gold coinage were being prepared in London. The Sydney Branch Mint of the Royal Mint was completed and officially opened on May 14, 1855.

The obverse of the First Bust type half-sovereign from the new mint was very similar to the existing Royal Mint design being struck in London, which was the work of James Wyon, whereas the reverse was a very different new Australian design by his nephew Leonard Wyon. The reverse, except for AUSTRALIA that was placed centrally across the whole of the coin, was very similar to the then current English shilling. The First Type bust was only issued as currency for the years of 1855 and 1856 and was widely known as the filleted head, but from then on it failed to meet with approval.

A new Second type bust was introduced in 1857 and both obverse and reverse are the work of Leonard Wyon; the slightly smaller bust this time features the hair of Victoria gathered up into a knot behind with a wreath of native Banksia. The reverse is the same as the First Type coinage and this Second type half-sovereign continued to be struck until 1866.

The First Type of the Sydney Branch Mint (Australia) half-sovereigns consists of only two issues, 1855 and 1866, and because only 21,000 half-sovereigns were issued bearing the date of 1855, it is an extremely rare coin and is the rarer of the two dates by far, and it seldom appears at auctions or on dealers' lists. If an example does appear, even in the lowest of grades, it will cost a very large sum to acquire. The second coin of 1856 is very rare, especially if found in the better grades, but with 470,000 of these half-sovereigns being struck they do occasionally appear, so at least the type collector may be lucky. However, if it appears in any of the top grades it will cost at best a large four figure sum.

The Second Type half-sovereigns from this Branch Mint are much more interesting for the enthusiast and they do produce a larger choice, but even though there are thirteen different varieties and dates the collector will need a deep pocket for sure, but at least coins from this series will be available. The major rarity of this group is the 1858 M.383A with the extraordinary error that shows an R in place of the first E in the denomination and so reads HALF SOVRREIGN, which is simply beyond belief. It must have been spotted back in London at the Royal Mint very quickly, and new dies would have been prepared immediately and sent off to Sydney, therefore not many examples of this error will exist. It seems this particular error coin was first discovered by the Sydney dealer Barry Sparkes and published in the *Australian Coin Review* of December 1994.

It is interesting to record some details from the Royal Mint Report of 1870 which includes a report from the Deputy Master C. Elouis of the Sydney Branch Mint. In this report it states that in 1867 62,000 half-sovereigns were struck and then in 1869 a further 154,000 of the same coins were again prepared. However, in spite of these known facts relating to these particular years, no half-sovereigns bearing the dates of 1867 and 1869 are known, so it is very likely that earlier existing dies may well have been used. This suggestion is perhaps endorsed because we know that Royal Mint records state that no half-sovereigns were issued for 1862, 1864 and 1866. However, the Sydney Branch Mint struck just over eight million sovereigns for these same years, so it is not unreasonable to suggest that half-sovereign dies may well have been provided also for this period. Therefore if these dies were actually used then perhaps it would account for the Australian mintage figures given for these years. What we do know for certain is that half-sovereigns bearing all three of these year dates do exist.

Some early Sydney Branch Mint gold coins appear to be different and vary in colour due to alloy composition for these coins. The important part is the 8.33% alloy of silver, and it is this that gave a different, more yellow, colour and finish. The inclusion of silver was simply because it was already in the raw gold, but it still produced the required (22 carat 916.6 fine) specification even though it could not be removed. However, an assayer at the Sydney Branch Mint, Francis Bowyer Miller, eventually developed a method to remove the silver content. So from then on all Imperial gold coinage struck at the Branch Mints remained at 22 carat 916.6 fine, but the alloy of 8.33% silver was removed and replaced with the same quantity of copper giving a more reddish tinge.

The first of the Imperial Type ID half-sovereigns to be struck at the Sydney Branch Mint bears the date of 1871, and it is well worth quoting the Royal Mint Report of 1872. In the text a separate report of the Sydney Branch Mint is included, submitted by the Deputy Master C. Elouis, dated September 6, 1872. The second to last paragraph on page 50, reads as follows: *"On the 14 January 1871 a Royal Proclamation was issued, giving currency to gold coins made at the Branch Mint at Sydney, New South Wales, of the like designs as those approved for the corresponding coins of the currency of the United Kingdom, and in accordance therewith, the gold coins issued from this Branch of the Royal Mint are (with the exception of an identifying Mint mark) identical with the gold coins issued from the parent establishment"*.

For these Imperial sovereigns there were five types of obverse used by the Sydney Branch Mint between 1871 and 1887.

Type 1 was used at the start for the dates 1871 and 1872 only and was concurrent with the second, larger young head of the London series of this period. The relative position of the bust has the nose of Queen Victoria point towards the left side of the O in VICTORIA, variety 2B. A variation occurs for the year 1872 in that the alignment is slightly rotated with the nose then pointing towards the T of the Queen's name. The inner rim of these obverses carries 117 denticles in the border.

1872 also marks the juncture of what is the Type 2 obverse, a one date only occurrence where the inner border rim has an increased number of denticles to a total of 123 giving the impression of finer graining to the rim.

There is then a gap in half-sovereign production until the date of 1875 which introduces a new obverse, Type 3, again for the one date only, which has a slightly increased size to the bust coupled with an even finer appearance to the border rim as it now contains 146 denticles.

As half-sovereigns were clearly not needed every year there was then another gap in production until the date of 1879 which again produced a new obverse, Type 4, also of a larger bust type but now with a narrower front hair band.

The subsequent date of 1880 then introduces another new obverse, Type 5, which then continues until 1887, the end of the Young Head period. In this type, the bust again appears a little larger and this can be seen by the lack of a definable gap between the hair bun and the G of GRATIA, and the front of the truncation descends very close to the 1 of the date. For 1883 and for some of the 1882-dated issue this type of head is struck in a lower relief.

The reverses of the Sydney issues during this period also have a few minor variations. Those dated 1871 and 1872 have the raised dot on the cross bar of the shield divisions as shown on page 184. From 1875 onwards this dot disappears. For the dates 1880, 1881, 1882, and 1883 the reverse legend and flower stops move a little closer to the rim border and the cross on top of the crown can be either buried in that border, or on a variation it can be clear of the border. For the final dates of 1886 and 1887 the cross is always buried in the border. Another reverse variation that has emerged from recent research by Les Robinson is the broken letter I in REGINA which gives the impression of the use of an "Arabic 1" in the legend. This variety occurs for half sovereigns dated 1880, 1881, 1882 and 1883.

A new Branch Mint of the Royal Mint was officially opened in Melbourne on June 12, 1872. The Royal Mint Report of 1873 includes two reports from the new Deputy

Master, Mr E. W. Ward, for the years of 1872 and 1873, and it appears from the first report that no half-sovereigns were struck in this opening year, although 748,000 sovereigns were produced. However, Ward's report for 1873 indicates that a total of 165,034 half-sovereigns were struck along with 752,000 sovereigns, so it seems that this new Branch Mint of Melbourne was quickly getting into its stride. But a gap of three years then elapsed before the next issue in 1877. However, similar circumstances again occurred and as a result the next half-sovereign was not struck until 1881. Except for 1883 the coin was then struck for each consecutive year until 1887, the year in which the special Golden Jubilee issue also appeared.

It is interesting to note that during the final six years of the Melbourne Type IE series of half-sovereigns the mintage figures are very low, and the total number issued was in fact only 310,564 pieces. The Sydney Branch Mint mintage figures for the same coins are higher but they too can only be considered as mostly on the low side, and analysis of these figures has endorsed the rarity of both these Branch Mint half-sovereigns.

Description and details of the Queen Vctoria Sydney Branch Mint AUSTRALIA type half-sovereign with First type bust

First Type bust 1855 and 1856 engraved by James Wyon; reverse by L. C. Wyon.

Obverse: Young head of Victoria to left. Hair bound with double fillet and collected into a knot behind. Legend: VICTORIA D:G: BRITANNIAR:REGINA F:D: Date below truncation.

Reverse: AUSTRALIA across the centre with a small crown above. A branch of laurel leaves on either side at the bottom held by a knotted bow. HALF SOVEREIGN at the bottom, and SYDNEY MINT shown across the top.

Edge: Milled.

The coin is struck with a reverse die axis ↑↓.

SYDNEY BRANCH MINT HALF-SOVEREIGNS OF QUEEN VICTORIA
AUSTRALIA REVERSE. FIRST TYPE BUST

No.	Date	Type/Variety	Mintage	Rating
378	1853	Pattern	Very few	R7
379	1855	Pattern	Very few	R7
380	1855	Normal	21,000	R3
381	1856	Normal	470,000	R
381A	1856	Rev. no berry above L of HALF in wreath	Incl. in above	R4
381AA	1856/5	Overdate 6 over 5	Incl. in above	R4

THE GOLD SOVEREIGN SERIES

Description and details of the Queen Victoria Sydney Branch Mint AUSTRALIA type half-sovereign with Second type bust

Obverse and reverse engraved by Leonard C. Wyon.

Obverse: Smaller Young head of Victoria to left. Hair collected by a wreath of native Banksia part of which drops down the face, and then secures knot behind. Legend: VICTORIA D:G: BRITANNIAR: REG:F:D: Date below truncation.

Reverse: AUSTRALIA across the centre with a small crown above. A branch of laurel leaves on either side at the bottom held by a knotted bow. HALF SOVEREIGN at the bottom, and SYDNEY MINT shown across the top.

Edge: Milled.

The coin is struck with a reverse die axis ↑↓.

SYDNEY BRANCH MINT HALF-SOVEREIGNS OF QUEEN VICTORIA
AUSTRALIA REVERSE, SECOND TYPE BUST

No.	Date	Type/Variety	Mintage	Rating
381B	1856	Pattern	Very few	R6
382	1857	Normal	537,000	C
382A	1857/5	Obv. Overdate 7 over 5	Incl. in above	R4
382B	1857	Plain edge proof	Very few	R6
382C	1857	Inverted A for V in VICTORIA error	Incl. in above	R3
383	1858	Normal	483,000	C
383A*	1858	SOVRREIGN error legend on reverse	Incl. in above	R4
383B	1858	RFG for REX error on obverse	Incl. in above	R3
383C	1858	Inverted A for V in SOVEREIGN error	Incl. in above	R3
383D	1858	Inverted A for V in VICTORIA error	Incl. in above	R3
384	1859	Normal	341,000	S
384A	1859/8	Obv. Overdate 9 over 8	Incl. in above	R4
385	1860	Normal	156,000	R
386	1861	Normal	186,500	R
386A	1861/0	Obv. Overdate 1 over 0, or rotated 6	Incl. in above	R3
386B	1861	First D on obverse struck over a rotated D	Incl. in above	R3
386C	1861	Rev. no berry above L of HALF in wreath	Incl. in above	R3
387	1862	Normal	210,000	S
387A	1862	Obv. High 6 in date	Incl. in above	R2
388	1863	Normal	348,500	R
389	1864	Normal	282,000	S
389A	1864	Obv. Roman I in date, probably over inverted 1 (?)	Incl. in above	R4
390	1865	Normal	100,000	R2
391	1866	Normal	216,000	R

* This error spelling has had an attempt to correct it with E struck over the first erroneous R.

HALF-SOVEREIGNS OF VICTORIA, 1837–1901

Description and details of the Queen Victoria Type ID Shield reverse type half-sovereign, Sydney Branch Mint (mint mark S)

Obverse: Young head of Victoria to left by William Wyon. Hair bound with double fillet and collected into knot behind. Legend: VICTORIA DEI GRATIA. Date below truncation.

Reverse: The Ensigns Armorial of the United Kingdom within a garnished shield surmounted by a crown, with dot A small flower stop appears in the field either side of the lower garnishing at the bottom of the coin. Legend: BRITANNIARUM REGINA FID:DEF. Mint mark S below.

Edge: Milled.

The coin is struck with a reverse die axis ↑↓.

TYPE ID. SYDNEY BRANCH MINT HALF-SOVEREIGNS OF QUEEN VICTORIA, SHIELD REVERSE (MINT MARK "S")

No.	Date	Type/Variety	Mintage	Rating
460	1871	Obv. 1. (117 denticles) Second larger young head. Date below. Rev. Garnished shield with dot	160,000	S
461	1872	Obv. 1. Victoria's nose points to T in legend*	356,000	S
461A	1872	Obv. 2. (123 denticles)	Incl. in above	S
462	1875	Obv. 3. (146 denticles) Slightly larger bust. Rev. no dot	312,000	S
463	1879	Obv. 4. Larger bust. Hair ribbon narrow	220,000	S
464	1880	Obv. 5. Legend and flower stops close to heavier border. Rev. cross on crown buried in border	80,000	R
464A	1880	Obv. 5. Rev. cross on crown clear of border	Incl. in above	R3
464B	1880	Proof	Very few	R6
464C	1880	Rev. Arabic 1 in REGINA	Incl. in above	R3
465	1881	Rev. cross on crown buried in heavier border	62,000	R2
465A	1881	Rev. cross on crown clear of border	Incl. in above	R3
465B	1881	Rev. Arabic 1 in REGINA	Incl. in above	R3
466	1882	Rev. cross on crown buried in heavier border	52,000	R
466A	1882	Obv. 5. Struck in low relief. Date below. Rev. cross on crown clear of border	Incl. in above	R7
466B	1882	Rev. Arabic 1 in REGINA	Incl. in above	R3
467	1883	Rev. cross on crown buried in heavier border	221,000	S
467A	1883	Obv. 5. Struck in low relief. Date below. Rev. cross on crown clear of border	Incl. in above	R2
467AA	1883	Rev. Arabic 1 in REGINA	Incl. in above	R2
467B	1883	Proof	Very few	R6
468	1886	Obv. 5. Struck as normal. Rev. cross on crown buried in heavier border	82,000	R
469	1887	Rev. cross on crown buried in heavier border	33,500**	S
469A	1887	Obv. 5 with Rev. 3 cross cleat of border	Incl. in above	R3
469B	1887	Pattern in silver	2	R7

*This slight turning of the bust position occurs only in this year.

**Total mintage for 1887 is 134,000, i.e. 33,500 Young head plus 100,500 Jubilee bust.

Description and details of Queen Victoria Type IE Shield reverse half-sovereign, Melbourne Branch Mint (mint mark M)

Obverse engraved by William Wyon, reverse by J. B. Merlen.

Obverse: Young head of Victoria to left. Hair bound with double fillet and collected into knot behind. Legend: VICTORIA DEI GRATIA. Date below truncation. As Type IA.

Reverse: The Ensigns Armorial of the United Kingdom within a garnished shield (no dot) surmounted by a crown. A small flower stop appears in the field either side of the lower garnishing at the bottom of the coin. Legend: BRITANNIARUM REGINA FID:DEF: Mint mark M below garnishing.

Edge: Milled.

The coin is struck with a reverse die axis ↑↓.

TYPE IE SHIELD REVERSE HALF-SOVEREIGNS OF QUEEN VICTORIA (MELBOURNE MINT: MINT MARK "M")

No.	Date	Type/ Variety	Mintage	Rating
470	1873	Obv. 3	165,034	S
471	1877	Obv. 3. Larger bust with narrow hair ribbon	80,016	R
471A	1877	Obv. 4	Incl. in above	R
472	1881	Obv. 5. Largest bust in low relief	42,081	R2
473	1882	Obv. 5. 146 denticles in beaded border, thicker truncation at right	107,522	R
473A	1882	Obv. 6. 144 denticles in beaded border, bust with thinner truncation. Indent to truncation above upright of 1 in date	Incl. in above	R3
474	1884	Obv. 5	48,084	R2
474A	1884	Proof	Very few	R6
475	1885	Obv. 5	11,085	R3
476	1886	Obv. 5	38,086	R2
476A	1886	Proof	Very few	R6
477	1887	Obv. 5 combined with Rev 4	9,155*	R3
477A	1887	Obv. 5 combined with Rev 3	Incl. in above	R6

*Total mintage for 1887 is 64,013, i.e. 9,155 Young head plus 54,858 Jubilee bust.

OBVERSE AND REVERSE VARIATIONS OF THE BRANCH MINT HALF SOVEREIGN

Obverse Type 1. nose pointing below O of VICTORIA. 117 short denticles, widely spaced

Obverse Type 2. Legend repositioned, nose pointing below T of VICTORIA. 123 denticles

Obverse Type 3. Legend again repositioned with nose pointing below O but I of DEI now above second hair ribbon. 146 denticles

Obverse Type 4. Narrow ribbon. 1879S and 1877M have 146 denticles, 1882M has 144 denticles

Obverse Type 5. Low relief, wide head, top of hair close to G of GRATIA. Wide, coarse border, thicker lettering and date. No tragus lobe. 136 denticles

Reverse Type 1. Top of cross clear of border. Dot on vertical line of shield. 120 denticles

Reverse Type 2. Top of cross touches border. Redesigned shield with dot missing from vertical line. 122 denticles

Reverse Type 3. As Type 1 but without dot. Cross touches border. 147 denticles

Reverse Type 4. Wide coarse border of 148 denticles. Top of cross buried in border. Bottom rosettes close to border

249

JUBILEE HALF-SOVEREIGNS OF QUEEN VICTORIA

The first half-sovereign bearing the new Boehm bust, introduced for the Queen's Golden Jubilee, shows the Queen facing left wearing a small crown, veiled and with ribbon and star of the Order of the Garter and the Order of Victoria and Albert. Boehm's initials, J.E.B. (Joseph Edgar Boehm), appear at the bottom on the Queen's shoulder. The reverse once more displays the heavily garnished shield surmounted by the crown, but the flower stops have been omitted to allow space for the date, 1887, which is now moved to the reverse. The legend remains the same as before.

The Golden Jubilee half-sovereigns were struck at the Royal Mint in London from 1887 to 1893 but none were struck for 1888 or 1889. The Melbourne Branch Mint also struck the Jubilee half-sovereigns, but only for the years 1887 and 1893. The Sydney Branch Mint produced Jubilee issue half-sovereigns for the years 1887, 1889 and 1891.

As in the sovereign series the engraver's initials that appear on the obverse of all the coins are an interesting area for study as there are several variations to note which have all been defined further by David Iverson and Steve Hill in *The Jubilee Head Gold Half-Sovereign 1887–93* published by Sovereign Rarities in 2019. For example smaller letter punches for J.E.B. have been used on some of the first issues, including both Melbourne and Sydney coins, also the spacing of the initials varies on some coins.

There are two different reverse types, the normal "High shield" type and the "Low Shield" types and it is interesting to note that both are coins struck in London and so neither displays a mint mark. The raising of the shield has been done quite deliberately to accommodate the Australian mint marks below the garnishing.

Mintage figures relating to the Royal Mint Jubilee half-sovereigns are very high as one would expect, and they do in fact reveal that well over 22 million were struck for the period of issue. Perhaps surprisingly the first year, 1887, produced the lowest figures of 841,200 coins struck, so in general the collector should be able to acquire these coins quite easily although it is becoming scarce. However, coins from the branch mints of Melbourne and Sydney will not be easy for the collector to acquire, mainly because the mintage figures for both of these branch mints were quite low.

Victoria Jubilee Head half-sovereign varieties

London—J.E.B. truncation varieties

| No. 478A | No. 478B | No. 478C | No. 478D |
| (DISH L502) | (DISH L503) | (DISH L504) | (DISH L505) |

No. 478E
(DISH L506)

No. 478F
(DISH L508)

Melbourne, Australia—J.E.B. truncation varieties

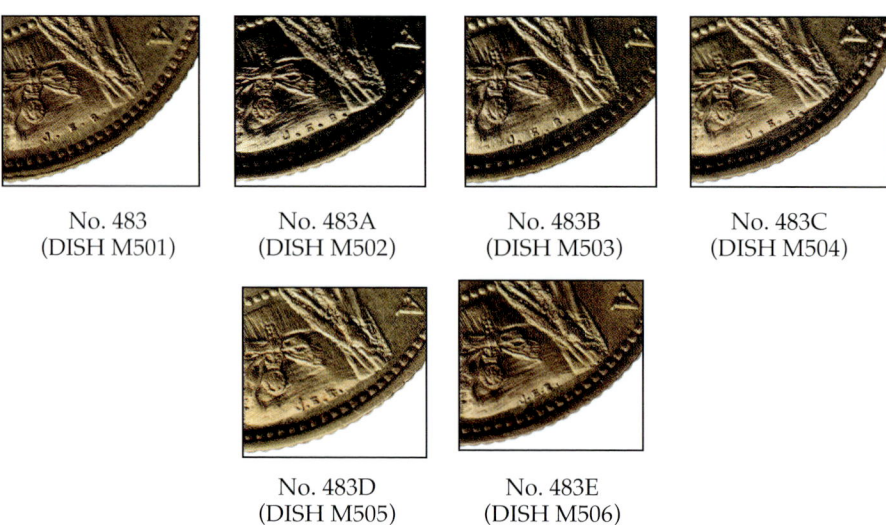

| No. 483 | No. 483A | No. 483B | No. 483C |
| (DISH M501) | (DISH M502) | (DISH M503) | (DISH M504) |

No. 483D
(DISH M505)

No. 483E
(DISH M506)

Victoria Jubilee Head half-sovereign varieties *continued*

Sydney, Australia—J.E.B. truncation varieties

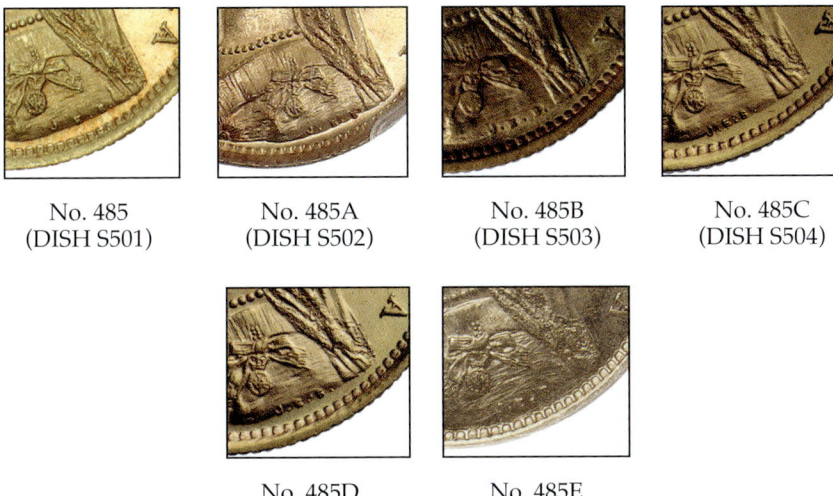

No. 485
(DISH S501)

No. 485A
(DISH S502)

No. 485B
(DISH S503)

No. 485C
(DISH S504)

No. 485D
(DISH S505)

No. 485E
(DISH S506)

Description and details of Queen Victoria Jubilee Head half-sovereign, London Mint (no mint mark)

Obverse: The bust of the Queen facing left wearing a small crown, veiled and with ribbon and star of the Order of the Garter and the Order of Victoria and Albert. Boehm's initials J.E.B. are shown in relief on the bottom of the shoulder. Legend: VICTORIA DEI GRATIA.

Reverse: The Ensigns Armorial within a garnished shield surmounted by an imperial crown. Legend: BRITANNIARUM REGINA FID:DEF: The date is shown below the shield.

Edge: Milled.
The coin is struck with medal die axis ↑↑.

JUBILEE HALF-SOVEREIGNS OF QUEEN VICTORIA
(LONDON MINT: NO MINT MARK)

No.	Date	Type/Variety	Mintage	Rating
478	1887	Obv. no initials on truncation, high shield on reverse (DISH L501)	c. 10,188	R2
478A	1887	Obv. hooked J type, close initials on truncation, stops at junction with field (DISH L502)	c. 3,397	R5
478B	1887	Obv. hooked J type, close initials on truncation, bottom of letters and stops at junction with field (DISH L503)	c. 3,397	R5
478C	1887	Obv. hooked J type, wider spread initials on truncation, the J only at junction with field (DISH L504)	c. 3,397	R6
478D	1887	Obv. hooked J type, close initials on truncation, E. only at junction with field, J double struck (DISH L505)	c. 3,397	R6
478E	1887	Obv. hooked J type, close initials on truncation, J. lower than E.B. (DISH L506)	c. 3,397	R6
478EE	1887	Obv. hooked J. type, spread initials on truncation (DISH L507)	—	R7
478F	1887	Obv. imperfect J type initials, rev. high shield (DISH L508)	841,200	C
478G	1887	Proof (WR362)	797	S
479	1890	Obv. no initials, rev. high shield (DISH L509)	1,586,217	C
479A	1890	Obv. no initials, rev. low shield (DISH L511)	c. 339,903	R
479B	1890	Obv. imperfect J type initials, rev. low shield (DISH L512)	c. 339,903	R
480	1891	Obv. no initials, rev. low shield (DISH L513)	1,087,884	S
480A	1891	Obv. no initials, rev. high shield (DISH...)	Incl. in above	R5
480B	1891	Obv. imperfect J type initials, rev. low shield (DISH...)	Incl. in above	R6
481	1892	Obv. no initials, rev. high shield (DISH L514)	684,024	R
481A	1892	Obv. no initials, rev. low shield (DISH L516)	12,971,499	C
481B	1892	Obv. imperfect J type initials, rev. low shield (DISH L517)	24,963	R6
482	1893	Obv. no initials, rev. low shield (DISH L518)	186,218*	S

*This figure is 4.2% of the mintage of 1893 half sovereigns, the remaining 95.8% were made up of Old head type.
Note: The existence of DISH L510 and L515 (1890 and 1892 imperfect J, high shield types) are unconfirmed at the time of publication.

HALF-SOVEREIGNS OF VICTORIA, 1837–1901

Description and details of Queen Victoria Jubilee Head half-sovereign, Melbourne Branch Mint (mint mark M)

Obverse: The bust of the Queen facing left wearing a small crown, veiled and with ribbon and star of the Order of the Garter and the Order of Victoria and Albert. Boehm's initials J.E.B. are shown in relief on the bottom of the shoulder. Legend: VICTORIA DEI GRATIA.

Reverse: The Ensigns Armorial within a garnished shield surmounted by an imperial crown. Legend: BRITANNIARUM REGINA FID:DEF: The date is shown below the shield. Mint Mark M below lower garnishing bisecting date.

Edge: Milled.

The coin is struck with medal die axis ↑↑.

JUBILEE HALF-SOVEREIGNS OF QUEEN VICTORIA (MELBOURNE MINT: MINT MARK "M")

No.	Date	Type/Variety	Mintage	Rating
483	1887	Obv. hooked J type, wide spread initials on truncation, B. intrudes into field (DISH M501)	c. 9,143	R4
483A	1887	Obv. hooked J type, widespread initials on truncation, B. at junction of truncation with field (DISH M502)	c. 9,143	R4
483B	1887	Obv. hooked J type, closer initials on truncation E. at junction of truncation with field (DISH M503)	c.9,143	R4
483C	1887	Obv. hooked J type, closer initials on truncation B. intrudes into field (DISH M504)	c. 9,143	R4
483D	1887	Obv. hooked J type, very close initials on truncation E. intrudes into field (DISH M505)	c. 9,413	R4
483E	1887	Obv. hooked J type, very close initials, letters at junction of truncation with field (DISH M506)	c. 9413	R4
483F	1889	Proof, plain edge	Very few	R7
483G	1890	Proof, with initials, low shield	Very few	R6
484	1893	Obv. imperfect J initials, rev. low shield (DISH M507)	110,024	R2

Detail showing the position of the "High" and "Low" shields on the reverse of the London Mint half-sovereigns.

255

THE GOLD SOVEREIGN SERIES

Description and details of Queen Victoria Jubilee Head half-sovereign, Sydney Branch Mint (mint mark S)

Obverse: The bust of the Queen facing left wearing a small crown, veiled and with ribbon and star of the Order of the Garter and the Order of Victoria and Albert. Boehm's initials J.E.B. are shown in relief on the bottom of the shoulder. Legend: VICTORIA DEI GRATIA.

Reverse: The Ensigns Armorial within a garnished shield surmounted by an imperial crown. Legend: BRITANNIARUM REGINA FID:DEF: The date is shown below the shield. Mint Mark S below lower garnishing.

Edge: Milled.

The coin is struck with medal die axis ↑↑.

HALF-SOVEREIGNS OF QUEEN VICTORIA (SYDNEY MINT: MINT MARK S)

No.	Date	Type/Variety	Mintage	Rating
485	1887	Obv. hooked J, wider spread initials, higher J (DISH S501)	c. 20,100	R4
485A	1887	Obv. hooked J, wider spread initials, B intrudes into field (DISH S502)	c. 20,100	R4
485B	1887	Obv. hooked J, closer initials, B more distant (DISH S503)	c. 20,100	R2
485C	1887	Obv. hooked J, closer initials, J intrudes into field (DISH S504)	c. 20,100	R4
485D	1887	Obv. hooked J, closer initials, B intrudes into field (DISH S505)	c. 20,100	R4
485F	1887	Proof, plain edge, imperfect angled JEB	Very few	R6
486	1889	Obv. imperfect J initials, rev. low shield (DISH S507)	64,000	R2
487	1891	Obv. no initials, rev. high shield (DISH S508)	130,900	R
487A	1891	Obv. imperfect J initials, rev. high shield (DISH S509)	23,100	R3
487B	1893	Proof, plain edge	Very few	R7

Note: DISH S506 remains physically unconfirmed.

OLD OR VEILED HEAD HALF-SOVEREIGNS OF QUEEN VICTORIA

Queen Victoria herself chose the effigy by Thomas Brock which featured on the half-sovereign for the first time dated 1893. The Queen is seen in much older form, veiled and draped. The legend includes, for the first time, IND. IMP. (Empress of India). These letters were added because of a Proclamation of 1876 concerning the Provisions of Royal Titles. For the first time the reverse of the half-sovereign now portrays Benedetto Pistrucci's legendary design of St George slaying the dragon. However, it should be noted that Pistrucci's initials B.P. do not appear on the half-sovereigns.

The half-sovereigns for this last period of Victoria's reign were struck at the London Mint, Melbourne Mint, Sydney Mint and, for the first time, at the new Branch Mint in Perth, Western Australia. The collector should not find a problem in acquiring any of the half-sovereigns struck at the London Mint, and this is because for every new year of issue mintage figures were never less than two million coins and some years were in fact well in excess of four million. However, even with these very high mintage figures, today, coins of this type can be very difficult to find in choice condition.

All the coins from the branch mints may present problems because in the main their mintage figures were quite low. The Melbourne Branch Mint half-sovereign of 1893 (M.497) is probably one of the rarest in the whole series—the Royal Australian Mint does have an example of it, but few other pieces are known. In his report for 1893, George Anderson, Deputy Master of the Melbourne Branch Mint, does in fact reveal, in Appendix D, that only 110,024 half-sovereigns were issued. The 1896 issue from this mint may be relatively easy to find but the two later issues could well be very costly. The three Sydney Branch Mint half-sovereigns are all rare, especially in high grades, but they are available although the cost could prove prohibitive.

Description and details of the Queen Victoria Old Head half-sovereign, London Mint (no mint mark)

Obverse: The bust of the Queen facing left, crowned, veiled and draped, wearing ribbon and star of the Order of the Garter. The small letters T.B. appear below the bust. Legend: VICTORIA.DEI.GRA. BRITT.REGINA.FID.DEF.IND.IMP.

Reverse: St George slaying the dragon with sword. The date is shown below the exergue/ground line. The initials B.P. for Benedetto Pistrucci do not appear on this type.

Edge: Milled.

The coin is struck with medal die axis ↑↑.

OLD HEAD HALF-SOVEREIGNS OF QUEEN VICTORIA (LONDON MINT: NO MINT MARK)

No.	Date	Type/Variety	Mintage	Rating
488	1893	Normal	4,392,418	C
488A	1893	Proof (WR363)	773	S
489	1894	Normal	3,794,591	C
490	1895	Normal	2,869,183	C
491	1896	Normal	2,946,605	C
492	1897	Normal	3,568,156	C
493	1898	Normal	2,868,527	C
494	1899	Normal	3,361,881	C
495	1900	Normal	4,307,372	C
496	1901	Normal	2,037,664	C

Description and details of the Queen Victoria Old Head half-sovereign, Melbourne Branch Mint (mint mark M)

Obverse: The bust of the Queen facing left, crowned, veiled and draped, wearing ribbon and star of the Order of the Garter. The small letters T.B. appear below the bust. Legend: VICTORIA.DEI.GRA. BRITT.REGINA.FID.DEF.IND.IMP.

Reverse: St George slaying the dragon with sword. The date is shown below the exergue/ground line. The initials B.P. for Benedetto Pistrucci do not appear on this type. Mint mark M in ground line.

Edge: Milled.
The coin is struck with medal die axis ↑↑.

OLD HEAD HALF-SOVEREIGNS OF QUEEN VICTORIA (MELBOURNE MINT: MINT MARK M)

No.	Date	Type/Variety	Mintage	Rating
497	1893	Normal (132 denticles in beaded border on obv.)	110,024	R6
497A	1893	Proof	Very few	R7
498	1896	With 1893 obv. (132 denticles in beaded border with D of DEF and I of IND pointing to bead)	218,946	R3
498A	1896	Normal (134 denticles in beaded border with D of DEF and I of IND pointing to space)	Incl. in above	S
498B	1896	Proof (134 denticles as M498A)	4	R6
498C	1898	Proof	4	R6
499	1899	Normal (132 denticles)	97,221	R2
499A	1899	Normal but with 134 denticles	Incl. in above	R5
499B	1899	Proof	Miniscule	R7
500	1900	Normal	112,920	R2
500A	1900	Normal, rev. with M mint mark central above 90 of date	Incl. in above	R2
500B	1901	Proof	2	R7

Description and details of the Queen Victoria Old Head half-sovereign, Perth Branch Mint (mint mark P)

Obverse: The bust of the Queen facing left, crowned, veiled and draped, wearing ribbon and star of the Order of the Garter. The small letters T.B. appear below the bust. Legend: VICTORIA.DEI.GRA.BRITT.REGINA.FID.DEF.IND.IMP.

Reverse: St George slaying the dragon with sword. The date is shown below the exergue/ground line. The initials B.P. for Benedetto Pistrucci do not appear on this type. Mint mark P in ground line.

Edge: Milled.

The coin is struck with medal die axis ↑↑.

OLD HEAD HALF-SOVEREIGNS OF QUEEN VICTORIA (PERTH MINT: MINT MARK P)

No.	Date	Type/Variety	Mintage	Rating
500C	1899	Proof	Unique	R7
501	1900	Normal	59,688	R2
501A	1901	Proof	c. 8	R7

Note: The P mint mark is often blundered and unclear.

HALF-SOVEREIGNS OF VICTORIA, 1837–1901

Description and details of the Queen Victoria Old Head half-sovereign, Sydney Branch Mint (mint mark S)

Obverse: The bust of the Queen facing left, crowned, veiled and draped, wearing ribbon and star of the Order of the Garter. The small letters T.B. appear below the bust. Legend: VICTORIA.DEI.GRA. BRITT.REGINA.FID.DEF.IND.IMP.

Reverse: St George slaying the dragon with sword. The date is shown below the exergue/ground line. The initials B.P. for Benedetto Pistrucci do not appear on this type. Mint mark S in ground line.

Edge: Milled.

The coin is struck with medal die axis ↑↑.

OLD HEAD HALF-SOVEREIGNS OF QUEEN VICTORIA (SYDNEY MINT: MINT MARK S)

No.	Date	Type/Variety	Mintage	Rating
502	1893	Normal	125,000	R
502A	1893	Proof, plain edge	Very few	R7
503	1897	Normal but with 1893 obv. (132 denticles in beaded border with D of DEF and I of IND pointing to bead)	Not known	R3
503A	1897	Normal (134 denticles in beaded border with D of DEF and I of IND pointing to space)	Not known	R
503B	1897	Proof (134 denticles)	3	R6
504	1899	Normal but with 1893 obv. (132 denticles in beaded border with D of DEF and I of IND pointing to bead). Exists?	Not known	R7
504A*	1900	Normal but with 1893 obv. (132 denticles in beaded border with D of DEF and I of IND pointing to bead)	130,000	R3
504B*	1900	Normal (134 denticles in beaded border with D of DEF and I of IND pointing to space)	Incl. in above	R
504C*	1900	Normal, rev. with S mint mark central above 90 of date	Incl. in above	R2

Note: The mintage figures for 1893 and 1900 are confirmed by the Deputy Master, E. H. S. Von Arnheim, in the Sydney Branch Mint reports for these years. However, similar reports were also submitted for the years of 1898 and 1899, and these indicate a further issue of 50,000 and 65,000 half-sovereigns, respectively. As no half-sovereigns are known to exist with dates for these years, it has been suggested that possibly existing dies dated 1897 may have been used. Although Von Arnheim's report for 1897 does not include any half-sovereigns being issued, there is ample evidence that half-sovereigns dated 1897 do exist.

* These were previously incorrectly numbered 505, 505A and 505B (they correctly appear as part of the Edward VII series).

Reverse A of the Edward VII half-sovereign. Note the ground line is well away from the edge.

Reverse B of the Edward VII half-sovereign. Note the initials B.P. now appear.

EDWARD VII, 1901–10

The first half-sovereign for Edward VII was struck in 1902 featuring the bust of the monarch to the right with the initials of the engraver, De S for De Saulles, below the truncation. There are two different reverses which are referred to simply as A and B.

Reverse A. 1902–04. On this first reverse of St George slaying the dragon a clear space can be seen all around the image, and this is very noticeable behind the rear of the flowing cloak. This is again apparent in front of the dragon's lower foot, and the exergue line stops well short of the border leaving a clear space at each end. The same line is also shown considerably thicker, and the two reins coming from under the horse's head quickly merge into one. The date is below the exergue line but Pistrucci's initials B.P. do not appear on this type A reverse.

Reverse B. 1904–10. This time the design of St George slaying the dragon has been slightly enlarged, and so the rear folds of the cloak are now almost touching the border as does the lower foot of the dragon. The exergue line is thinner and now almost touches the border on both sides, and the reins of the horse continue as a pair right up to the horse's chest. The dragon's wings have been re-designed, and the one nearer to the head is increased in size causing it to touch the dragon's neck. St George's sword is shown at a slightly lower angle, and Pistrucci's initials B.P. are placed to the right of the date below the exergue line.

The half-sovereigns dated 1904 from the London Mint and the Perth Branch Mint can both be found with either A or B reverse. The Melbourne Branch Mint only used Reverse B whilst the two reverses are found on the half-sovereigns from Perth and Sydney.

Good examples of all dates struck by the London Mint are readily available. However, the branch mint coins can be a problem, especially any of the three dates from the Perth Branch Mint in extremely fine or better grades. The first of the Melbourne or Sydney issues are also rare and in extremely fine or better grade will be quite difficult to find.

Description and details of the Edward VII half-sovereign, London Mint (no mint mark}

Obverse. The bare head of the King facing right. The small letters De S (for De Saulles) below the truncation in relief. Legend: EDWARDVS VII D:G:BRITT:OMN:REX F:D:IND:IMP:
Reverse: A or B. St George slaying the dragon. Date below the exergue line.*
Edge: Milled.
The coin is struck with medal die axis ↑↑.

HALF-SOVEREIGNS OF EDWARD VII (LONDON MINT: NO MINT MARK)

No.	Date	Type/Variety	Mintage	Rating
505*	1902	Rev. A no B.P.	4,244,457	C
505A*	1902	Matt proof (WR411)	Not known	N
505B*	1902	Non-matt finish proof (WR410)	Not known	R6
506	1903	Normal	2,522,057	C
507	1904	Normal	1,717,440	N
507A	1904	Rev. B with B.P.	Not known	R
508	1905	Rev. B with B.P.	3,023,993	C
509	1906	Normal	4,245,437	C
509A	1906	Matt proof (WR412)	Not known	R6
510	1907	Normal	4,233,421	C
511	1908	Normal	3,996,992	C
512	1909	Normal	4,010,715	C
513	1910	Normal	5,023,881	C

* These numbers were previously additionally allocated to what are now 504A, 504B and 504C in the Victoria series.

HALF-SOVEREIGNS OF EDWARD VII, 1901–10

Description and details of the Edward VII half-sovereign, Melbourne Branch Mint (mint mark M}

Obverse. The bare head of the King facing right. The small letters De S (for De Saulles) below the truncation in relief. Legend: EDWARDVS VII D:G:BRITT:OMN:REX F:D:IND:IMP:

Reverse: B. St George slaying the dragon. Date below the exergue line. Mint mark M in centre of exergue line.*

Edge: Milled.

The coin is struck with medal die axis ↑↑.

HALF-SOVEREIGNS OF EDWARD VII
(MELBOURNE MINT: MINT MARK M)

No.	Date	Type/Variety	Mintage	Rating
514	1906	Rev. B with B.P.	82,042	R
515	1907*	Normal	Not known	N
516	1908	Normal	405,034	C
517	1909	Normal	186,094	N

***Note**. No official mintage figures are given for this date so it is likely that the figure for 1908 would have included those bearing the date of 1907.

Description and details of the Edward VII half-sovereign, Perth Branch Mint (mint mark P}

Obverse. The bare head of the King facing right. The small letters De S (for De Saulles) below the truncation in relief. Legend: EDWARDVS VII D:G:BRITT:OMN:REX F:D:IND:IMP:

Reverse: A or B. St George slaying the dragon. Date below the exergue line. Mint mark P in centre of exergue line.*

Edge: Milled.

The coin is struck with medal die axis ↑↑.

HALF-SOVEREIGNS OF EDWARD VII
(PERTH MINT: MINT MARK P)

No.	Date	Type/Variety	Mintage	Rating
518	1904	Rev. A no B.P.	60,030	R
518A	1904	Rev. B with B.P.	Not known	R
519	1908	Rev. B	24,668	R2
520	1909	Rev. B	44,022	R

Description and details of the Edward VII half-sovereign, Sydney Branch Mint (mint mark S}

Obverse. The bare head of the King facing right. The small letters De S (for De Saulles) below the truncation in relief. Legend: EDWARDVS VII D:G:BRITT:OMN:REX F:D:IND:IMP:
Reverse: St George slaying the dragon. Date below the exergue line. Mint mark S in centre of exergue line.*
Edge: Milled.
The coin is struck with medal die axis ↑↑.

HALF-SOVEREIGNS OF EDWARD VII
(SYDNEY MINT: MINT MARK S)

No.	Date	Type/Variety	Mintage	Rating
521	1902	Rev. A no B.P.	84,000	R
521A	1902	Matt proof	Not known	R6
522	1903	Rev. A	231,000	S
523	1906	Rev. B with B.P.	308,000	S
524	1908	Normal	538,000	N
525	1910	Normal	474,000	N

GEORGE V, 1910–36

The new half-sovereign of George V was first issued bearing the date of 1911, and the obverse displays the King bareheaded facing left with the initials of B.M. for Bertram Mackennal, the designer, shown in relief at the rear of the truncation. The reverse once more features Pistrucci's legendary design of St George slaying the dragon; the date is placed centrally below the exergue line and the initials B.P. for Benedetto Pistrucci appear on the far right side of the date.

No more currency half-sovereigns were struck at the Royal Mint for this reign after 1915 but they continued to be issued by the Australian branch mints of Melbourne, Perth and Sydney as well as at the new branch mint of Pretoria in South Africa. This new branch mint began business on January 1, 1923 but it is not until 1925 that the report of the Deputy Master, Mr R. Pearson, reveals the striking of 946,615 half-sovereigns. The following year, 1926, was to be the last year that half-sovereigns were struck there and although several million sovereigns were later struck, up to 1932, it ceased to operate as a branch mint in 1941. A branch mint also opened in Bombay in 1918, but no half-sovereigns were struck there .

Most of the George V half-sovereigns will not be difficult for the collector to find although there are a few dates which may be a little more difficult. However, coins from the branch mint of Perth deserve special mention as they only produced half-sovereigns for five years between 1911 and 1920 although they only bear three dates: 1911, 1915 and 1918. Those struck in 1919 and 1920 bear these earlier dates with the 1918 (M.534)—the existence of which was only discovered about 50 years ago—amongst the rarest within this small group, and although several examples exist, little else is known about them. However, the relevant Royal Mint reports for the branch mint of Perth includes some very useful information. In his report for 1918, under the heading *"Issues of gold"*, Deputy Master J. F. Campbell mentions an issue of *"3,812,884 sovereigns, half-sovereigns nil, gold bullion £7,327"*. This last item might well refer to the 1918 half-sovereign as no other information on this coin appear in the report. Campbell's report for 1919 does reveal, in the *"Issues of gold"* list, an issue of 113,572 half-sovereigns, presumably dated 1919. However, it is interesting to note in detail what he goes on to say: *"A considerable amount of coin and bullion produced at the Perth branch has, it is understood, been exported in the interests of the Gold Producers' Association. This includes the whole of the half-sovereigns produced and the whole of the Gold Bullion for Export. The exportation of half-sovereigns is unusual, and attention has been drawn to the fact that questions of policy might be involved if the demand reached large proportions"*.

Finally, Campbell's report for 1920 again reveals very interesting details, and in the *"Issues of gold"* section there is reference to an issue of 106,416 half-sovereigns. So these half-sovereigns were without doubt struck and there is no indication in the report to suggest that they were exported, as was the 1919 coinage. So only one question remains about these last two issues of half-sovereigns, and that is just how many of these two very small mintages have survived? These Half-Sovereigns from the outputs of mint activity for 1919 and 1920 were all with certainty struck dated 1918, as has been proven from the research by Howard Hodgson on the subject in *Coin News* April and May 2019, and most if not all of the mintage was exported to Asia (there is no export account for 55,000 of the quantity only). There was seemingly no output in the year 1918 itself, and some 1920-dated dies that were ordered from London arrived two months too late for the two January 1920 production journeys that account for the whole 1920 output. The 1918 Perth Half-Sovereign therefore has the highest mintage of Half-Sovereign from this mint, but the lowest survival rate, which remains an enigma.

The iconic St George and the dragon design also made an appearance on the £1 banknote issue of George V that effectively replaced the gold sovereign. The banknote illustrated was printed in 1917 and was the third issue signed by the then Chief Cashier John Bradbury. The reverse design depicts a superb engraving of the Houses of Parliament.

Description and details of the George V half-sovereign, London Mint

Obverse: The bare head of the King facing left. The small letters B.M. for Bertram Mackennal are shown in relief on the lower truncation towards the rear. Legend: GEORGIVS V D.G.BRITT:OMN:REX F.D.IND:IMP:

Reverse: St George slaying the dragon. Date is shown below the exergue line with the small letters B.P. for Benedetto Pistrucci to the right in relief.

Edge: Milled.

The coin is struck with medal die axis ↑↑.

GEORGE V HALF-SOVEREIGNS
(LONDON MINT: NO MINT MARK)

No.	Date	Type/Variety	Mintage	Rating
526	1911	Normal	6,104,106	C
526A	1911	Proof (WR418)	3,764	S
526B	1911	Matt proof (WR419)	Not known	R7
527	1912	Normal	6,224,316	C
528	1913	Normal	6,094,290	C
529	1914	Normal	7,251,124	C
530	1915	Normal	2,042,747	N

Description and details of the George V half-sovereign, Melbourne Branch Mint

Obverse: As London Mint.
Reverse: As London Mint except with mint mark M in centre of ground line above date.
Edge: Milled.
The coin is struck with medal die axis ↑↑.

GEORGE V HALF-SOVEREIGNS
(MELBOURNE MINT: MINT MARK M)

No.	Date	Type/Variety	Mintage	Rating
531	1915	Normal	125,664	N

Description and details of the George V half-sovereign, Perth Branch Mint
Obverse: As London Mint.
Reverse: As London Mint except with mint mark P in centre of ground line above date.
Edge: Milled.
The coin is struck with medal die axis ↑↑.

GEORGE V HALF-SOVEREIGNS
(PERTH MINT: MINT MARK P)

No.	Date	Type/Variety	Mintage	Rating
532	1911	Normal	130,373	R
533	1915	Normal	136,219	S
534	1918	Normal	Incl. below	R3
535	1919*	Normal	113,572	R3
536	1920*	Normal	106,416	R3

*All coins for these years were struck with the date 1918. See note on Perth half-sovereigns on page 269.

Description and details of the George V half-sovereign, Sydney Branch Mint

Obverse: As London Mint.
Reverse: As London Mint except with mint mark S in centre of ground line above date.
Edge: Milled.
The coin is struck with medal die axis ↑↑.

GEORGE V HALF-SOVEREIGNS (SYDNEY MINT: MINT MARK S)

No.	Date	Type/Variety	Mintage	Rating
537	1911	Normal	252,000	N
538	1912	Normal	278,000	N
539	1914	Normal	322,000	N
540	1915	Normal	892,000	C
541	1916	Normal	448,000	C

THE GOLD SOVEREIGN SERIES

Description and details of the George V half-sovereign, Pretoria Branch Mint
Obverse: As London Mint.
Reverse: As London Mint except with mint mark SA in centre of ground line above date.
Edge: Milled.
The coin is struck with medal die axis ↑↑.

GEORGE V HALF-SOVEREIGNS
(PRETORIA MINT, SOUTH AFRICA: MINT MARK SA)

No.	Date	Type/Variety	Mintage	Rating
541A	1923	Proof	655	R
542	1925	Normal	946,615	C
543	1926	Normal	806,540	C

EDWARD VIII (JANUARY–DECEMBER 1936)

No gold half sovereigns were struck for the reign of Edward VIII

GEORGE VI, 1936–52

No currency half-sovereigns were struck during the reign of George VI but a gold proof half-sovereign bearing the bust of George VI was issued for the Coronation and bears the date of 1937. The denominations struck were a five pound piece, two pound piece, sovereign and half-sovereign. All were plain edge proofs although technically they are patterns as they were never officially proclaimed as currency and only 5,501 pieces of each were struck.

The effigy for the obverse of these gold coins was modelled by Thomas Humphrey Paget (1893–1974) and the reverse once more features Pistrucci's iconic St George slaying the dragon.

Description and details of the George VI half-sovereign

Obverse: The bare head of the King to the left. The small letters H.P. standing for Humphrey Paget below truncation at rear. Legend: GEORGIVS VI D:G:BR:OMN:REX F:D:IND:IMP.
Reverse: St George slaying the dragon. Date below exergue line with B.P. for Benedetto Pistrucci to the right.
Edge: Plain.
The coin is struck to proof standard with mirror like fields, and medal die axis ↑↑.

GEORGE VI HALF-SOVEREIGNS LONDON MINT

No.	Date	Type/Variety	Mintage	Rating
543A	1937	Plain edge Proof (WR442)	5,501	S
543B	1937	Matt proof (WR443)	Miniscule	R6

ELIZABETH II, 1952–2022

The first gold coins struck for the reign of Elizabeth II were all proof coins bearing the date of 1953. These consisted of a five pound piece, two pound piece, sovereign and half-sovereign and only a few of each were struck for the National collections. The new obverse of Elizabeth II was the work of Mary Gillick. The reverse features Benedetto Pistrucci's famous design of St George slaying the dragon.

In 1957 the first bullion-type sovereigns were struck for the reign, however, no bullion-type half-sovereigns were struck for this period.

In 1974 a new bust of the Queen was introduced, the work of sculptor Arnold Machin (1911–99). The first half-sovereign of the reign bearing this portrait was a proof dated 1980; the currency issue dated 1982 is the only one of its kind from the third issue.

The fourth issue in 1985 saw the introduction of the third new portrait of the Queen with a new effigy designed by Raphael David Maklouf. The gold coinage of the new Maklouf busts consisted of a five pound piece, two pound piece, sovereign and half-sovereign, and most of the denominations were issued every year from 1985 to 1997 but some were used in the Royal Mint sets. However, all of these gold issues were only struck as proof coins, as was the Britannia pound series of gold, and none included any bullion issues of half-sovereigns.

1989 marked the 500th anniversary of the gold sovereign and to mark this special year the Royal Mint struck a five pound piece, two pound piece, sovereign and half-sovereign, all of the same design portraying Her Majesty the Queen seated on the Coronation throne, whilst the reverse shows the royal arms surmounted on a double rose. The coins, which were the work of sculptor Bernard Sindall, were struck to proof standard.

In 1998 the fifth bust, the work of sculptor and medallist Ian Rank-Broadley, FRBS, was introduced. He worked from photographs taken specially for coinage purposes by permission of Her Majesty. The new bust featured the Queen facing right wearing a tiara, with the letters I R B placed below the truncation. The new gold coinage was first struck bearing the date 1998, and it consisted of a five pound piece, two pound piece, sovereign and half-sovereign, and all were proof coins that were in the main issued in Royal Mint sets.

In 2000, for the first time since 1982, a bullion type half-sovereign was struck. The coin carries the Rank-Broadley bust of the Queen and has been struck for every year since, except 2002 when a special issue for her Majesty's Golden Jubilee with a shield-type reverse by Timothy Noad was issued and 2005 when there was another special issue, with a modern depiction of St George and the dragon, again by Timothy Noad, on the reverse. Once again in 2012 a special issue with a fanciful portrayal of St George by Paul Day, was issued in place of the bullion coin of that year.

In 2014 the bullion coin market was given a boost when permission was granted for sovereigns and half-sovereigns bearing an "I" mint mark to be struck in India exclusively for the Indian market.

The following year a new effigy by Royal Mint designer Jody Clark was introduced and used on coins dated 2015 and 2016 before another portrait by James Butler was used for those issued in late 2016 in celebration of Her Majesty the Queen's 90th birthday. However, the 2017 special issue to mark the 200th anniversary of the "modern" sovereign carries Jody Clark's portrait once more, with a reverse based on the first sovereign of 1817 with the Garter and legend surrounding Pistrucci's iconic St George and the dragon design with the streamer reinstated on St George's helmet.

What our coins could have looked like—plaster model of the unadopted design by Cecil Thomas for the first coinage of Her Majesty Queen Elizabeth II (courtesy of the Royal Mint Museum).

Description and details of the Elizabeth II half-sovereign (Proof type only)
First coinage 1953

Obverse: Bare head of Queen right, with tie at the back of the hair. Legend: ELIZABETH II DEI GRA:BRITT:OMN:REGINA F:D:+

Reverse: St George slaying the dragon. Date below the exergue line with the small letters B.P. to the right.

Edge: Milled.

The coin is struck to proof standard with mirror-like fields, and medal die axis ↑↑.

HALF SOVEREIGNS OF ELIZABETH II (FIRST ISSUE)

No.	Date	Type/Variety	Mintage	Rating
543C	1953	Proof only (WR454)	Small number	R6

Description and details of the Elizabeth II half-sovereign. Second bust type, First Decimal period

Obverse: Bust of the Queen facing right and wearing a coronet. Legend: ELIZABETH · II · DEI · GRATIA · REGINA · F:D:
Reverse: St George slaying the dragon. Date below exergue line with small letters B.P. to right.
Edge: Milled.
The coin is struck with a medal die axis ↑↑.

HALF-SOVEREIGNS OF ELIZABETH II (SECOND BUST, FIRST DECIMAL PERIOD)

No.	Date	Type/Variety	Mintage (+included in sets)	Rating
543D	1980	Proof	76,700 (+10,000)	C
544	1982	Normal	2,500,000	C
544A	1982	Proof	19,090 (+2,500)	N
544B	1983	Proof	17,710	N
544C	1984	Proof	12,410 (+7,095)	N

Description and details of the Elizabeth II half-sovereign. Third bust type (Proof issues only)

Obverse: Bust of the Queen facing right and wearing a diadem, the letters R.D.M. are placed at the rear of the truncation. Legend: ELIZABETH · II · DEI · GRATIA · REGINA · F:D:
Reverse: St George slaying the dragon. Date below exergue line with small letters B.P. to right.
Edge: Milled.
The coin is struck with a medal die axis ↑↑.

HALF-SOVEREIGNS OF ELIZABETH II (THIRD BUST, PROOF ISSUES ONLY)

No.	Date	Type/Variety	Mintage (+included in sets)	Rating
544D	1985	Proof	9,951 (+5,849)	N
544E	1986	Proof	4,575 (+12,500)	N
544F	1987	Proof	8,187 (+12,500)	N
544G	1988	Proof	7,074 (+11,192)	N
544H	1989	See special issues for details*		
544I	1990	Proof	4,231 (+3,658)	N
544J	1991	Proof	3,588 (+2,488)	N
544K	1992	Proof	3,783 (+2,132)	N
544L	1993	Proof	2,910 (+1,741)	N
544M	1994	Proof	5,000 (+2,167)	N
544N	1995	Proof	4,900 (+1,830)	N
544O	1996	Proof	5,730 (+1,610)	N
544P	1997	Proof	7,500 (+1,677)	N

*As this design carries the obverse and reverse by Bernard Sindall, strictly speaking it should not be included with the fourth type.

THE GOLD SOVEREIGN SERIES

Description and details of the Elizabeth II half-sovereign. Fourth bust type, first reverse

Obverse: Bust of the Queen facing right and wearing a diadem, the letters I R B for Ian Rank-Broadley appear at the rear of the truncation. Legend: ELIZABETH · II · DEI · GRATIA · REGINA · F:D:
Reverse: St George slaying the dragon. Date below exergue line with small letters B.P. to right.
Edge: Milled.
The coin is struck with a medal die axis ↑↑.

HALF-SOVEREIGNS OF ELIZABETH II
(FOURTH BUST TYPE, FIRST REVERSE)

No.	Date	Type/Variety	Mintage (+included in sets)	Rating
544Q	1998	Proof. Ian Rank-Broadley bust	6,147 (+1,349)	N
544R	1999	Proof	7,500 (+1,903)	N
545	2000	Normal	146,822	C
545A	2000	Proof	7,458 (+2,250)	N
546	2001	Normal	94,763	N
546A	2001	Proof	4,596 (+1,891)	N
547	2002	See special issues for details		
547A	2002	See special issues for details		
548	2003	Normal	47,818	C
548A	2003	Proof	4,868 (+3,787)	N
549	2004	Normal	34,924	C
549A	2004	Proof	4,446 (+2,510)	N
550	2005	See special issues for details		
551	2005	See special issues for details		
552	2006	Normal	Not known	N
552A	2006	Proof	4,173 (+2,290)	N
New re-engraved reverse for 2007 in lower relief, small date				
553	2007	Normal	75,000*	N
553A	2007	Proof	2,442 (+3,219)	N
Modified reverse with larger date for 2008				
554	2008	Normal	75,000*	N
554A	2008	Proof	2,465 (+3,137)	N

* These figures are the edition limit, it is not known how many were actually issued.

Description and details of the Elizabeth II half-sovereign. Fourth bust type, second reverse

Obverse: Bust of the Queen facing right and wearing a tiara, the letters I R B for Ian Rank-Broadley appear below the truncation. Legend: ELIZABETH · II · DEI · GRA REGINA · FID · DEF

Reverse: St George slaying the dragon but the new reverse introduced in 2009 is based on the 1893 design with less ground below and there is no BP in exergue. Date below exergue line.

Edge: Milled.

The coin is struck with a medal die axis ↑↑.

HALF-SOVEREIGNS OF ELIZABETH II (FOURTH BUST TYPE, SECOND REVERSE)

No.	Date	Type/Variety	Mintage (+included in sets)	Rating
555	2009	Normal, no B.P. initials in exergue	50,000	N
555A	2009	Proof, no B.P. initials in exergue	2,996 (+2,416)	N
556	2010	Normal, no B.P. initials in exergue	16,485	N
556A	2010	Proof, no B.P. initials in exergue	3,351 (+2,019)	N
557	2011	Normal	50,000	N
557A	2011	Proof	4,259 (+1,028)	N
558	2012	See special issues for details		
558A	2012	See special issues for details		
559	2013	Normal	1,051 (+124)	N
559A	2013	Proof	1,863 (1,915)	N
560*	2014	Normal	672	N
560A	2014	Proof	1,367 (+1,350)	N
560B	2014	Normal. Indian minting	62,000	N
561*	2015	Normal	500	N
561A	2015	Proof	1,704 (+1,499)	N

* BU editions also known with reverse design frosted like a proof, though grading services are grading them as proof with unfrosted obverse die

Description and details of the Elizabeth II half-sovereign. Fifth bust type

Obverse: Bust of the Queen facing right and wearing a crown, the letters JC standing for Jody Clark appear below the truncation. Legend: ELIZABETH · II · DEI · GRA · REGINA · FID · DEF ·
Reverse: St George slaying the dragon, with no streamer. Date below exergue line with small letters B.P. to right.
Edge: Milled.
The coin is struck with a medal die axis ↑↑.

HALF-SOVEREIGNS OF ELIZABETH II (FIFTH BUST TYPE)

No.	Date	Type/Variety	Mintage (+included in sets)	Rating
562	2015	Proof	1,046 in sets only	N
563*	2016	Normal	472	R
564	2016	See special issues for details (James Butler obverse)		
565	2017	See special issues for details (200th Anniversary)		
565A	2017	See special issues for details (200th Anniversary)		
566	2018	Proof, with special 65 privy-mark	1,878 (+2,566)	N
566A	2018	Normal	Not known	N
567	2019	Proof	1,523 (+2,103)**	N
567A	2019	Normal	Not known	N
568	2020	Proof. Rev. with George III Royal cypher	2,000 (+1,878)	N
568A	2020	Normal	Not known	N
569	2021	Proof, with special 95 in crown privy-mark	1,483 (+1,739)	N
569A	2021	Normal	Not known	N
570	2022	See special issues for details (Platinum Jubilee)		
571	2022	See special issues for details (Platinum Jubilee)		
571A	2022	See special issues for details (Platinum Jubilee)		

* Some if not the majority of these are struck to a high standard with some frosting like a proof.

** An additional four proof Half-Sovereigns from the Trial of the Pyx were sold to the public.

ELIZABETH II HALF-SOVEREIGNS —SPECIAL ISSUES

500th ANNIVERSARY OF THE GOLD SOVEREIGN. Obverse and reverse by Bernard Sindall

No.	Date	Type/Variety	Mintage (+included in sets)	Rating
544H	1989	Proof	8,888 (+12,936)	S

Note. The legend inscriptions are in Lombardic style lettering.

GOLDEN JUBILEEE OF HER MAJESTY QUEEN ELIZABETH II.
Obverse by Ian Rank-Broadley. Shield reverse by Timothy Noad

No.	Date	Type/Variety	Mintage (+included in sets)	Rating
547	2002	Normal	61,347	N
547A	2002	Proof	10,000 (+6,947)	S

The Jubilee gold coinage was approved by Royal Proclamation on December 11, 2001.

THE GOLD SOVEREIGN SERIES

MODERN INTERPRETATION OF ST GEORGE. New reverse for 2005 by Timothy Noad

No.	Date	Type/Variety	Mintage (+included in sets)	Rating
550	2005	Normal	30,299	N
551	2005	Proof	5,011 (+2,958)	S

DIAMOND JUBILEE OF HER MAJESTY QUEEN ELIZABETH II. Stylised reverse by Paul Day

No.	Date	Type/Variety	Mintage (+included in sets)	Rating
558	2012	Normal	edition 2,137 (+119)	N
558A	2012	Proof	2,303 (+2,597)	S

90th BIRTHDAY OF HER MAJESTY QUEEN ELIZABETH II. Obverse portrait by James Butler

No.	Date	Type/Variety	Mintage (+included in sets)	Rating
564	2016	Proof	1,995 (+1,666)	N

HALF-SOVEREIGNS OF ELIZABETH II, 1952–2022

**200th ANNIVERSARY OF THE MODERN SOVEREIGN. Obverse by Jody Clark.
Reverse 1 as 1817 half-sovereign. Reverse 2 normal with privy mark**

No.	Date	Type/Variety	Mintage (+included in sets)	Rating
565	2017	Proof	2,492 (+2,198)	N
565A	2017	Normal but with special "200" privy mark	Not known	S

**PLATINUM JUBILEE OF HER MAJESTY QUEEN ELIZABETH II. Royal arms reverse
by Timothy Noad**

No.	Date	Type/Variety	Mintage (+included in sets)	Rating
570	2022	Normal	Not known	C
571	2022	Proof	Edition 2,000 (+2,200)	N
571A	2022	Proof, piedfort	70	R3

THE GOLD SOVEREIGN SERIES

CHARLES III, 2022–

Following much speculation all day, the death of Her Majesty Queen Elizabeth II aged 96 was finally announced in the early evening of Thursday, September 8, 2022. Her 73-year-old son, Charles, Prince of Wales, immediately became King Charles III, the oldest Monarch to ascend the throne in British history. Because of the Queen's advanced age, preparations for a seamless changeover of Monarch had been ongoing for some time and that included work on coins banknotes and stamps. Sculptor Martin Jennings had been charged with the new coinage portrait (which has also been applied as the new stamps) and he designed two new effigies, entirely on computer, both a bare-head effigy similar to that used by the 20th century kings, and a crowned head for the special Coronation issues. The special edition reverse designs for Sovereign series gold have, so far, been a Memorial to the Late Queen in 2022 and the aforementioned Coronation reverse in 2023. The St George and dragon design by Benedetto Pistrucci made a return for the 2024-dated issues.

Description and details of the Charles III bare head half-sovereign, Memorial Reverse

Obverse: Bare head effigy of King Charles III left by Martin Jennings, raised initials below neck MJ. Legend CHARLES III. DEI. GRA. REX. FID. DEF.

Reverse: Royal heraldic coat of arms with crowned lion and unicorn supporters, crowned helm above, banner motto below DIEU ET MON DROIT with date.

Edge: Milled.
The coin is struck with a straight upright die axis ↑↑

MEMORIAL FOR THE LATE QUEEN
Martin Jennings obverse, Jody Clark Royal Arms reverse.

No.	Date	Type/Variety	Mintage	Rating
572	2022	Normal	Not known	C
573	2022	Proof	2,866 (+3,127)	C

Description and details of the Charles III Crowned head half-sovereign,

Obverse: Crowned head effigy of King Charles III left by Martin Jennings, raised initials below neck MJ. Legend CHARLES III. DEI. GRA. REX. FID. DEF.

Reverse: Pistrucci's St George armed with sword slaying the dragon. The date in the exergue below the ground line with B.P. in small raised letters to upper right.

Edge: Milled.

The coin is struck with a straight upright die axis ↑↑.

CORONATION OF KING CHARLES III
Crowned bust left by Martin Jennings.

No.	Date	Type/Variety	Mintage	Rating
574	2023	Normal	Not known	C
575	2023	Proof	Edition 2,500 (+2,875)	C
576	2023	Matt Proof	Edition as a set 23	R3

Description and details of the Charles III bare head half-sovereign

Obverse: Bare head effigy of King Charles III left by Martin Jennings, raised initials below neck MJ. Legend CHARLES III. DEI. GRA. REX. FID. DEF.

Reverse: Pistrucci's St George armed with sword slaying the dragon. The date in the exergue below the ground line with B.P. in small raised letters to upper right.

Edge: Milled.
The coin is struck with a straight upright die axis ↑↑.

REGULAR HALF-SOVEREIGN DESIGN KING CHARLES III
Bare head left by Martin Jennings. Reverse Pistrucci's St George and dragon with date in exergue

No.	Date	Type/Variety	Mintage	Rating
577	2024	Normal	Not known	C
578	2024	Proof	Edition 1,250 (+1,450)	C

THE QUARTER-SOVEREIGN

In 2009 a gold quarter-sovereign was issued for the first time in the United Kingdom by the Royal Mint, although there had been earlier pattern pieces which had not been adopted. Its design and production is exactly the same as its larger counterparts, with the current effigy of the reigning monarch on the obverse and Benedetto Pistrucci's St George slaying the dragon on the reverse of the standard coins, although as with the larger coins, the special issues carry their own reverses. Since its introduction there have been a number of different types, including the issues for Her Majesty Queen Elizabeth II's Diamond and Platinum Jubilees in 2012 and 2022, one for the 200th Anniversary of the Sovereign in 2017, a memorial design after Her Majesty passed away in 2022, and a Coronation design the following year.

There have been five different obverses to date: the definitive Queen Elizabeth II effigies by Ian Rank-Broadley and Jody Clark, the special issue by James Butler, and two King Charles III portraits, both by sculptor Martin Jennings. There is a bare headed version, reminiscent of the 20th century kings, which appeared first on the Memorial coin and appears on the series going forward (as well as the definitive coinage and stamps) and a crowned head design that featured on the Coronation issue of 2023.

This small gold coin has proved very popular and it is anticipated that it will continue in production, just as the sovereign and the half-sovereign have done for the past 200 years. Most of these coins have been issued as parts of two-coin or three-coin sets.

Specifications of the Quarter Sovereign:
Weight: 1.997 grams
Fineness, 22 carat: 11/12 fine gold, 1/12 alloy.
Millesimal fineness: 916.66.
Thickness: less than 1mm.
Diameter: 13.50mm.

The introduction of the Quarter Sovereign in 2009 completed the Sovereign "family" of Five Pounds, Double Sovereign, Sovereign, Half Sovereign and, of course, Quarter Sovereign—seen here issued as a complete, boxed Sovereign set.

Description and details of the Elizabeth II quarter-sovereign. Fourth bust type, first reverse

Obverse: Bust of the Queen facing right and wearing a diadem, the letters I R B for Ian Rank-Broadley appear at the rear of the truncation. Legend: ELIZABETH · II · DEI · GRATIA · REGINA · F:D:
Reverse: St George slaying the dragon. Date below exergue line with small letters B.P. to right.
Edge: Milled.
The coin is struck with a medal die axis ↑↑.

ELIZABETH II QUARTER-SOVEREIGN FOURTH TYPE BUST

No.	Date	Type/Variety	Mintage (+included in sets)	Rating
600	2009	Normal	50,000	N
600A	2009	Proof	11,745 (+1,750)	N
601	2010	Normal	8,985	N
601A	2010	Proof	4,546 (+1,461)	N
602	2011	Normal	50,000	N
602A	2011	Proof	6,736 (+1,028)	N
603	2012	See special issues for details		
603A	2012	See special issues for details		
604	2013	Normal	1,729	N
604A	2013	Proof	1,696 (+1,535)	N
605	2014	Normal	Not known	N
605A	2014	Proof	1,886 (+1,044)	N
606	2015	Proof	1,808 (+1,171)	N

There is an earlier proposal and subsequent pattern for a gold Quarter Sovereign in the reign of Queen Victoria (1837–1901) dated 1853 which utilised the obverse die of the maundy twopence with a reverse stating the denomination and date around a crowned shield. The coin is approximately 17mm in diameter and weighs about 2 grammes and is listed by *Wilson & Rasmussen* as number 365. There is also an article by Graham Dyer in the *British Numismatic Journal* of 1997, "Quarter-Sovereigns and Other Small Gold Patterns of the Mid-Victorian Period".

THE GOLD SOVEREIGN SERIES

Description and details of the Elizabeth II quarter-sovereign. Fifth bust type

Obverse: Bust of the Queen facing right and wearing a crown, the letters JC for Jody Clark appear below the truncation. Legend: ELIZABETH · II · DEI · GRA · REGINA · FID · DEF ·
Reverse: St George slaying the dragon. Date below exergue line with small letters B.P. to right.
Edge: Milled.
The coin is struck with a medal die axis ↑↑.

ELIZABETH II QUARTER-SOVEREIGN FIFTH TYPE BUST

No.	Date	Type/Variety	Mintage (+included in sets)	Rating
607	2015	Proof	550 (+598)	N
608	2016	See special issues for details		
609	2017	See special issues for details		
610	2018	Proof, with special 65 privy-mark	1,321 (+2,034)*	N
611	2019	Proof	1,312 (+1,757)*	N
612	2020	Proof, with GR cypher privy mark	1,878	N
613	2021	Proof, with special 95 in crown privy-mark	1,739	N

*An additional six pieces for 2019 were sold as the Trial of the Pyx pieces to the public.

QUEEN ELIZABETH II QUARTER SOVEREIGNS SPECIAL ISSUES

DIAMOND JUBILEE OF HER MAJESTY QUEEN ELIZABETH II. Stylised reverse by Paul Day

No.	Date	Type/Variety	Mintage (+included in sets)	Rating
603	2012	Normal	137	R
603A	2012	Proof	7,579 (+2,262)	N

90th BIRTHDAY OF HER MAJESTY QUEEN ELIZABETH II. Obverse by James Butler

No.	Date	Type/Variety	Mintage (+included in sets)	Rating
608	2016	Proof	1,727 (+1,316)	N

200th ANNIVERSARY OF THE SOVEREIGN. Obverse by Jody Clark. Reverse as 1817 sovereign

No.	Date	Type/Variety	Mintage (+included in sets)	Rating
609	2017	Proof	2,442 (+1,746)	N

QUARTER-SOVEREIGNS OF ELIZABETH II, 1952–2022

PLATINUM JUBILEE OF HER MAJESTY QUEEN ELIZABETH II. Royal Arms reverse
by Timothy Noad

No.	Date	Type/Variety	Mintage (+included in sets)	Rating
614	2022	Normal	Not known	C
615	2022	Proof	Edition 2,200 in sets only	N
615A	2022	Proof, piedfort	70	R3

The Sovereign 2024 Five-Coin Gold Proof Set brings together the Five-Sovereign, Double-Sovereign, Sovereign, Half-Sovereign and Quarter-Sovereign. This year marks the first time the definitive coinage portrait of His Majesty King Charles III has been paired with Benedetto Pistrucci's St George and the dragon design on a Proof Sovereign.

295

Description and details of the Charles III bare head quarter-sovereign, Memorial Reverse

Obverse: Bare head effigy of King Charles III left by Martin Jennings, raised initials below neck MJ. Legend CHARLES III. DEI. GRA. REX. FID. DEF.

Reverse: Royal heraldic coat of arms with crowned lion and unicorn supporters, crowned helm above, banner motto below DIEU ET MON DROIT with date.

Edge: Milled.
The coin is struck with a straight upright die axis ↑↑.

MEMORIAL FOR THE LATE QUEEN
Martin Jennings obverse, Jody Clark Royal Arms reverse.

No.	Date	Type/Variety	Mintage	Rating
616	2022	Normal	Not known	C
617	2022	Proof	2,701 (+3,127)	C

Description and details of the Charles III Crowned head quarter-sovereign

Obverse: Crowned head effigy of King Charles III left by Martin Jennings, raised initials below neck MJ. Legend CHARLES III. DEI. GRA. REX. FID. DEF.

Reverse: Pistrucci's St George armed with sword slaying the dragon. The date in the exergue below the ground line with B.P. in small raised letters to upper right.

Edge: Milled.
The coin is struck with a straight upright die axis ↑↑.

CORONATION OF KING CHARLES III
Crowned bust left by Martin Jennings.

No.	Date	Type/Variety	Mintage	Rating
618	2023	Normal	Not known	C
619	2023	Proof	Edition 1,7500 (+2,875)	C
620	2023	Matt Proof	Edition as a set 23	R3

QUARTER-SOVEREIGNS OF CHARLES III, 2022–)

Description and details of the Charles III bare head quarter-sovereign

Obverse: Bare head effigy of King Charles III left by Martin Jennings, raised initials below neck MJ. Legend CHARLES III. DEI. GRA. REX. FID. DEF.

Reverse: Pistrucci's St George armed with sword slaying the dragon. The date in the exergue below the ground line with B.P. in small raised letters to upper right.

Edge: Milled.

The coin is struck with a straight upright die axis ↑↑.

REGULAR QUARTER-SOVEREIGN DESIGN KING CHARLES III
Bare head left by Martin Jennings. Reverse Pistrucci's St George and dragon with date in exergue

No.	Date	Type/Variety	Mintage	Rating
621	2024	Normal	Not known	C
622	2024	Proof	In sets only 1,450	C

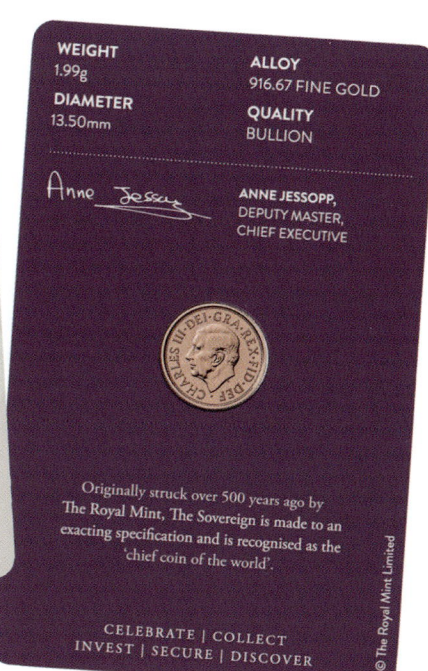

The 2024 quarter-sovereign gold bullion coin in blister pack.

297

FINALLY

Today the gold sovereign is a collector's piece, an investment piece, a gift, but the coin's roots were, of course, as money, as a circulating coinage handled by some, familiar to all. Just as our money today has items intrinsically associated with it (wallets, purses, coin counters in supermarkets, "change" bags for banks, scales, etc, so there are historical items that owe their very existence to the sovereign and half sovereign.

Most commonly encountered are sovereign cases, often beautifully crafted pieces made by a professional goldsmith or silversmith (although also found in nickel, pewter, gold plate, silver plate, brass, copper, leather and even wood), that were placed in a pocket or on the end of a watch chain and used just as you would expect: to carry sovereigns (or half-sovereigns) separate from one another rather than have them clattering around in a purse or pocket. Indeed one of the reasons the relatively soft gold coins are usually found in reasonable condition today is the fact that the use of sovereign cases, which prevented the coins rubbing against each other, was so prevalent.

Such cases are still to be found today, and some are highly collectable. Particularly highly sought after are those that were made, or adapted, to fit both sovereigns and half sovereigns, or coins and cigarettes, coins and visiting/business cards, coins and matches, or indeed coins and anything else! There are even those that are a combination of sovereign case and pocket watch . . .

In addition to cases, sovereign balances and scales are also highly collectable today and they too served a vital role at a time when a sovereign was still a great deal of money. Anyone who has ever taken change in a little plastic bag in to the bank will know that bank staff do not count out the coins they are to exchange for notes or pay into an account, but rather they rely on the weight of the bag. The same practise has been in use for 200 years with brass scales and accurate weights produced to weigh the gold coinage so that both bank staff and merchants knew that the sovereigns they were getting were indeed the real thing. Several examples of coin weights were made by the Royal Mint although other manufacturers produced their own versions—one must assume that these manufacturers were trusted enough in the world of banking and commerce to be relied on to produce weights that were accurate!

On the following pages we have illustrated an interesting selection of sovereign cases, weights and scales, and are indebted to Tony Davis for allowing the use of his superb photographs.

FINALLY . . . .

THE GOLD SOVEREIGN SERIES

300

FINALLY . . . .

THE GOLD SOVEREIGN SERIES

FINALLY . . . .

To conclude, we must mention counterfeit sovereigns and half-sovereigns because alas they do still exist, and there are still many that appear these days. There are a few points that may help if you are confronted with a possible counterfeit coin from the sovereign series: the colour is often far too yellow and can also create a "soft" hazy-like impression. Check the weight and study the design of the bust carefully; what at first glance appears to be wear may well be weakness in parts of the striking, which is often one of the major faults of a counterfeit; another is the field area of the coin that should be very flat and without any blemish. Also look carefully at the reverse designs of St George and the dragon. Examples have been seen when the streamer should not have been flowing from the helmet, as well as more folds than there should be on St George's cloak—these are just a few of the points to look for, but the easiest way by far to identify a forgery is by checking the weight. However, there is no substitute for experience so handle as many examples of the real thing so that it becomes second nature to spot the bad one!

Examples of forgery errors are illustrated below. These errors include the letters B.M. on the truncation that do not look correct (especially the letter M) and several irregularities in the field areas. In this particular case the coin's status as forgery was confirmed by its specific gravity (only 16.08 where if it was correct for 22 carat gold it would be 17.5), its milling count of 120 and its weight 7.9765gms, both of which are low. The other illustration is of a Melbourne Mint coin from 1895—again the specific gravity is low, as is the weight and milling count and indeed the colour is too yellow. However, the surest sign that the coin is counterfeit is the fact that the Melbourne Branch Mint struck no Jubilee sovereigns beyond 1893!

ENGRAVERS OF THE SOVEREIGN SERIES

Obverse	Engraver	Reverse	Engraver
GEORGE III			
Laureate	Benedetto Pistrucci	St George	Benedetto Pistrucci
GEORGE IV			
Laureate	Benedetto Pistrucci	St George	Benedetto Pistrucci
Bare Head	William Wyon	Shield	Jean Baptiste Merlen
WILLIAM IV			
Bare Head	William Wyon	Shield	Jean Baptiste Merlen
VICTORIA			
Young Head	William Wyon	Shield	Jean Baptiste Merlen
AUSTRALIA rev.			
First Head	James Wyon	Wreath	James Wyon
Second Head	Leonard C. Wyon	Wreath	James Wyon
Young Head	William Wyon	St George	Benedetto Pistrucci
Jubilee Head	Joseph Edgar Boehm	St George	Benedetto Pistrucci
Old Head	Thomas Brock	St George	Benedetto Pistrucci
EDWARD VII			
Portrait	George William De Saulles	St George	Benedetto Pistrucci
GEORGE V			
Portrait	Bertram Mackennal	St George	Benedetto Pistrucci
EDWARD VIII			
Portrait	Humphrey Paget	St George	Benedetto Pistrucci
GEORGE VI			
Portrait	Humphrey Paget	St George	Benedetto Pistrucci
ELIZABETH II			
First Portrait	Mary Gillick	St George	Benedetto Pistrucci
Second Portrait	Arnold Machin	St George	Benedetto Pistrucci
Third Portrait	Raphael Maklouf	St George	Benedetto Pistrucci
Seated monarch	Bernard Sindall	Rose & Crown	Bernard Sindall
Fourth Portrait	Ian Rank-Broadley	St George	Benedetto Pistrucci
Fourth Portrait	Ian Rank-Broadley	Shield	Timothy Noad
Fourth Portrait	Ian Rank-Broadley	St George	Timothy Noad
Fourth Portrait	Ian Rank-Broadley	St George	Paul Day
90th Birthday	James Butler	St George	Benedetto Pistrucci
Fifth Portrait	Jody Clark	St George	Benedetto Pistrucci
Fifth Portrait	Jody Clark	Platinum Jubilee	Timothy Noed
CHARLES III			
Bare Head	Martin Jennings	Memorial	Timothy Noed
Crowned Head	Martin Jennings	St George	Benedetto Pistrucci
Bare Head	Martin Jennings	St George	Benedetto Pistrucci

Bibliography

BONAR, J., "Ottawa Branch Mint Report", *Royal Mint Report*, 1908.

BROWN, I. D. and COMBER, C., "Notes on the Gold Coins of Elizabeth I", *British Numismatic Journal*, Volume 59, 1989.

CAMPBELL, J. F., "Perth Branch Mint Report", *Royal Mint Report*, 1899.

CHALLIS, C. E. (Ed.)., *A New History of the Royal Mint*, Cambridge, 1992.

CLANCY, Dr Kevin, *A History of the Sovereign Chief Coin of the World*, Royal Mint Museum, Llantrisant, 2015.

CRAIG, Sir John, KCVO, CB, LLD, *The Mint, A History of the London Mint from AD 287 to 1948*, Cambridge, 1953.

CULLIMORE ALLEN, J. J., Sovereigns of the British Empire, London, 1965.

DIX, NOONAN WEBB, "George Holloway Collection of Fine Sovereigns of Elizabeth I", Auction 198, November 17, 2021.

DUVEEN, Sir Geoffrey and STRIDE, H. G., *The History of The Gold Sovereign*, London, 1962.

DYER, Graham P., et al, *Royal Sovereign 1489–1989*, Royal Mint, 1989.

DYER, Graham P., "The Existence of 1923 S A Currency Sovereign", *Spink Numismatic Circular*, March 1985.

EIMER, Christopher, *The Pingo Family and Medal Making in 18th Century Britain*, London, 1998.

FORRER, L., *Biographical Dictionary of Medallists*, Spink & Son, London, 1902.

GLENDINING'S, "Herbert M. Lingford Collection, Part II", June 20, 1951.

GRIERSON, Philip, "The Origins of the English Sovereign and the Symbolism of the Closed Crown", *British Numismatic Journal* 1964, Volume 33.

IVERSON, David and HILL, Steve (Ed.), *The Jubilee Head Gold Sovereigns 1887–1893*, Baldwin's, London, 2015.

DISH—can now refer to any of the Jubilee Head publications by David Iverson and edited by Steve Hill. The sovereign one listed, but also updated version from Sovereign Rarities in 2018.

The Jubilee Head Gold Half-Sovereign, published by Sovereign Rarities in 2019.

The Jubilee Head Gold Two Pounds of 1887, published by Sovereign Rarities in 2020.

KAHAN, R. R., "Bombay Branch Mint Report", *Royal Mint Report*, 1918.

LINECAR, Howard W. A. and STONE, Alex G. *English Proof and Pattern Crown-Size Pieces 1658-1960*, published by Spink & Son 1968.

MACKAY, Dr James, *The Sovereign, the World's Most Famous Coin, A History and Price Guide*, Hillden Publications, 2001.

MARSH, Michael A., *Benedetto Pistrucci Principal Engraver & Chief Medallist of the Royal Mint 1783–1855*, Cambridge, 1996.

MARSH, Michael A., "Rare Victorian Sovereigns", *Coin Monthly*, February 1982.

MARSH, Michael A., "A Sovereign Overdate from the Melbourne Mint", *Coin Monthly*, December 1982.

NORTH, Jeffrey J., *English Hammered Coinage, Volume 2*, published by Spink & Son.

PEARSON, R., "Pretoria Branch Mint Report", *Royal Mint Report* 1923.

POTTER, W. J. W. and WINSTANLEY, E. J., "The Coinage of Henry VII Part 3", *British Numismatic Journal* 1963, Volume 32.

SHARPLES, J., "Sovereigns of the Overseas Branches", *Royal Sovereign 1489–1989*, Royal Mint, 1989.

SHARPLES, J., "The Story of the 1872/1 Sovereign", *Australian Coin Review*, December 1985.

WILSON, Alex and RASMUSSEN, Mark, *English Pattern, Trial and Proof Coins in Gold 1547–1968*, Cambridge, 2000.

WHITTON, C. A., "The Coinage of Henry VIII and Edward VI in Henry's Name", *British Numismatic Journal*, 1949–51, three parts in Volume 26.

WOODHEAD, Peter, The Herbert Schneider Collection, Volumes one and two, published by Spink & Son, 1996 and 2002 respectively.

Addendum

The melting of gold sovereigns by the Bank of England in 1930–31

by Howard Hodgson

LIKE most industrialised countries, Britain was on the Gold Standard at the beginning of 1930. This was an economic policy which encompassed a system of fixed exchange rates with the value of each country's currency being expressed in terms of a fixed weight of gold. Under the policy, the Bank of England was required to sell gold in unlimited quantities to anyone who wished to acquire it but only in the form of 400 ounce bars. The price was fixed at £3 17s 10½d per ounce of 22 carat gold (.916 fineness). The reason for selling gold in the form of bars rather than sovereigns was to prevent the latter from re-entering circulation, something which the country could no longer afford after World War I. Towards the end of the 1920s the pound's exchange rate came under pressure and there developed what today would be described as "a run on sterling". As a result of the pound repeatedly falling below its official exchange rates, substantial amounts of gold were purchased from the Bank, exported to Europe and elsewhere, and sold at a profit. As the "run" developed, the Bank found itself requiring ever greater numbers of gold bars in order to meet its obligations.

The melting programme

In November 1929 Sir Frederick Phillips of the Treasury wrote to Sir Robert Johnson, the Deputy Master of the Royal Mint, to say that the Bank of England *"may be wanting some sovereigns melted down to gold bars—I suppose of approximately 400 oz troy of fine gold. Will you let me know pretty soon what you can do for them"*[1]. The Royal Mint replied to say that they were willing to help but pointing out that they had no refinery of their own and therefore were only able to produce bars of 22 carat gold, the same fineness as sovereigns. (A Royal Commission established in 1848 had recommended separating the roles of refining and coining and the Mint's refinery, located alongside it on Tower Hill, was leased to Anthony de Rothschild in 1852.) If bars of fine gold were required then it was a job for refiners. Nonetheless, the Mint added that for security reasons it would be unwise to send gold sovereigns directly to refiners and eventually it was agreed that bars of 22 carat gold were acceptable.

At the beginning of 1930 the Bank of England held £98.5 million in sovereigns but only £45.0 million in gold bars[2] and, as pressure on sterling increased, it was clear that the melting process needed to get underway quickly. By early April 1930 the Bank had drawn up a detailed protocol setting out how the process was to operate. This included sending sovereigns to the Mint in bags of 1,000 coins each by tale (meaning that the contents were determined by count not weight). The Mint was to weigh each bag on arrival in the presence of an accompanying representative from the Bank and jointly agree the weight. Thereafter the Mint was to account to the Bank for the weight of gold received thus rendering it unnecessary for anyone from the Bank to supervise the melting. However, the Mint immediately spotted an obstacle in that the Bank specified that 1,750 sovereigns should be melted to make each bar. The Mint therefore asked that the sovereigns should be delivered in bags of 1,750 saying that they did not have the resources available to sort them into the necessary quantities for melting. A compromise was eventually reached with the Bank still sending bags of 1,000 sovereigns but accompanied by three members of staff to help with sorting.

It was also agreed that "new" sovereigns should be melted, "new" meaning coins that were uncirculated or, more pertinently, of full weight. Under the Gold Standard a sovereign contained

307

exactly 20 shillings of fine gold. Melting worn coins which had fallen below their standard weight would have resulted in a loss thereby increasing the cost of the programme. For numismatists this is crucial as it gives an enticing insight into what may have been melted. The protocol also specified that the bars were to be impressed with a Royal Mint stamp, their exact fineness (as determined by the Assay Department of the Mint) and a serial number supplied by the Bank. The Mint was tasked with a weekly production target of 600 bars, which required 1,050,000 sovereigns. Work got underway on April 24, 1930 and the initial plan called for 20 million sovereigns to be melted. However, in what turned out to be the first phase of a three-phase operation, a total of 24,990,000 sovereigns were melted, the task being completed by November 21, 1930. During this period pressure on sterling continued and the Mint was melting sovereigns at full capacity. The Treasury thought it prudent to seek additional help and Rothschild (owner of the former Mint refinery) and another London refiner, Johnson Matthey & Co, were approached and asked to assist. During this first phase, they each melted 1,050,000 sovereigns bringing the total number of coins destroyed to 27,090,000.

Although the Mint had now completed its original task, the economic situation had not improved and a second phase was required. This ran through to June 29, 1931 by which time the Mint, Rothschild and Johnson Matthey & Co had melted a further 48,300,000, 1,365,000 and 8,356,000 sovereigns respectively meaning that an additional 58,021,000 coins had disappeared into the furnace. During the summer of 1931 the UK's exchange rate difficulties continued to mount and a third and, as it turned out, final melt was commenced, starting on July 27, 1931. This time worn sovereigns and half-sovereigns were brought within the scope of the programme.

The sterling crisis intensified and on August 24, 1931 the ruling Labour Government collapsed as the Cabinet was unable to agree on the drastic cuts in government spending that would have been required to save the sterling exchange rate. A cross-party National Government was formed but it was too slow to take the necessary steps to resolve the crisis. Gold continued to flow overseas and eventually the government's borrowing lines were fully drawn down. On Friday, September 18, 1931 the Bank concluded that it could no longer sustain the outflow of gold. The Prime Minister was recalled from Chequers where he had gone for the weekend and at 9.45pm that evening in London the decision was taken to abandon the Gold Standard and to devalue sterling. The decision was kept secret until Sunday, when all financial markets were closed, and the following day, Monday, September 21, 1931, emergency legislation was rushed through Parliament and given the Royal Assent. This revoked the obligation on the Bank to sell gold at a fixed price, stopping the outflow of gold and enabling sterling to be devalued. It was a turning point in history. The Gold Standard, in place since 1821, had been discarded and Britain was forced to acknowledge that it was no longer the world's chief economic power.

On October 5, 1931 the Mint was told to cease the melting programme. During this third phase 9,450,000 "new" sovereigns, 5,880,000 "old" sovereigns and 5,460,000 "old" half-sovereigns had been melted, making a total of 20,790,000 coins with a face value of £18,060,000. Across all three phases of the programme 100,441,000 sovereigns and 5,460,000 half-sovereigns amounting to £103,171,000 had been melted:

	No. of Coins	Face Value
Sovereigns		
Royal Mint—new	82,740,000	£82,740,000
Royal Mint—old	5,880,000	£5,880,000
Rothschild—new	2,415,000	£2,415,000
Johnson Matthey & Co—new	9,406,000	£9,406,000
Total Sovereigns	100,441,000	£100,441,000
Half-Sovereigns		
Royal Mint—old	5,460,000	£2,730,000
Overall Total	105,901,000	£103,171,000

To put matters into context, nearly 106 million coins had been melted, containing 24 million ounces of fine gold with a value of around £35 billion at today's prices. As the average total value of gold coin in circulation in the United Kingdom during the ten years from 1905 to 1914 is estimated to have been £107 million, this means that the number of coins melted was equivalent to the entire pre-War circulation of gold[3]. It also represented 10.1 per cent and 2.8 per cent respectively of the total number of sovereigns and half-sovereigns that had been struck between 1817 and 1931. (Several books[4] on sovereigns say that 91,350,000 were melted. However, this is the face value of the coins melted by the Royal Mint which, as we have seen, included half-sovereigns, and excludes coins melted by refiners.)

The coins melted

So which coins were melted? Sadly, we will never know for certain. The melting process was an economic and political matter carried out by personnel who had neither the time, resources nor, in all probability, the inclination to record the exact details of the dates and mintmarks of the coins melted. In addition, one has to take into account that many sovereigns had been melted over the years by, for example, the Mint as part of its continuous recoinage of light gold coin since the 1890s, by other mints, by bullion dealers, jewellers, dentists and private individuals. Therefore any discussion on this topic risks seeking to impose undue order on what was a random, continuous and fragmented process. Nevertheless it is possible to gain an insight into those coins most likely to have come within the scope of the programme.

The Royal Mint Annual Reports for 1930 and 1931 both contain helpful comments and the most significant is that of H. W. L. Evans, the Superintendent of the Operative Department, who noted at the conclusion of the programme that *"while the majority of coins melted had been struck at the London Mint, other coins were received which had been struck at the Branch Mints in Sydney, Melbourne, Perth and Pretoria; some of those from Pretoria being the issue of 1931"*[5]. Also helpful is a note sent by the Bullion Office of the Bank of England to the Chief Cashier in October 1930 summarising its gold holdings and noting that *"between 11 and 31 October £3,000,000 sovereigns are due from Australia and £1,000,000 from South Africa"*. Another factor to consider is that the sovereign was an international coin extensively used in world trade and those struck prior to the World War I had been widely distributed. Those which came within the scope of the programme are more likely to have been recently struck coins which were sitting in the vaults of central banks as part of gold reserves and had never entered circulation. Armed with these thoughts we can take a look at what may have been melted.

London

As noted by Evans, the majority of coins included in the programme were London sovereigns. Mintages towards the end of Queen Victoria's reign up to World War I had been substantial and none of the sovereigns of that period are particularly rare today. However, there are a couple of coins that require special mention.

1917: Sovereigns had ceased to circulate in Britain by the summer of 1915 and the small mintages undertaken in 1916 and 1917 must therefore have gone to the Bank of England to form part of government reserves. It has been speculated by others[6] that these coins were melted down in the United States in 1934 under the terms of its Gold Reserve Act of the same date but no documentary evidence has been put forward to support this. Such a theory is undermined by the discovery of large numbers of 1916 sovereigns in a London bank vault in the 1970s and the coin, which used to be considered rare, is today relatively common. It also ignores the fact that five million sovereigns were melted by the US Mint in San Francisco in July and August 1926. London sovereigns of 1917 are undoubtedly scarce today but for most of them to have been melted down in the USA in 1934 would have required them to avoid the earlier culls in San Francisco and London. In the absence of any documentary evidence to the contrary it seems just as plausible, if not more so, that many of the 1917 sovereigns were melted in 1930–31. As we have already seen, the Bank held 98.5 million sovereigns in its vaults at the beginning of 1930 and there is no evidence to suggest that those of 1917 were not amongst them.

1925: A total of 3,518,000 sovereigns were struck in 1925 using light gold coin which had accumulated at the Bank of England, who tendered them to the Royal Mint for recoinage. The new sovereigns were returned to the Bank after striking. The 1925 sovereign was regarded as rare in the period between the wars and it seems likely that they were melted down as part of the programme. Subsequently, a total of 886,000 1925 sovereigns, still bearing the effigy of George V, were struck in 1949, 1951 and 1952. The 1925 sovereign is now regarded as a reasonably common coin and it seems probable that those surviving today are from the post-war mintage. (Some coin dealers assert that original 1925 sovereigns can be distinguished from those minted after World War II as the latter are said to be better struck with more pronounced rims.)

Australia

The right of individuals to bring gold to the Australian Branch Mints and demand that it be coined into sovereigns was suspended in 1916 as a wartime measure which remained in force until 1925 to enable the Australian Government to control the supply of gold. Sovereigns struck during this period by Melbourne and Sydney were therefore mostly minted for the Australian Government as part of its Note Issuance Reserve and many of them would have been sitting in the vaults of the Commonwealth Bank. The Perth Mint struck larger numbers of sovereigns at this time but these were mainly exported and therefore widely dispersed. As we have seen, at least three million sovereigns were sent from Australia to London to be melted down which likely included many Melbourne and Sydney coins of the 1920s.

South African sovereign 1931, one of the issues partially melted.

South Africa

None of the regular currency issues from Pretoria are particularly scarce (excluding the tiny mintages of 1923 and 1924) and the numbers struck were generally substantial. As we have seen, some of the coinage of 1931 was melted but the mintage that year was 8,511,792 and surviving numbers do not seem to have been significantly impacted. Incidentally, it is not often realised that South Africa, then the world's largest gold producer, remained on the Gold Standard after Britain and Australia had departed. This was to prove detrimental to the South African economy and the country was forced to abandon it just over a year later on December 27, 1932. Nonetheless, it explains why Pretoria alone struck sovereigns in 1932 after all the other Branch Mints had ceased production.

Conclusion

The melting of sovereigns for the Bank of England was an economic and political matter undertaken as one of a number of measures designed to avoid the devaluation of sterling. Sadly, it ended in ignominious failure. The 1931 devaluation was to prove to be the first of a series of UK currency crises throughout the 20th century which ultimately led to today's sterling exchange rates. Numismatics suffered collateral damage from the events of 1930-1 as the number of sovereigns destroyed was roughly equivalent to the entire pre-War circulation of gold in the United Kingdom and represented more than 10 per cent of all sovereigns ever minted to that point. The dates most heavily impacted are likely to have been the more recent strikings which had small mintages. These would include Australian sovereigns of the 1920s, the London mintage of 1917 and the original London mintage of 1925.

Britain's abandonment of the Gold Standard was to begin a process whereby today no country bases its currency on gold. At a lunch in London in June 1933, Sir Robert Johnson stated that as far as the Mint was concerned gold coinage as currency was for ever dead and that, with the Royal Mint and its branches having struck something like 1,000,000,000 sovereigns, "we feel we have earned our rest". A fitting epitaph to the end of an era.

The author is grateful to Graham Dyer, Senior Research Curator at the Royal Mint Museum, for his advice and comments.

Footnotes:
[1] TNA MINT 20/1180: Sovereigns Melted into Ingots for the Bank of England.
[2] Bank of England Archive C43/134: Exercise in Melting Down New Sovereigns into Bars.
[3] Capie and Webber, "Total Coin and Coin in Circulation in the United Kingdom", 1868–1914 (*Journal of Money, Credit and Banking*. Vol/ 15, No. 1, 1983), pp. 24–39.
[4] See, for example, Sir Geoffrey Duveen and H. G. Stride, *The History of the Gold Sovereign* (London 1962), pp. 91 and 106; and Michael A. Marsh, *The Gold Sovereign*—Revised Edition by Steve Hill (Exeter 2017), p. 78.
[5] Royal Mint, 62nd Annual Report 1931 (London 1932) p. 30.
[6] Op. cit. 4.

This article first appeared in COIN NEWS, March 2021.

From sovereigns to gold bars:

The London Bullion Market Association (LBMA) oversees the trading of gold in London, including the specifications of gold bars. Surprisingly, so-called 400 ounce bars are not required to weigh an exact amount but can vary from 350 to 430 fine troy ounces. Until relatively recently gold refining could achieve a maximum purity of only .996 and so the minimum requirement for "fine" gold bars is .995. Bars are required to have sloping sides and dimensions of about 10" long, 3" wide and a depth of 1¾".

The decision to melt exactly 1,750 sovereigns per bar resulted in ingots whose gross weight was about 450 ounces. These were of a fineness of .916 and contained approximately 411 ounces of fine gold. They met LBMA specifications as to weight but not fineness and were consequently dubbed "coin bars" rather than "fine bars". The Bank of France initially refused to accept such bars resulting in some having to be melted, refined and recast into fine bars by Rothschild and Johnson Matthey & Co.

Where money talks

Subscribe from just £10

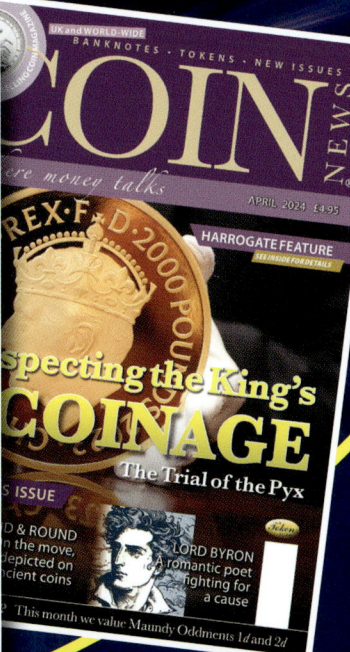

TRY BEFORE YOU BUY!
Get your FREE sample copy

Both print and digital subscriptions are available

COIN NEWS is Britain's biggest selling Coin and Banknote magazine. Every month it is crammed full with over 90 pages of news, views, articles and insights into the fascinating world of coin and banknote collecting. Every issue features all the latest numismatic news, auction results and comments on the hobby as well as a wealth of interesting articles on all things coin and banknote—from hammered to modern from treasury notes to polymers—all are covered!

For more information please call 01404 46972
or visit www.tokenpublishing.com

COINS OF THE REALM
AUCTIONS

Simply Bid. Simply Buy. Simply Sell.

0%
Buyers premium

bidlive.coinsoftherealm-auctions.com

Accepting Consignments, call today:
0800 169 1066

www.coinsoftherealm.com

Download the App searching 'Coins of the Realm'

Buy & Sell Gold Coins and Bars

Baldwin's have over one hundred and fifty years experience of buying and selling gold coins. We can help you put together a holding of gold, or silver, at the best market prices. Uncover timeless value and security in every bar, coin, and purchase opportunity we offer.

Sell your gold and silver! Looking to obtain a fair price for your precious metals? We buy all gold and silver.

GET IN TOUCH AND ASK US HOW

BALDWIN'S
BULLION

Are you in search of a trusted partner to guide you through the world of buying and selling gold & silver bullion?
Ask a trusted numismatic dealer, we've been doing it since 1872

For more information call 020 7930 6879 or email info@baldwinsbullion.com
www.baldwinsbullion.com | 399 Strand, London WC2R 0LX

 /BullionBaldwins   Baldwins_Bullion

COLONIAL COINS & MEDALS

Located in the heart of Brisbane, Colonial Coins and Medals is Australia's leading specialists in Coins (Ancient, British & World), Military Medals (Australian & British Commonwealth), and Medallions & Banknotes (British Commonwealth).

EST. 1966

WWW.COLONIALCOINS.COM.AU

We invite you to visit our retail website to experience our extensive numismatic inventory - we look forward to providing you with our bespoke, professional service.

218 Adelaide Street, ANZAC Square Building
Brisbane City, 4000, Australia

EMAIL: Info@ColonialCoins.com.au   TEL: +617 3229 3949

 @Colonial.Coins    @ColonialCoinsAndMedals

Mark Rasmussen Numismatist

Specialising in Coins of Great Britain, Scotland, Ireland and the Islands

A small selection of notable coins handled in recent years

Twenty Pound Piece of James VI of Scotland

Sovereign of Henry VII

Sovereign of Henry VIII

Ryal of Elizabeth I

Triple Unite of Charles I

Five Guineas of Charles II

Countermarked U.S. Dollar of George III

Proof Gold Penny of George III

1933 Penny of George V

1935 Proof Crown in Gold

1937 Penny of Edward VIII

1819 Sovereign of George III

1952 Penny of George VI

1937 Threepence of Edward VIII

P. O. Box 42, Betchworth, Surrey RH3 7YR
Telephone/Fax: 01306 884 880
Mobile: 07798 611006
e-mail: mark.rasmussen@rascoins.com   www.rascoins.com

SOVEREIGN RARITIES LTD

DEALERS in RARE COINS from 1000 YEARS of BRITISH HISTORY
Resident British Coin Specialist STEVE HILL the author of this book.

Proof Half-Sovereign, 1817

Half-Sovereign, 1821

Proof Half-Sovereign, 1831

Two-Pounds, 1823

Two-Pounds, 1887

Proof Two-Pounds, 1893

Matt Proof Two-Pounds, 1902

Proof Five-Pounds, 1826

"Una and the Lion", Proof Five-Pounds, 1839

17-19 MADDOX STREET, LONDON, W1S 2QH
TEL: +44 (0)20 3019 1185   INFO@SOVR.CO.UK

WWW.SOVR.CO.UK

THE ROYAL MINT
THE ORIGINAL MAKER

THE GREAT SEALS
OF THE REALM

The Golden Seal of Henry VIII

For centuries, seals have been used in Britain to symbolise the official will and authority of the monarch. Henry VIII is the only English monarch to have used a golden seal, or 'bulla', and it was specially created to seal his confirmation of the Treaty of Amiens between himself and Francis I, King of France, in 1527. In 1901, the Deputy Master of The Royal Mint was appointed Ex Officio Engraver of Royal and Government Seals and now, using specimens housed at The Royal Mint Museum, we have remastered Henry VIII's golden seal in gold, silver and cupro-nickel for the modern day.

royalmint.com

Scan the Code

OUR HISTORY IN YOUR HANDS

THE LONDON MINT OFFICE

CALL US ON **0808 133 3772** OR VISIT
WWW.LONDONMINTOFFICE.ORG/**GOLD-SOVS**

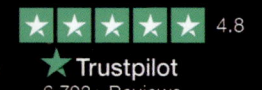

SCAN ME

FOUNDED 1666

SPINK

WHERE HISTORY IS VALUED

For your Numismatic Icon.
Trust our Quintessential Global Auctioneers.

Polish-Lithuanian Commonwealth,
Sigismund III Vasa,
"Treaty of Deulino"
Commemorative 10 Ducats, 1618

Estimate
£80,000 – £120,000

Elizabeth I,
Fine Sovereign,
1584-1586

Estimate
£70,000 – £90,000

George I,
'Prince Elector'
Guinea, 1714

Estimate
£25,000 – 30,000

Vespasian, 'Judaea Capta' Aureus,
December AD 69 - early AD 70,
Tarraco Mint
Found at March, Cambridgeshire,
Autumn 2017

For assistance in recording your historic discoveries, to simply getting commitment-free advice and valuations for landowners

Please contact:
Gregory Edmund | gedmund@spink.com | 020 7563 4048
Tim Robson | trobson@spink.com | 020 7563 4007

WWW.SPINK.COM

SPINK UK | 69 Southampton Row
Bloomsbury | London | WC1B 4ET

#SPINK_AUCTIONS

Trust Your Coins to the Experts

Founded in 1987, NGC is the world's largest third-party coin authentication, grading and encapsulation service. Collectors and dealers around the world trust NGC for its accurate and consistent grading, its commitment to impartiality and its industry-leading guarantee.

Serving UK collectors from our office in Bloomsbury, London
(located in the same building as Spink)

For more information,
contact Certified Collectibles Group – International UK Limited (CCG UK):

📞 (+44) (0) 20 3968 3848
✉ Service@CollectiblesGroup.uk

Learn more at
NGCcoin.uk/about

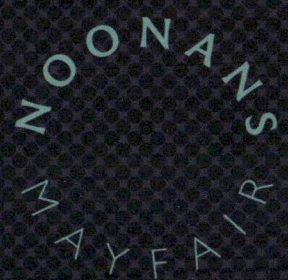

LOOKING TO SELL OR BUY GOLD SOVEREIGNS? TRUST OUR EXPERTS

ALL ENQUIRIES PLEASE CONTACT CHRIS WEBB OR BRADLEY HOPPER
ON 020 7016 1700 OR EMAIL COINS@NOONANS.CO.UK

LOT 440: GEORGE III (1760–1820)
NEW COINAGE, SOVEREIGN, 1817
SOLD IN APRIL 2024
HAMMER PRICE: £4,200

LOT 1: AN EXCEPTIONAL FIRST ISSUE FINE GOLD
SOVEREIGN OF THIRTY SHILLINGS
SOLD AS PART OF THE GEORGE HOLLOWAY
COLLECTION OF FINE SOVEREIGNS OF
ELIZABETH I IN NOVEMBER 2021
HAMMER PRICE: £140,000

IF YOU'RE INTERESTED IN SELLING AND YOU'D LIKE A FREE VALUATION
OUR EXPERTS ARE HERE TO HELP

NOONANS MAYFAIR • 16 BOLTON STREET MAYFAIR LONDON W1J 8BQ
WWW.NOONANS.CO.UK

AVERE COINS

To **Buy** or **Sell** Sovereigns

visit our website or contact us directly

averecoins.co.uk

📞 01243 915 155

✉ info@averecoins.co.uk

AVERECOINS

BNTA